The Strategic Presidency
HITTING THE GROUND RUNNING

Second Edition, Revised

James P. Pfiffner

 University Press of Kansas

© 1996 by the University Press of Kansas.

The first edition was published in 1988 by the Dorsey Press.

Published by the University Press of Kansas (Lawrence, Kansas 66049), which was organized by the Kansas Board of Regents and is operated and funded by Emporia State University, Fort Hays State University, Kansas State University, Pittsburg State University, the University of Kansas, and Wichita State University

Library of Congress Cataloging-in-Publication Data

Pfiffner, James P.
   The strategic presidency : hitting the ground running / James P.
Pfiffner. — 2nd ed., rev.
     p. cm. — (Studies in government and public policy)
   Includes bibliographical references and index.
   ISBN 0-7006-0768-4 (cloth)   — ISBN 0-7006-0769-2 (pbk.)
   1. Presidents—United States—Transition periods. 2. United
States—Politics and government—1945–1989. I. Title. II. Series.
JK518.P45   1996
353.03'4—dc20   96-4536

British Library Cataloguing in Publication Data is available.

Printed in the United States of America

10 9 8 7 6 5 4 3 2

For Deb and our children:
Megan Cyr (1982)
Katherine Courtney (1985)
Morgan Meehan (1987)

Contents

Preface to the Second Edition

The premise of the first edition of *The Strategic Presidency* was that a new president must move quickly in order to achieve a policy agenda. The argument was that moving quickly would take advantage of any perceived mandate and relatively high public approval at the beginning of an administration. It is also necessary to organize the administration, court Congress, and narrowly focus the agenda in order to maximize the opportunity for success. As in the first edition, the focus here continues to be not on the "interregnum" between election and inauguration but on the broader dimensions of taking control of the government and accomplishing policy goals at the beginning of a presidency.

This second edition updates the analysis of presidential transitions by taking up the cases of George Bush in 1988–1989 and Bill Clinton in 1992–1993. Most of the original text remains intact, though a new section on the political appointments quagmire has been added to the conclusion. The Bush and Clinton cases are illuminating in their contrasts. George Bush was elected as a conserver of the "Reagan revolution" and faced a heavily Democratic Congress; his policy agenda was minimal. In contrast, Bill Clinton was elected as the voters opted for change (counting Ross Perot's 19 percent) along with a solidly Democratic Congress, and he had an ambitious policy agenda. What do these two new cases tell us about presidential transitions? Neither president "hit the ground running"—Bush because he did not try and Clinton because he was not prepared and had not focused his policy priorities.

The model for hitting the ground running still remains the Reagan administration in 1981. Its organized approach, legislative tactics, focus of agenda, and the president's political leadership enabled it to accomplish greater policy change than anyone had expected. This judgment does not imply that Reagan's 1981 agenda was good for the country. While one could argue that defense needed beefing up (as Carter's final budget recommended), the fiscal consequences of

$2 trillion added to the national debt and $200-billion deficits "as far as the eye can see" (David Stockman's phrase) will haunt the United States well into the twenty-first century.

Neither does the judgment that George Bush did not try to hit the ground running imply that he should have had an active policy agenda or that his presidency was not successful (though these points could be argued separately). His performance in foreign and national security policy was impressive. But his was a presidency of consolidation, and he did not choose to pursue an active domestic policy agenda. One could argue, however, that his stewardship role should have included an initial effort to reduce the large deficits he had inherited. Nor does Bill Clinton's failure to hit the ground running imply that he did not have important policy victories. He confronted the budget deficit in his first months in office and courageously fought his deficit-reduction package through a reluctant Democratic Congress with active opposition from a united Republican party. In addition, Clinton convinced Congress to pass NAFTA, among other laws, and the first session of the 103rd Congress was a productive one.

Charles O. Jones, in his important book *The Presidency in a Separated System*, invites us to reconsider whether the advice to hit the ground running is always appropriate. He calls our attention to the broad political circumstances under which presidents come to office, particularly the nature of the election and partisan support in Congress. He argues that not all presidents should be judged by the same standard, and that we should not expect each new president to hit the ground running. Rather, we should judge them according to their opportunities. Thus George Bush, facing a strongly Democratic Congress and no plausible mandate, should not be expected to pursue an active policy agenda.

The strategic approach to the presidency in recent decades may have been unique to the Reagan presidency. He had a plausible mandate, a specific policy agenda, and he was determined to make the most of it. Bush had little opportunity and did not try. Clinton had an ambitious agenda but was not prepared, and his political opportunities were less than was apparent at first.

This second edition of *The Strategic Presidency* critically examines how the Bush and Clinton transitions did on these dimensions of presidential leadership. My analysis benefits from the scholarship of Jones and others who call attention to the ways in which differing opportunities affect the ability of different presidents to act strategically. Neither Bush nor Clinton had the same opportunity that Reagan had in 1981, but neither was as organized nor did either act strategically as did the Reagan administration in 1981. Political accomplishment depends upon both opportunity and the ability to take advantage of that opportunity.

Jones raises another reason not to unreservedly endorse a hitting-the-ground-running approach: it might not lead to wise policy. He argues that too hurried an approach can lead to policy escalation in which a new president pushes the system further than is electorally justified by magnifying the mandate beyond its legitimate bounds. As examples here he cites Lyndon Johnson's plethora of new programs in 1965 and Ronald Reagan's fiscal agenda, which brought us such huge deficits. Bill Lammers also points out the costs of moving too quickly in a president's first year in office when there is so little time for the careful deliberation that ought to go into major policy change. He agrees with Jones that our evaluation of a president's first year ought to take into account political opportunity as well as policy performance. In these caveats Jones and Lammers echo the concern of Richard Neustadt when he warned of the hopefulness and arrogance that tempt newly victorious administration into hubris (see p. 7). In the first edition I also warn that "the complexities of governmental structure and policy militate against quick solutions" (p. 4).

In this edition I maintain that hitting the ground running is still appropriate advice if a newly elected president has a specific policy agenda and wants to maximize the chances of achieving those policy goals. Reservations about the substance of the policies are certainly relevant. Effective tactics and strategy can be used on the part of poorly conceived goals. But from the perspective of a newly elected president, the best opportunity for policy success is at the beginning of an administration when a mandate can be claimed and a honeymoon with the public or Congress may exist. Opportunity alone is not enough; one must take concerted advantage of the opportunity.

Despite reservations about the wisdom of policies pursued at the beginning of new administrations, the advice to hit the ground running is still relevant. The alternative to acting strategically is to take things ad hoc, as they come. Given the vagaries of fortune, this reactive approach is often followed of necessity. But if a new administration wants to have a modicum of control over its destiny, it is well advised to choose a policy agenda (ambitious or modest) and focus its energy on pushing it through the political system. Aside from pursuing the policy agenda, the rest of the advice proffered in *The Strategic Presidency* concerns what any new administration must do: get control of the government. That is, it must organize the White House, establish relations with the cabinet, recruit competent appointees, court Congress, tackle the budget, and win the support of career civil servants. Rather than a prescription for precipitous policy change, this is commonsense advice. But behind the obviousness of these tasks lies the complexity and difficulty of performance in the political cauldron of a presidential transition. That is the challenge of presidential transitions, and that is why an examination of the successes and failures of recent presidents is a worthwhile undertaking.

ACKNOWLEDGMENTS

For this second edition of *The Strategic Presidency* I owe thanks to a number of friends and scholars. First of all, I would like to thank Fred Greenstein, who wrote me in 1994, "The Strategic Presidency is too good to let go out of print," and suggested that a second edition would be justified. Were it not for Fred's encouragement, this edition might not have been written, and for this he has my lasting gratitude. My thanks also go to Fred Woodward of the University Press of Kansas, who saw merit in the project, gave me wise advice, and shepherded the book through the publication process.

My thanks to Harrison Wellford for teaching me about the practical aspects of presidential transitions and for sharing with me documents from the transitions (actual or planned) of 1976–1977, 1980–1981, 1988–1989, and 1992–1993. Anne Wexler was generous in her willingness to tutor me in the subtleties of the political dimensions of transitions. Chase Untermeyer was gracious in granting me a number of interviews during a time he was extremely busy with his official duties as Assistant to the President for Presidential Personnel.

For comparative data on the pace of presidential appointments of Presidents Carter, Reagan, Bush, and Clinton, I owe special thanks to Ron Geisler, the executive clerk to the president (now enjoying a well-deserved retirement), and his colleagues in the Executive Clerk's Office, Tim Saunders (now executive clerk), and Sarah Emory. Their faxes kept me up-to-the-minute on the appointments process in 1993.

Several colleagues allowed me to use their scholarship before final publication. For this I would like to thank Joel Aberbach, Hugh Heclo, Chuck Jones, Bill Lammers, Burdett Loomis, Marty Lipset, Cal Mackenzie, Bob Maranto, David Mervin, Judith Michaels, and Bert Rockman. Roz Kleeman, Tom McFee, and Dona Wolf gave me the benefit of their careers in public service by sharing insights from each of their unique perspectives on the political appointments process. Other friends and colleagues gave me the benefit of comments on the ideas and earlier versions of my manuscripts. These friends include Jim Carter, Tim Conlan, Matthew Dickenson, Bob Dudley, Scott Harris, Cynthia Harrison, Chris Hill, John Mauthe, Bob Maranto, Priscilla Regan, Bert Rockman, Tom Stanton, Katie Dunn Tenpas, Richard Waterman, Margaret Wrightson, and Amy Zegart. Mark Rozell gave my manuscript a thorough going-over before publication, for which I thank him. Louise White, the chair of the Department of Public and International Affairs at George Mason University, was generous in arranging teaching schedules that were most conducive to my research and writing, and I want to thank her for her thoughtfulness.

Finally, my deepest debt is to my family for their love and encouragement over the years that I have been working on this project. It is to them that I dedicate this book.

Preface to the First Edition

In 1980 I was working in the director's office of the Office of Personnel Management, the central management agency that handles civilian personnel for the executive branch, then under Carter. Shortly after the election I noticed that we were having some difficulty scheduling our agency drivers to take the director to meetings across town. After some investigation I discovered that the Reagan transition team was also using the motor pool, and the drivers were being responsive to their potential new bosses. The director, even though he still had legal control of the agency, had become a lame duck along with the president.

Watching the 1980–1981 transition from inside the government sparked my interest in presidential transitions. The more I studied presidential transitions, the more I became convinced that the toughest job for a new administration was to take control of the government. I had always assumed that a new president automatically had control of the government after January 20, but when in the late spring of 1981 the Reagan administration still had not made many of its key personnel appointments, I realized that the transition was a process rather than an event and that it was still under way.

This book is intended to provide some insight into how governmental power in the United States is transferred. Those who run future presidential transitions into office may not agree with my conclusions, but they should benefit from considering the successes and failures of recent presidents. Students can gain some insight into the nuts and bolts of how the presidency works on the inside. How can a new president put his own stamp on the budget? How are presidential appointees recruited and selected? How can the bureaucracy best be led and directed? How can the president's agenda be most effectively promoted in Congress? As with most human endeavors, there are no easy formulas for success, but looking at the experience of others is a good place to start.

This book is also about the presidency in a broader sense because those things that must be done during the transition (hiring people, making budgets, dealing with Congress, etc.) are major concerns throughout every presidency. But during a transition these tasks become acutely important because the time period is so compressed. It is a time when everything seems new to the incoming administration. it is a time of euphoria when the stakes are high and the tone for the rest of the administration is set. So this book is really about the presidency in general, but the lens through which I focus my analysis is the transition period.

This study is also intended to add further raw material and interpretations to scholarship on the presidency. After a two-decade hiatus, scholarly attention is again being focused on presidential transitions. The subject is important because the essence of a democracy is the ability to change leadership peacefully at the will of the electorate. But beyond the lack of violence there must be cooperation to assure continuity between the outgoing and incoming administrations. Important developments in this "presidential common law" have marked the transitions of the past two decades.

To an incoming president the transition period is crucial because the tone for the whole administration can be set during transition. Successes can provide momentum for the president's agenda and failures can come back to haunt an administration. The transition period is a time to savor the election victory, but it is also a time of frustration because the timetable is so tight, and all of the important tasks of transition must be accomplished simultaneously.

While the legal and symbolic transfer of the authority of the president takes place at the inauguration ceremony at noon on January 20 when a new president is sworn into office, the process of taking power extends forward and backward from this moment. Preparation for transition into office begins before the election (and sometimes before the nominating convention) and extends six months or more into the first year of the new administration. This study argues that if new presidents want to implement their policy agendas and not merely be caretakers in office, they must consciously plan their transitions into office. That is, they must take a strategic approach to the presidency.

This strategic approach entails careful preparation to take control of the key levers of governmental power, each of which is the subject of one chapter in this book. It begins with the task that must be done first and over which the president has most control, choosing and organizing the White House staff (Chapter 1). Next in importance is the relationship between the White House and the president's cabinet (Chapter 2), for this relationship will determine whether presidential programs and priorities will be implemented with enthusiasm or will be lost in backbiting and destructive competition. Presidential appointments to the sub-cabinet (Chapter 3) will have much to do with control of the executive branch as well as with the president's relationship with Congress.

New presidents traditionally are suspicious of the career bureaucracy, but must depend upon its members to carry out faithfully the administration's programs. How presidents and their appointees can best lead the bureaucracy is the subject of Chapter 4. The budget is the official administration statement of priorities as well as an important driver of the economy. The range of constraints and options that new presidents have with the budget will be discussed in Chapter 5. Finally, much of what presidents try to do must first pass Congress in one way or another. The partisan balance in Congress is not under presidential control, but there are some positive actions presidents can take to improve their legislative chances. These opportunities and pitfalls are considered in Chapter 6.

These key areas of presidential concern are generic to all phases of a presidential administration, but they take on a unique intensity during transition. The administration is doing them for the first time, and mistakes at the beginning are particularly costly and can shut off future options. The approach of this book is thematic and analytical, not chronological. Rather than spend equal time on each administration, the focus is on the experiences of recent administrations that seem to best illuminate the special problems of the transition of power. This book is concerned with control of the *government,* not broader aspects of presidential power such as foreign policy, press relations, or public opinion.

I have tried to capture a sense of what is involved in establishing a presidential administration by asking the people who have done it. While working at the Office of Personnel Management I dealt with many political and career executives of both parties during the 1980–1981 transition. After I left OPM to return to teaching I began to interview former and current White House officials to ask their advice for future presidential transitions. My questions to these officials pertained to their own areas of responsibility, but the main emphasis was: "What did you learn about effective presidential transitions?" "How would you do things differently if you were to do it again?" My purpose was to see what lessons could be learned from their experience in the transition of the presidency.

I interviewed more than fifty officials who participated in presidential administrations, from Truman to Reagan, and I have tape recordings of virtually all of these interviews. When I have quoted a person I have been careful not to take the quote out of context, but it should be emphasized that the quoted person would not necessarily agree with the line of reasoning that I am following or my conclusions. I have also used memoranda and internal documents that came across my desk when I was in the government and that I discovered in presidential libraries. In addition, former government officials and fellow scholars have opened their files for my research. These sources, along with the published work of other scholars, form the basis of this book.

This book's normative bias, if there is one, is that in my democratic process there are no final answers. Thus a president ought to leave intact the infrastructure of governmental machinery so that a new president and new Congress can change the direction of public policy. Paradoxically, there can be no change unless there is a certain amount of stability in institutions and personnel. This perspective does not imply that no agencies ought to be shut down, but rather

that the enduring institutions of government—the professional personnel systems, the Office of Management and Budget, and so on—ought to be left
intact, if not unchanged. As Hugh Heclo has put it: "The test of a staff serving
the presidency as an ongoing institution is not its responsiveness to one set of
demands, but its ability to respond to one set of demands without diminishing
its capacity to respond to the next."*

ACKNOWLEDGMENTS

During the course of this four-year project, I have accumulated many debts to
friends, colleagues, and others who have helped me in my research and writing.
First of all I must express my thanks to the members of presidential administrations whom I interviewed and who gave so generously of their time. I was continually amazed at their graciousness and willingness to help me with my
research. These interviews enabled me to get a sense of the presidency that
would not have been possible without their generosity and insights.

I would like to thank several people for opening up their personal files to
me. Bradley Patterson entrusted me with all of his transition files from his White
House days and shared his insights into the workings of the White House
gleaned from his fourteen years' experience there. Clark Clifford gave me access
to his personal files on the 1960 transition. Franklin Lincoln, Richard Nixon's
transition representative, generously shared with me his transition files and spent
a considerable amount of time helping me understand them.

A number of people gave me access to materials not otherwise public.
Theodore Sorensen let me quote from his confidential memoranda to George
McGovern and Carl Albert on their possible transitions to the presidency. Edwin
Meese and Harrison Wellford gave me permission to use their bipartisan study
of the 1980–1981 transition. This document is the best analysis of the practical
issues that must be addressed in any transition of the presidency. Their recommendations for improvements in the process deserve serious consideration. No
future administration should undertake a transition of the presidency without
careful study of this document.

I would like to thank Larry Berman for his help and trust in lending me his
personal research files on OMB and presidential transitions. Colin Campbell let
me read and quote from the manuscript of his book *Managing the Presidency:
Carter, Reagan, and the Search for Executive Harmony* (University of Pittsburgh
Press, 1986) before it was published. Samuel Kernell and Samuel Popkin let me
read and quote from the transcripts of "Twenty-Five Years of the Presidency," a
conference of former White House chiefs of staff, before publication by the Uni-

*Hugh Heclo, "Executive Budget Making," in *Federal Budget Policy in the 1980s,* ed.
G. B. Mills and J. L. Palmer (Washington, D.C.: The Urban Institute, 1984).

versity of California Press as *Chief of Staff*. The written and video records of this conference will be a valuable record for citizens and scholars for years to come.

I would like to thank Calvin Mackenzie, Project Director; Paul Light, Director of Research; and Ray Kline, President; of the National Academy of Public Administration for inviting me to work on the Presidential Appointee Project and for allowing me to use data from the study in my book. This project has accumulated the most important database on presidential appointees since the Brookings Institution studies of the early 1960s. Fritz Mosher let me use the manuscript of his book, *Presidential Transitions and Foreign Affairs* (Louisiana State University Press, 1987) before it was published. Ken Smorsten let me read portions of his manuscript on presidential transitions.

Several institutions have given me support during the writing of this book. A grant for the summer of 1983 from California State University, Fullerton, allowed me to travel and do most of the interviewing for the book. Julian Foster, Chair of the Political Science Department, was particularly helpful in providing me flexibility in my teaching schedule and released time for my research and writing. My colleagues at George Mason University have provided me with a stimulating atmosphere for research. The Chair of the Department of Public Affairs, Hal Gortner, and Jeremy Plant, Director of Public Administration Programs, were very accommodating in helping arrange my teaching schedule to give me maximum time to write.

The Brookings Institution hosted me as a visiting scholar for the summer of 1983, providing me with a Washington base from which to do my interviewing and a congenial atmosphere for research. Paul Peterson, Director of Governmental Studies, was particularly helpful and encouraging. Diane Hodges was her usual efficient self in helping me with institutional arrangements. Other colleagues at Brookings who helped me in thinking about the presidency include Lee Fritschler, Stephen Hess, Sam Kernell, Terry Moe, Bradley Patterson, James Reichley, Harold Seidman, James Sundquist, and Kent Weaver. I would like to thank Ken Thompson of the Miller Center for Public Affairs at the University of Virginia for inviting me to address a Center seminar, from which many useful comments emerged.

My experience at the Office of Personnel Management was invaluable in helping me to understand what goes on in the bowels of the bureaucracy during presidential transitions. I would like to thank Jule M. Sugarman, its first Deputy Director and later Acting Director, for his guidance and for the opportunity to watch a master at work. One of the first-rate career executives at OPM, Jan K. Bohren, gave me much useful advice about surviving in the bureaucracy. Debbie Loeb Bohren briefed me continually on the intricacies of the internal and external politics of running a large organization. They both provided outstanding leadership for the Managers Network Task Force.

For comments on my manuscript and other help I would like to thank my colleagues at Cal State Fullerton: Vince Buck and Alan Saltzstein; and my colleagues at George Mason University: Wayne Anderson, Joseph Fisher, Hugh Heclo, Jeremy Plant, and Richard Stillman. Others who helped me with comments and encouragement include Louis Fisher, Edie Goldenberg, Michael Hansen, Gordon Hoxie, John Kessel, Charles Levine, Chester Newland, Patrick McInturff, Paul Quirk, Michael Reagan, James Thurber, and Stephen Wayne.

Alana Northrop read each chapter carefully, and my rewriting benefited greatly from her insights and thoughtful comments. Roger Davidson went over the full manuscript with a fine-tooth comb and saved me from many embarrassments. His stylistic and substantive comments were invaluable. I would also like to thank the following scholars who reviewed my manuscript and whose comments significantly improved the book: Robert DiClerico, Barbara Hinckley, Samuel Hoff, William Lammers, Mark Peterson, and Norman Thomas. I would like to thank particularly one anonymous reviewer of an early draft who said: "Mr. P's prose has all the appeal of a coal dust sandwich. He has not yet found his voice. He may not this side of the grave. He writes like a reborn Roman bureaucrat. . . . He needs to uncork the Anglo-Saxon and let fly." But this was five drafts ago and *before* Roger Davidson took his finely honed editor's pen to the manuscript.

Finally, I would like to thank my wife, Deb, and my children, Megan Cyr and Katherine Courtney, whose love immeasurably lightened the load of writing this book.

Introduction:
Taking over the Government

In the last year of the Carter administration Hamilton Jordan had been one of the principal negotiators trying to free the American hostages in Iran. During the final hours of the Carter presidency he was constantly on the phone to negotiators in the Middle East. On January 20, 1981, while President Reagan's inauguration ceremony was still under way shortly after noon, Jordan called the White House Situation Room from Air Force One, which was at Andrews Air Force Base waiting to take President Carter back to Georgia. He asked for an update on the hostage situation but was told that since Jimmy Carter was no longer president he could not have access to classified information.[1]

The irony of this incident vividly reminds us of the abrupt changing of the guard prescribed in the Constitution. This is why Dwight Eisenhower insisted that there is really no *transition* of the presidency. Rather, presidential authority is *transferred* to the new president at noon on January 20 after a new president is elected.[2]

The problem of the succession of leadership is one of the most central issues in political theory and practice. In any polity the struggle for power will be intensified when there is any indication that the incumbent's power is eroding or that there may be a change of leadership. This makes the polity much more vulnerable to internal unrest or foreign intervention. The problem of succession throughout history has often been solved by the control of military force. Monarchies have dealt with the problem by inherited legitimacy. Modern democracies deal with the problem through elections, with the choice of new leadership determined by a campaign for votes and leadership succession determined by ballots cast.

In modern governments leadership succession involves the control of policy making and implementation. The United States is unique among modern governments in its separation-of-powers system. Most contemporary democracies

1

are constituted around a parliamentary system in which the executive, a prime minister and cabinet, is formed from members of the legislature. The permanent bureaucracy continues its work with only the very top administrative offices changing hands. Transitions of government are accomplished quickly, often within several weeks, with a minimum of disruption to the ongoing government.

Leadership of the U.S. government, however, does not change so simply. With presidential elections every four years, House elections every two years, and one-third of the Senate up for election every two years, a new president is not guaranteed a majority in the Congress. This lack of guarantee of a majority of his own party in Congress, and the lack of party discipline, even with a majority, presents a new president with major challenges in his attempt to take control of the government.

Other peculiarities of the separation-of-powers system present a new president with other problems. Cabinet members are selected for a variety of reasons, and may not have extensive experience in the area of their appointment. In a parliamentary system cabinet members would be experienced members of the legislature and would probably be part of the "shadow cabinet" waiting to take over agencies if the government were to change. The personnel appointments a new prime minister makes number between 50 and 500 in Western European countries. A new U.S. president can make more than five thousand appointments. European bureaucracies are usually headed by "permanent undersecretaries" who remain in office to work with the new cabinet head. In the United States the whole top leadership of a department changes, with recent administrations reaching more deeply into the permanent bureaucracy to make political appointments.

These peculiarities in the American system of government make the problem of transition of the presidency particularly difficult and complex. Presidential succession in the United States can occur in a number of ways. A president can be succeeded by the vice president or another member of his own political party. In this case the transition to a new administration is likely to be gradual, with some members of the previous administration asked to stay on either permanently or merely to provide some continuity until the new president has chosen his own team.

It is the party turnover transitions, however, that present the greatest challenge to the U.S. system and contain the greatest danger of confusion and vulnerability for national security. In these cases virtually the entire top level of the government changes hands. The new president must, after long months (or years) of campaigning, immediately grasp the levers of power and take control of the government. These extreme cases of governmental change in the United States are the focus of this book, because they present the greatest challenge to our democracy. Within-party transitions can be seen as much smaller versions of these transitions, but without much of the bitterness engendered by party rivalry.

The presidency has changed hands eight times since 1960, five times with a change in party control. The within-term transitions of Presidents Johnson and

Ford presented their own challenges, with Johnson emphasizing continuity ("Let us continue"), and Ford discontinuity ("Our long nightmare is over"). George Bush's succession to the presidency by election in his own right was the first time a sitting vice president had been elected to the presidency since 1836. He faced dual challenges: he had to demonstrate continuity with the Reagan administration, yet he had to define his own approach to the presidency.

Lessons will be drawn from these experiences, but the emphasis will be on the party turnovers of 1961, 1969, 1977, 1981 and 1993. These transitions embody sharp contrasts in policy and priorities and take the longest before the new president is in relatively complete control of the government. In 1960 and 1968 the incumbent was not a candidate, and the transfer was eased somewhat, since the permanent government could prepare for a transition without seeming to be disloyal. But all of these transitions involved a change from one party to its challenger, with changes in policy and style.

A narrow definition of transition includes at least the period of time from the election to inauguration, about eleven weeks. During this time a newly elected president must, at the very least, designate his cabinet and set up appointment procedures for the rest of his administration. But this period is not long enough to do the range of things that must be done if the president is to take effective control of the government on January 20. Despite Eisenhower's insistence on the finite nature of the transfer of presidential authority, in reality the shift of power between administrations extends from the election until the new president has established his control over the government. Thus the effective period of transition actually extends well into the new president's first year in office.

For this study the period of transition includes preelection activities undertaken by candidates to prepare for the possibility of election. It also includes the period between election and inauguration, the "interregnum," or narrowly defined transition period. But this study also includes the postinauguration phase in which the new administration takes the reins of power and attempts to put its own stamp on the government. This period can last from a few months to a year, or until the administration begins to worry seriously about the upcoming midterm elections.[3] An effective presidential transition requires serious preparation even before the election and concerted efforts six to eight months after inauguration. But the specific time period is not crucial; what is important is the ability of a new administration to take control of the government.

This book begins with the premise that power is not automatically transferred, but must be seized. Only the *authority* of the presidency is transferred on January 20; the *power* of the presidency—in terms of effective control of the policy agenda—must be consciously developed. This book will analyze the key levers of presidential power in the United States. The analysis will proceed from those levers in the president's most immediate control to those over which he has important influence, but not complete control. The president first must organize his White House staff (Chapter 1) and establish its relationship with his cabinet officers (Chapter 2). Next he can appoint the top levels of the executive branch bureaucracy (Chapter 3) who will work directly with the career Civil Service (Chapter 4), who will actually carry out his policies. But in order to secure his policy agenda he must also gain control of the budget (Chapter 5) through the budgetary process in the executive branch and in Congress. Finally a new president must work with Congress (Chapter 6) if he is to be successful in accomplishing his major priorities. Chapters 7 and 8 will analyze how these challenges were met in the Bush and Clinton transitions.

By "strategic presidency" is meant a self-conscious approach to planning the assumption of governmental control after an election. This strategic approach was undertaken systematically by Jimmy Carter and Ronald Reagan. Carter devoted considerable resources to planning his transition into office, and Reagan assembled a large bureaucracy to assist in his transition. Presidents-elect Bush and Clinton each allowed some planning, but neither took the planning efforts very seriously, or put significant resources into them.

It is the argument of this book that serious planning is necessary if an administration is to "hit the ground running." If a policy agenda is to be implemented, a new president cannot afford to rely on the formal powers of office. The levers of governmental power must be grasped deliberately. While this may seem like common sense, it is by no means easy, because the pressures of the campaign are often overwhelming, and the rush of events after an election cannot be slowed.

Presidents-elect face several dilemmas in their attempts to take over the government.

1. They must act quickly to accomplish their objectives, but the complexities of governmental structure and policy militate against quick solutions. In order to take advantage of the narrow "window of opportunity" to accomplish administration goals, people and programs must be put into place quickly. But the size and complexity of the huge programs and organizations of contemporary U.S. government argue for a more deliberate approach. With time and experience come added competence as the new administration matures and learns how to manipulate the governmental levers of power.

2. Each new president after a party turnover seems to reject automatically the previous administration's approach. Sometimes this leads to reinventing the wheel, and sometimes it leads to improved performance. New presidents who have just won an election and have run on the platform that the incumbent administration was incompetent and misguided are likely to feel that they have nothing to learn from the outgoing administration that they were elected to replace. This often leads to an out-of-hand dismissal of any advice proffered and to the rejection of methods, organizations, and policies of the predecessor merely because of association with the discredited administration.

3. After winning an election a new president and his cohorts must change gears from campaigning and shift to the much different task of governing. This is a difficult transition, and tough choices must be made in making the trade-off between loyalty and competence in staffing the administration. In the world of politics loyalty is highly regarded. No president could have become elected without years of hard work by loyal aides and allies. When the president is elected, it is expected that this loyalty will be paid back with jobs in the government. But campaigning is not the same as governing, and people well suited to one are not necessarily good at the other. While loyalty cannot be neglected, it is in the president's best interest to have a competent administration.

THE LAME-DUCK ADMINISTRATION

When control of the presidency changes parties the lame-duck administration has eleven weeks to tidy up its affairs and prepare the way for the new administration. Immediately after the election power begins to shift noticeably. Senior career executives begin to distance themselves from their bosses, To be identified too closely with the discredited administration could mean bureaucratic limbo after January 20. The bureaucratic machine begins to slip into neutral gear because its present leaders cannot guarantee any commitments beyond January 20. The lame-duck budget must be finalized, but people's hearts are not in it, because they know it will soon be moot. "A lame duck President might look at his authority to govern in the transition period as if it were a large balloon with a slow leak . . . the leak will initially be small. . . . But he must recognize that the balloon is ineluctably shrinking with each passing week. . . . By the end of the year, he will have lost the attention of the permanent government and can accomplish very little."[4]

Meanwhile, the lame-duck political appointees are hunting for jobs for themselves. The disappointment of rejection by the voters is compounded by uncertainty about their own futures. It is always possible that the outgoing administration will try to tie the hands of the new administration by last-minute policy commitment or appointments, but this can be made less likely by vigilance on the part of the victors and forebearance on the part of the outgoing administration leadership.

Since the bitterness that marked the 1952 transition from Truman to Eisenhower, outgoing administrations have taken steps to smooth the way for their successors. In 1960, when it was certain that a new president would be elected, Eisenhower gave orders that the Bureau of the Budget was to make preparations for the transition. A BOB memorandum stated the purpose of briefing incoming officials: "The emphasis will be on careful selection of subjects for purposes of assisting the coming administration in the interval between the Presidential elections and the inauguration."[5] In 1968 President Johnson in a December 7 cabinet meeting said: "It is neither desirable or equitable to bind the hands of the next Administration in major program areas unless there is overriding necessity to do so. We should not needlessly foreclose the options of the new Administration to initiate their own program changes. It would be particularly unfair to take actions now which must be implemented over a long period of time." He further urged his officials not to take any "rash, eleventh hour actions" to spite the new administration.[6]

In 1980 the Carter administration took careful steps to assure that no improper actions were taken during the election year. On January 4, 1980, the director of the Office of Personnel Management sent out a bulletin to agencies reminding them that during an election year they ought to "carefully review all personnel actions to be certain they meet all civil service rules and regulations and also that these actions are free of any stigma of impropriety." The bulletin urged agency personnel directors to review carefully any actions that would place incumbents of positions in the excepted service in the competitive service.[7] Jack Watson, President Carter's deputy for transition, sent out a memo establishing guidelines for the transition: "Our guideline is simply to be helpful and forthcoming in every way possible, without burying the new people under mountains of briefing books and paper."[8]

Party turnover transitions from 1960 on have shown a marked improvement over the previous interparty transfers of 1952 and 1932.[9] Despite efforts such as the ones discussed above, there is always the potential for friction and bitterness when there is a party turnover of the presidency. Several other things can be done to reassure the incoming administration that the incumbents are not attempting any "midnight" maneuvers and the outcoming administration that it is dealing with the legitimate representatives of the president-elect. In 1976 and 1980 care was taken to establish one point of contact between the government and the transition team of the president-elect in order to avoid any confusion about who spoke for the new team. A bipartisan study of the 1980–1981 transition recommended that a lame-duck president consider placing a freeze on personnel appointments and government regulations in order to reassure the incoming administration.[10]

THE NEED TO "HIT THE GROUND RUNNING"

While the outgoing administration is tying up loose ends and political appointees are trying to find new jobs for themselves, the incoming victors are filled with euphoria and exhausted from the campaign. They must shift gears from campaigning to governing, and they are faced with the gigantic task of taking over the U.S. government. They want to take advantage of the "mandate" from the voters and create a "honeymoon" with Congress. Clark Clifford advised John Kennedy: "The first problem of the new Administration, of course, is to get off the mark quickly with its New Frontier program."[11] Early victories may provide the "momentum" for further gains. This desire to move fast is driven by the awareness that power is fleeting. According to H. R. Haldeman: "You've got the power now, don't listen to anyone else. Your power is going to start eroding from January 20th on."[12]

The need to "hit the ground running" is also important because of what scholar Paul Light calls the circle of decreasing influence. He argues that there is a consistent pattern in recent decades that presidents decline in power as they move into their first terms. The transition period provides a window of opportunity that will not occur again. The president's popular approval is high; Congress is open to new leadership, and tough choices that will alienate some have not yet been made. It is time of opportunity and change. Ironically, this cycle of decreasing influence is mirrored by a cycle of increasing effectiveness that results from learning on the job.[13] The president's greatest opportunity to work his will comes when he has the least ability to do it effectively; this is what makes planning an effective transition so crucial.

While the transition provides the opportunity for early victories, it is also a time of danger. Richard Neustadt, who has participated in several, argues that new administrations, like that of Kennedy in 1961, are marked by ignorance and hopefulness. "The ignorance was tinged with innocence, the hopefulness with arrogance."[14] The hopefulness stems from the victory of the campaign and the feeling that "they" couldn't do the job, but "we" can. The ignorance is born of inexperience. Winners of elections consistently tend to exaggerate their mandates from the voters and overplay the importance of their victories.[15]

Neustadt also warns of the syndrome that leads the American public and the new administration to expect "another Hundred Days."[16] The combination of high expectations and lack of experience can lead to early mistakes on the part of a new administration; and the mistakes can sometimes be dangerous for the country. Soon after entering office President Kennedy authorized a CIA-backed invasion of Cuba by expatriates. The planners seriously underestimated the power and popularity of Fidel Castro. The invasion failed, causing severe embarrassment to the new Kennedy administration.[17]

Other, less dangerous, blunders can have lasting effects on a presidency and can keep it from achieving its fullest potential. So Neustadt urges caution: "I argue for postponement. . . . Transitions are not forever, ignorance wears off, hopefulness cools down . . . it should be worth a forfeit of presumptive gains to skirt the losses lurking where one's ignorance and hopefulness combine."[18] But Neustadt is unusual among those with White House experience. Most argue along with H. R. Haldeman that if you want to achieve specific policy goals, the best opportunity lies early in your first term.

THE INSTITUTIONALIZING OF TRANSITIONS

Before 1963 transitions were conducted by "presidential common law, confirmed by custom."[19] But as the role of the federal government has grown and the complexity of national policy has increased, the presidency has increased in size and has become more centralized. This trend has accelerated since 1960, and the formalization of transition organizations followed.

Franklin Roosevelt in 1944 began the tradition of briefing his opponent on national security and foreign policy matters, a tradition that still stands. Dwight Eisenhower met personally with President-elect Kennedy in 1960. His graciousness was in sharp contrast with the Wilson-Harding transition of 1920–1921 when President Wilson had no contact with the president-elect and did little to ease the transition.[20] In 1960 Eisenhower and Kennedy established another precedent in designating General Wilton B. Persons and Clark Clifford as liaison between the incoming and outgoing administrations. Later President Johnson broke new ground in briefing candidates and inviting liaison designees to the White House before the election.

In the 1960–1961 transition John Kennedy spent over $300,000 provided by the Democratic National Committee and his own personal funds. The government provided some office space for agency head designates, but many of the people working on his transition had to donate their time and pay their own way. After taking office President Kennedy established a commission on transition costs that recommended governmental financing. Accepting the argument that it is in the national interest to have an orderly transition of the presidency, Congress passed the Presidential Transition Act of 1963.[21] The act provided that "to promote the orderly transfer of a President and the inauguration of a new President," the administrator of General Services (GSA) would provide office space wherever the president-elect wanted as well as staff, travel, communication, and printing expenses. The act authorized $900,000 to be spent for transitions.

In 1968 the act was used for the first time, and President Johnson decided to split the $900,000 equally, with $375,000 going to the incoming and outgoing presidents and $75,000 for the incoming and outgoing vice presidents.[22] President-elect Nixon used all of the funds allotted plus another million dollars raised by private donations.[23] Franklin Lincoln, who ran President Nixon's transition, argued in 1969 that the funds provided by the Transition Act were "manifestly insufficient" and recommended an increase.[24] In 1976 the sums provided for transition were increased for $2 million for the incoming administration and $1 million for the outgoing administration. In 1977 the Ford and Carter administrations each turned back $300,000 of the $1 million and $2 million provided for their transitions, respectively.[25] In 1981 the Reagan administration used the full amount of funds and spent another $2 million raised from private donations.[26]

Kennedy

In 1960 John Kennedy took some steps to prepare for a possible transition into office, though his efforts were quite small by the standards of 1976 and 1980. In addition to not wanting to divert precious campaign dollars from the campaign,

Kennedy was inhibited from a too explicit preparation by not wanting to be "needlessly defiant of fate," remembering the experience of "President Dewey" in 1948.[27] His main preparations consisted of asking Clark Clifford and Richard Neustadt to write memos for a possible transition and establishing a series of task forces during the fall of 1960. In addition, the Brookings Institution prepared a series of memos for each candidate in 1960.

In the first week of August 1960 Senator Kennedy called Clark Clifford to his home and said, "If I am elected, I do not want to wake up on the morning of November 9 and have to ask myself, 'What in the world do I do now?' "[28] What Kennedy wanted was "a treatise on what it is that my associates and I do in order to get the new government in operation."[29] Kennedy also asked Richard Neustadt to prepare some memoranda on transition, but stipulated that Neustadt and Clifford were not to consult with each other.

Clifford's "Memorandum on Transition" (now in Clifford's files) was dated November 9, 1960. It covered White House organization, the role of the cabinet, and warned of the pressures for patronage that would begin immediately. The Neustadt memoranda included "Staffing the President-Elect (10/20/60)," "Cabinet Departments: Some Things to Keep in Mind (11/3/60)," and "Organizing the Transition: A Tentative Check-List for the Weeks between Election and Inaugural."[30] The memos singled out a few positions that Neustadt recommended be filled immediately, but emphasized maintaining flexibility by not committing the president too early to a specific White House staff. "It is trouble enough to build a staff group for the President-Elect out of a campaign organization. It would be a waste of time—and you won't have the time—to shake your organization up again as you cease being President-Elect and become President."[31]

On November 10, 1960, Kennedy asked Clark Clifford to represent him with the Eisenhower administration and to assist him in the transition. Clifford accepted but stipulated that he would not accept a position with the new administration. When Kennedy asked why, Clifford said that by keeping himself out of the competition for a position with the administration "I think I can be of a lot more service for you, for now the power struggle around the throne will start. The tugging and the pulling, the jockeying for position. Every man becomes a competitor or even an enemy. So I can avoid all of that if they know . . . that I'm not going back into government . . . and I think they'll be glad to come to me with their problems."[32] This may have helped prevent some of the internal rivalries that were to plague the Carter transition in 1980.

Kennedy also began the systematic use of task forces intended to study and report on different policy areas to help in his transition. In late summer of 1960, after his nomination, he designated seven task forces, then added nineteen more after the election and three more in January. By the inauguration, twenty-four of the twenty-nine had reported to him. Out of the reports he developed ideas for legislative initiatives early in the administration. In addition the reports were used to brief the president, to enlarge his circle of advisers, and as a source of personnel for the administration. When asked about the overlap in subject matter among some of the task forces, Kennedy replied: "I simply cannot afford to have just one set of advisers."[33]

Early in 1960 the Brookings Institution initiated a study of the problem of presidential transition that it intended to make available to the winning candidate in 1960. The purpose of the project was "to bring about greater public understanding of the problems of organizing a new administration," but Brookings was "not concerned with substantive policy or with specific personnel questions."[34] The Brookings Advisory Committee met in September 1960, with Clark Clifford representing Kennedy and Bradley Patterson representing the White House. According to Patterson the discussion emphasized that the power of the new president would be at a peak during his first 90 days and proposed a more systematic recruitment effort for executive branch personnel than the usual "asking around among friends."[35] Later Brookings issued a series of papers on several issues pressing on a new president including one on personnel appointments that the new president would have to make.

In November Patterson did a survey of what departments and agencies were doing in preparation for the transition and concluded: "The spectrum of response varies from 'Why should we help this new guy do a better job? (Labor), to the most comprehensive collections of advance, written briefing materials (State). Most of the agencies are toward the State end of the spectrum."[36] This preparation on the part of the Eisenhower administration made the 1960 transition the smoothest in the twentieth century up to that time.

Nixon

The Nixon campaign in 1968, like Kennedy's in 1960, did not engage in any elaborate preelection preparation for transition. This was due in part to Nixon's experience as vice president, which made preparations less necessary. But also at work was the old superstition of not counting your chickens before they are hatched. H. R. Haldeman recalled: "We were working against the normal political superstition that you shouldn't start taking the steps of the victor until you've won the victory."[37] Another Nixon aide echoed that view: "We don't want to appear to be forming the Government before we've even been elected."[38]

Some preparations, however, were undertaken on the part of the candidate. In the summer of 1968 an associate from Nixon's New York law firm, Franklin Lincoln, put together a group of former military officers of flag rank to advise Nixon on national security issues.[39] Other Nixon aides appointed themselves to worry about the issues that would be involved in a transition into office while Nixon and his closest aides worried about the campaign.[40]

On October 4, 1968, Nixon designated Franklin Lincoln to be his representative for transition to the Johnson administration. Lincoln, who knew then Secretary of Defense Clark Clifford, was given access to Clifford's files on the 1960 transition in his preparation for a possible Nixon transition.[41] Lincoln wrote a memorandum for Nixon entitled "1968–69 Presidential Transition," dated October 25, 1968, to lay out the issues for a possible transition. The memo covered pre- and postelection issues, organization of the Executive Office, and a list of top-level appointments that should be designated shortly after the election.[42]

In other preparation activity Nixon appointed about twenty task forces, both before and after the election, under the supervision of Paul W. McCracken. The task forces developed policy issues, and many of their members ended up in the administration, though their proposals did not translate into a slate of legislative proposals in the early months of the administration. There was a project at Harvard under the leadership of Phillip Areeda to advise the Republican nominee on transition into office. The main thrust of the project's early meetings was to emphasize cooperation between President Johnson and the president-elect.[43] The Brookings Institution was also preparing a document entitled. "Agenda for the Nation" to advise the new president on major policy issues, but it did not have a significant impact on the Nixon agenda.

In preparation for the coming transition Lyndon Johnson set several precedents in helping the candidates. In July he invited the opposition candidates, Nixon and George Wallace, to the White House for personal consultations. And in September he invited Wallace and Nixon to designate representatives to meet with his representative for transition, Charles S. Murphy, for consultations on the coming transition. These steps taken prior to the election to ease a transition were a departure from precedent.

Franklin Lincoln met with Charles Murphy in October to arrange for FBI name checks for security clearances to be made for the Nixon campaign.[44] They also met on November 7 to arrange for FBI full-field investigations and arranged that the results would go directly to the Nixon people only, unless designees were to have access to classified materials before January 20.[45] Immediately after the election the "Plum Book," "Policy and Supporting Positions," which listed all political appointments available to the new administration, was given to Franklin Lincoln.[46] Lincoln, like Clifford, refused to accept a position with the administration after the inauguration, though he did accept an appointment to the president's Foreign Policy Advisory Board.

In addition to the unprecedented cooperation with presidential candidates before the election, President Johnson also broke new ground in coordinating foreign policy with President-elect Nixon and gaining his support for Vietnam policy. While marked by good faith on both sides, there were some disagreements with respect to other foreign policy issues.[47]

Carter

The first systematic preparation for the transition to the presidency was undertaken by Jimmy Carter's staff in the summer of 1976. In late spring Jack Watson, who was raising funds for the Carter campaign, and Jule Sugarman, who was county executive officer for Atlanta, decided that advance planning was necessary for a possible Carter victory. Planning for Carter's transition was essential because of his lack of experience with the federal government.[48] "It's hard to overestimate the dearth of information you have when you're running for the presidency as a non incumbent."[49]

Sugarman drafted a memo to Carter on the need for a systematic planning effort, and Jack Watson got the memo to Carter through Charles Kirbo. In June Carter directed them to go ahead with the project and set aside $150,000 from campaign funds to run a planning project. The dangers were that the effort would deprive the campaign of needed funds and that they would appear presumptuous, the reason why both the Kennedy and Nixon campaigns refused to do any elaborate preparation. But Carter decided that not being prepared to take over the presidency was a greater risk.[50]

The "Carter-Mondale Policy Planning Group" began to search for talented young people who could leave their jobs and work for very little pay. They ended up with about fifty people who were divided into the "Talent Inventory Program" (TIP) and policy planning study groups. Their goal was a list of possible nominees for every major government appointment and a series of briefing books that Carter could read immediately after the election. Watson and Sugarman took careful steps to keep their work very low profile and to keep the names being considered out of the press in order not to alienate any Carter supporters. But as the election drew near the press began to put more pressure on them for information, and leaks occurred that gave the Atlanta group more visibility than they wanted.

The transition planning group was intentionally segregated from the campaign organization in order to keep day-to-day brushfires from driving out long-range planning, but therein lay the seeds of discord that were to damage the transition planning effort after the Carter election victory. Friction began to develop between the transition planning group in Atlanta and the campaign organization. Hamilton Jordan's staff in the campaign came to see the Atlanta group as usurpers trying to steal from them the fruits of victory while they worked on getting the candidate elected. As Harrison Wellford put it: "Nothing is more destructive of unity among the candidate's troops than the rumor that while campaign activists are working round the clock to get the candidate elected, a group of 'planners' is sitting in a back room somewhere dividing up the spoils of the expected victory."[51]

Jack Watson said he saw the rift between the two groups of staff members developing, but there was not much he could do to stop it at that stage.[52] The priorities of the campaign were too pressing and the time of the candidate was too precious to settle the issue before the election. After the election valuable time was lost as Jordan's primacy was established.

The Carter transition efforts showed that personnel planning must maintain low visibility before the election and must be integrated with the campaign. One possible remedy for the rivalry present in the Carter transition is the declaration by the transition planner that he or she will not accept a position in the administration in order to preclude destructive competition. This was the position taken by Clark Clifford in 1960 and Franklin Lincoln in 1968. Another option is to designate as transition director a person who is clearly very close to the candidate and who has authority in both the campaign and transition planning. This was the path taken by Ronald Reagan in 1980. After the election the Carter transition effort, including personnel recruiters, policy advisers, and agency transition teams, numbered about 300, a modest effort compared with the Reagan transition bureaucracy in 1980.

Reagan

Ronald Reagan initiated planning for his transition into office earlier and conducted a more elaborate operation than any other president in history. In April of 1980 he asked a group of supporters to begin to plan for the first 100 days of a Reagan administration. That meeting resulted in two major efforts: Richard Allen headed a group of 132 people divided into 25 working groups; and 329 people in 23 issue-area groups were led by Martin Anderson.[53] No preelection central transition planning office was set up as Carter had done, but Edwin Meese oversaw several low-visibility planning operations including a personnel operation headed by Pendleton James.

President-elect Nixon chose to run his transition from the Pierre Hotel in New York City; Carter did most of this work from his home in Plains, and John Kennedy split his time between Palm Beach and Washington. President-elect Reagan chose a large government office building at 1726 M Street, N.W., in Washington, several blocks from the White House, for his transition headquarters, though he personally spent most of his time in California. In order to avoid the problems that the Carter transition experienced with two rival organizations, Reagan tried to be comprehensive in his appointments to his transition organization.

The elaborate superstructure was headed by an executive committee including William Casey, Anne Armstrong, Paul Laxalt, Caspar Weinberger, and Edwin Meese, who was also in charge of the operations sections of the organization. There were also seven deputy directors of the transition.[54] The operations group under William Timmons comprised 100 transition teams that spread throughout the government immediately after the election. They were supposed to report back to transition headquarters the status of agency operations and policy and prepare briefing books for appointees to the agencies. The teams were given office space in departments and agencies and had full access to budget and program files, though they were not given access to personnel files.

In addition to the overt purposes of the transition teams other functions were also important. The teams were a means of rewarding campaign workers without committing the administration to hiring them permanently. They served as watchdogs during the final days of the Carter administration. They performed the symbolic function in the bureaucracy of an occupying army. And they helped the leaders of the transition evaluate the performance of those who might be asked to stay on permanently with the administration.[55]

The teams stayed with their agencies until agency heads were designated by the president. At that time it was at the discretion of the new agency head to keep or dismiss the team. Some teams stayed on and agency appointments were made from their ranks; but some transition teams were dismissed as soon as the president's designee took over, as in the cases of the Departments of State and Defense.

The transition teams were thus of mixed utility. On the one hand, their use allowed the new agency head to absorb resentment if their members were fired, resentment that otherwise might be directed at the president. On the other hand, appointments to transition teams created expectations that people would be kept on and consequent disappointments if this did not happen. Control over the dispersed teams was a problem. Some teams did not feel they were having an impact at transition headquarters and resorted to leaks to the press in order to push one or another policy position.[56] Finally, Richard Neustadt has raised the question of the utility of elaborate transition teams, because policy and organizational planning is of little use if the new department head is not involved.[57]

A major problem with the Reagan transition operation was its size. There were 588 listings in the transition telephone directory, but the total number of those involved might have been twice that number.[58] At times it was not clear who was speaking for the administration. Even though transition teams had no policy authority, and public statements were supposed to be funneled through the transition hierarchy, there were a number of embarrassing leaks as representatives of various interests began to push their own policy preferences. On November 29 Richard Allen sent a memorandum to national security transition teams and the Foreign Policy Advisory Board warning them about unauthorized public statements on foreign policy issues.[59]

The Reagan transition effort was the largest and most elaborate in history, presumably based on the assumption that it takes a bureaucracy to take over a bureaucracy. But the 1980–1981 experience must be examined to judge which of the elements of the transition bureaucracy were essential to transition effectiveness and which were superfluous. In 1961 Clark Clifford thought that transitions should be more institutionalized; but in 1983 he felt that they had become too institutionalized.[60] The Bush transition was relatively small, since he was a sitting vice president. The Clinton transition operation, though large, was not as organized or elaborate as was Reagan's in 1980–1981.

OVERVIEW OF THE BOOK

In subsequent chapters we will examine how recent presidents have used the major levels of presidential power: the White House staff, the cabinet, personnel, the bureaucracy, the budget, and the legislative agenda. There will be no attempt to present a comprehensive administrative history of each administration. Rather the emphasis will be on lessons learned. The purpose here is to see what we can learn about the effective transition of the presidency.

Chapters 1 and 2 will examine how different presidents have organized the White House staff and how their staffs have interacted with cabinet appointees. Some recent presidents have promised to keep the White House staff in the background and operate under the principles of "cabinet government." They have ended up with dominant White House staffs and grumbling cabinet secretaries. President Reagan experimented with a system of cabinet councils to develop policy and integrate White House policy making with cabinet implementation. The cabinet council system and its abandonment in Reagan's second term will be evaluated.

One of the greatest challenges facing a new administration is making appointments, and no one seems completely satisfied with the process or the results. Chapter 3 will look at the recruitment system set up by recent administrations and the problems of defining the criteria for appointments and dealing with demands for patronage.

Most recent presidents seem to take office with an abiding distrust of the bureaucracy that will implement their priorities. Chapter 4 examines how different presidents have used the bureaucracy and the management tools that are available to a new administration to control policy implementation.

Recent presidents have come to office promising economic miracles, but have been frustrated in their attempts to control the budget and the economy. The constraints on presidents in fiscal and budget policy will be emphasized in Chapter 5, but lessons will be drawn from the significant budget victories of President Reagan.

Most of the policy priorities of presidents involve legislation that Congress must pass. Chapter 6 examines the importance of the early courting of Congress and the strategic choice of the rifle or the shotgun approach to the president's legislative agenda. It also examines the frustration of the Carter administration with Congress and the victories Ronald Reagan won in his first year in office. Chapter 7 will take up the within-party transition of President Bush in 1988–1989. It was the first transition in which a president was elected to succeed another president of the same party since 1928. Chapter 8 will analyze President Clinton's transition into office in 1992–1993, the first party-turnover transition since Reagan's in 1980–1981.

The emphasis throughout the book will be on the need to move on all fronts simultaneously and with dispatch. The failure to move expeditiously in any one of the areas may foreclose options or prevent the administration from achieving an important priority. Blunders in the early days of an administration may haunt it, while early victories may establish the necessary momentum to accomplish presidential goals. Our focus will be on lessons learned about how presidents can effectively take over the government in these six key areas. Illustrations will be drawn from all stages of recent presidencies, but the lessons will be applied to the transition period; for without an effective transition into office, much of the potential of a newly elected president may be dissipated.

1
Organizing the White House

"The most important decision the president has to make in the transition period, more important than deciding what his policy or his state of the union message will be or even his Secretary of State, is his choice of his principal White House staff."[1] If the president does not designate early who will be first among his White House staff, the hesitation becomes an invitation to struggle. Much is at stake because the president's program must necessarily wait while the battle for who is in charge is settled.

The Carter administration lost a lot of time while the relative positions of White House aides Hamilton Jordan (Carter's campaign director) and Jack Watson (Carter's transition planner) were established. This struggle negated some of the other elaborate preparations the administration had undertaken to prepare for office. In rejecting the strong chief of staff model of White House organization, Presidents Ford and Carter lost valuable time and energy while they experimented with a "spokes-of-the wheel" model of White House organization and refused to designate their chiefs of staff.

The urgency of this first order of business is matched by the complexity of making delicate judgments about human competence and chemistry. The president must blend factors of personal confidence, intelligence, experience, knowledge of the government, and compatibility with other members of the White House team. He must also balance the need for personal loyalty and familiarity with his need for people experienced with Congress and the Washington establishment as the winning team shifts from running the campaign to governing the country.

Recent presidents have solved the puzzle of White House organization in different ways, from the highly structured White House of Richard Nixon to the more fluid approach of John Kennedy. This chapter will examine the White House organizations of recent presidents. The emphasis will be on the role and functions of the White House staff and the importance of designating a chief of staff.

CHOOSING THE WHITE HOUSE STAFF

Presidents choose their White House staffs primarily from among those individuals who have worked with them on their campaigns and who understand best their personality and values. "You use your own campaign organization because people know each other" and are used to working together.[2] More importantly, the president has confidence in the judgment of the people who have weathered the storms of the campaign. According to John Ehrlichman, "The president's confidence is the only qualification for working in the White House."[3]

The Brownlow Committee, whose report led to the creation of the Executive Office of the President in 1939, envisioned a White House staff of individuals "possessed of high competence, great vigor, and a passion for anonymity," who would have "no power to make decisions or issue instructions in their own right."[4] But there is often a disjunction between the time-honored prescriptions for White House staff members and their actual behavior on the job.[5] In the contemporary presidency, White House staffers often seem to be "young, highly intelligent, and unashamedly on the make. They take chances, they cut corners, and unlike most politicians they sometimes have a little spontaneity and irreverence left in them. This accounts for much of their charm and most of their problems."[6]

The natural choice of campaign aides, however, may lead to problems because the nature of governing is different in important ways from the nature of political campaigns. Bradley Patterson, with fourteen years' working experience in the White House, argues that "the virtues needed in the crucible of a campaign—are almost the opposite of the preparation needed for life within the White House."[7]

In a political campaign issues are simplified and differences accentuated. In the White House, however, issues take on "infinite shades of gray."[8] Simplification does not help the president deal with the tough issues. In a campaign people are either for you or against you, and the latter are seen as the enemy. But in the White House coalitions must be built to gain support for the president's programs, and the country must be united behind the administration. In a campaign you can make points "if you make a strong speech or raise the right question or sound the alarm. None of that does you any good at all when you are in the White House and you are responsible for running the show. You have to come up with the answers."[9] The shift from campaigning to governing entails important changes in style, perspective, and attitude. Patterson asks: "Can a hard-driving, fast-moving bunch of egotists be so metamorphosed between November 5 and January 20?" His answer is only "perhaps."[10]

Richard Neustadt argues that one critical component in the qualifications of White House staffers is governmental experience, which engenders a respect for the traditions of the constitutional system and a sense that power in the U.S. government is shared among several institutions. He argues that in the Nixon administration the "new set" of advertising men and lawyers from the West Coast and their "beaver patrol" pushed out the "older set" of Washingtonians who were experienced in governing, such as Bryce Harlow, Arthur Burns, and Herbert Klein. The new staffers had no previous experience in government and were "loyal, empathetic, and ignorant. Ignorance and arrogance combined in Watergate."[11]

The combination of high-strung personality types in the presence of great power and the pressure to achieve short-term political goals combine to make the White House a peculiar cauldron fraught with danger as well as potential for good. Opportunities for greatness and abuse of power abound. "Policy differences, piled on top of personality clashes, multiplied by the time pressures, and heated by sometimes vindictive news leaks, can add up to an incandescent plasma of high-voltage conflict."[12] "I would provide a staff psychiatrist," one Carter staffer observed, "because it is a world of highfliers . . . there is a lot of competition between people. For instance, I have never worked before this in an atmosphere where information is hoarded. Part of your strength and position comes from hoarding and being very careful about whom you say things to."[13] With the particular personality types likely to be in the White House and the pressure-filled atmosphere, organizational issues take on extraordinary importance, with access to the president the prize.

EISENHOWER AND KENNEDY MODELS CONTRASTED

The two general models of White House organization in the contemporary presidency are the Eisenhower and the Roosevelt-Kennedy models. Eisenhower's participation in staff advisory systems in the military led him to conclude that the White House must be organized much more formally than Truman's and Roosevelt's. While good organization would not guarantee sound advice, Eisenhower felt it would enhance the likelihood of efficiency. "Organization cannot make a genius out of an incompetent. On the other hand, disorganization can scarcely fail to result in inefficiency."[14] Eisenhower insisted that as many issues as possible be settled below the presidential level and that issues be presented for his consideration on one-page memoranda.

The driving force behind the Eisenhower White House staff system was former New Hampshire Governor Sherman Adams, who came to dominate the White House with an iron hand. Adams said that his job was "to manage a staff that would boil down, simplify and expedite the urgent business that had to be brought to [Eisenhower's] personal attention and to keep as much work of secondary importance as possible off his desk."[15] He controlled who saw the president, and most cabinet officers reported to the president through him. He seemed to dominate White House policy so thoroughly that one newspaper ran a story headline declaring: "Adams Insists Ike Is Really President."[16]

When Theodore Sorensen, representing president-elect Kennedy, was briefed by General Persons, who had succeeded Sherman Adams, Persons told him: "With the exception of Press Secretary Hagerty, no member of the White House staff went in to see President Eisenhower except in General Persons' company or with General Persons' blessing, and no piece of paper went in to President Eisenhower without General Persons' okaying it in advance."[17] On the other hand, Eisenhower felt strongly that certain matters were cabinet rather than staff issues. According to Andrew Goodpaster, "I remember that when important issues came up in staff meetings, Eisenhower would interrupt and say, 'Excuse me, but this is not a staff matter. I will take that up with the secretary of defense, or interior.'"[18]

One of the useful functions Adams performed was to act as a lightning rod when the president made an unpopular decision on a minor matter. Adams could be seen as the "abominable no man" or the one who denied access to the president. This helped maintain Eisenhower's image as a benevolent leader not concerned with petty politics.[19] On the other hand, a chief of staff with tight control of access to the president can isolate him from diverse points of view and keep him from seeing people whom he ought to see. Greenstein argues that this was not the case with Adams and Eisenhower, though the issue was raised later with regard to the Nixon presidency.

After his election John Kennedy was strongly urged by his advisers to reject the Eisenhower model of White House organization and to adopt a system closer to that of Franklin Roosevelt. In his memorandum "Staffing the President-Elect," Richard Neustadt described the type of organization he thought Kennedy ought to adopt: "You would be your own 'chief of staff.' Your chief assistants would have to work collegially, in constant touch with one another and with you. There is room here for a *primus inter pares* to emerge, but no room for a staff *director* or arbiter, short of you. . . . [Y]ou would oversee, coordinate, and interfere with virtually everything your staff was doing. A collegial staff has to be managed; competition has to be audited."[20] Clark Clifford also urged Kennedy to reject the Eisenhower model with its dominant chief of staff.[21] In a memorandum to Kennedy he argued: "A vigorous President in the Democratic tradition of the Presidency will probably find it best to act as his own chief of staff, and to have no highly visible majordomo standing between him and his staff."[22]

These proposals of Neustadt and Clifford have been called the "spokes-of-the-wheel" model of White House organization. The president himself is the hub and his chief advisers the spokes, each of them having direct access to the president without their advice being "filtered" or "coordinated" by any single chief of staff. Kennedy followed this advice and ran a relatively loosely structured White

House with several senior aides having access to him. Although Theodore Sorensen became his principal adviser, he never became the keeper of the gate that Adams was for Eisenhower or H. R. Haldeman was for Nixon. But the lack of a chief of staff imposes a heavy burden on the president himself. After a long day and night of work during the transition, Kennedy remarked: "Now I know why Ike had Sherman Adams."[23]

Lyndon Johnson continued the Kennedy model of a fluid, unstructured White House staff. While Kennedy, like Roosevelt, dominated the White House staff with his intelligence and choice of which assignments to dole out to whom, Johnson carried his personal domination of White House staff members to extremes. Jack Valenti recalls how Johnson treated his staff.

> He brutalized them, always tried to shove spoonfuls of humility through their clenched teeth. He never named any of his aides to be chief of staff. He kept some aides unenlightened as to his thinking even as he instructed others in several directions at the same time. . . . He once said: "If anyone is going to make a big-ass blunder around here, I want it to be me and not some assistant to me who thinks he is running the country." He made sure everyone knew the source of their power: "Now you very important guys ought to keep one thing in mind. The folks tonight who tell you how smart you are and how charming you are don't give a pig's ass about you personally. They think you can get to me. They also know you won't be around this Oval Office one second longer than me."[24]

The lack of structure in Johnson's White House and Johnson's style of dominating his staff led Patrick Anderson to entitle a section of his chapter on the Johnson White House staff "Caligula's Court."[25] The White House under Johnson was so unstructured that when a new aide reported for duty and asked for an organization chart he was told by an amused career official who had been in the White House for thirty years: "We don't have any organization chart at the White House because we don't have any organization."[26]

NIXON'S WHITE HOUSE

Richard Nixon rejected the loosely structured styles of Presidents Kennedy and Johnson, and began his administration with a clear-cut White House organization. While staff members would change, the linchpin of the organization, H. R. Haldeman, maintained tight control over the White House. According to Haldeman, "You've got to establish a clear cut organizational structure" in order to keep staff rivalries and competition for the president's ear from dominating the policy process. "We all knew where we fit. There were five of us that were equal, but as [Bryce] Harlow said: there was a first among equals, and it was clearly me. Nobody questioned it. I never asserted it; I never argued it. I never had to."[27]

While others saw Haldeman as a barrier between them and the president and suspected that the White House staff was arrogating much power to itself, Haldeman saw his role as merely acting at the direction of the president. "If I told someone to do something, he knew it wasn't me—he knew exactly what it was; it was an order from the President. They knew an appeal wouldn't get anywhere."[28] According to this view every president needs someone who will make the tough decisions about protecting the president's time and who will shield the president from having to make unpleasant face-to-face decisions about personnel. Haldeman characterized himself: "Every President needs a son of bitch, and I'm Nixon's. I'm his buffer and I'm his bastard, I get done what he wants done and I take the heat instead of him."[29]

One of the assets of a close staff aide who is almost an alter ego to the president is that he can weigh what the president says and discount it if in his judgment the president made a poor or hasty decision out of pique. Haldeman often stalled and held petty or vindictive orders until Nixon had cooled down.[30] In one instance Haldeman refused to implement an order to plug up leaks in the State Department by subjecting each employee to lie detector tests. Haldeman argued that in such situations "It's the obligation of the staff . . . not to carry out the order until it has been at least reviewed once and then reordered by the president."[31]

Nixon also counted on Haldeman to protect his time and shield him from unnecessary demands. This was a valuable service in that it diverted hostility from disappointed seekers of appointments from the president to Haldeman. It also led to the dissatisfaction of some cabinet members, such as John Volpe and Walter Hickel, who complained that the White House staff was preventing them from seeing the president.

While others saw Haldeman's role as heavily influencing the president's decisions, Haldeman perceived his role to be free of politics and values. His function as he saw it was to "staff out" every issue that got to the president and scrupulously ascertain that all sides of the issues were presented fairly. While he consciously modeled himself after Sherman Adams, he saw himself as less involved in policy. "Adams spent little time with the President but a lot of time acting for him. I spend a lot of time with the President. I act at the President's direction. . . . I don't directly act in policy matters."[32] One of Haldeman's aides estimated that Nixon spent more than 70 percent of his staff time alone with Haldeman.[33]

The reaction in the country to the Watergate scandal was so strong that the next two presidents felt a need to distance themselves and their administrations from the Nixon legacy. This led Presidents Ford and Carter to begin their terms with promises of open access to the president and a spokes-of-the-wheel structure of White House organization. Each was forced to admit failure after a period of attempting to run the White House without a chief of staff.

THE FORD AND CARTER REACTIONS

Upon succeeding to the presidency, President Ford took pains to distinguish his administration from Nixon's.[34] He spoke of a return to "cabinet government" and an open presidency without a powerful White House staff standing between the president and his advisers or cabinet members. "A Watergate was made possible by a strong chief of staff and ambitious White House aides who were more powerful than members of the Cabinet but who had little or no practical experience in judgment. I wanted to reverse the trend."[35]

A survey of department and agency heads during the transition from Nixon to Ford found that virtually all felt that they were dominated by the Executive Office of the President and that their ideas did not receive a fair hearing. Nor did they have confidence that their proposals reached the president intact. The transition team thus recommended that Ford avoid "isolation of the President by providing a flow of information, access to the President, and a span of control that can be handled while still allowing time for reflection, and an orderly but inclusive decision making process."[36]

President Ford began his administration with nine people reporting to him and with the intention of running his White House without a chief of staff who might evoke the specter of H. R. Haldeman. As Robert Hartman described Ford's intentions: "The President doesn't want any Colonel House or Rasputin around here. He prefers something analogous to the Knights of the Round Table, where all are equal."[37] But in order to lend some sort of coherence to a White House staff of over 500 people, Ford designated Donald Rumsfeld to be "Staff Coordinator." After several months in office even Ford had to admit that something akin to a chief of staff was necessary in order to run the White House. Ford explained: "Someone, I decided, had to be responsible for scheduling appointments, coordinating the paper flow, following up on decisions I had made and giving me status reports on projects and policy development. I didn't like the idea of calling this person chief of staff, but that was the role he would fill."[38]

When Rumsfeld was appointed to be secretary of defense in the winter of 1975, his deputy Richard Cheney took over as Ford's chief of staff. Cheney perceived his role as chief of staff to be one of imposing order on presidential advice, but in a low-key manner that kept him out of the spotlight. Cheney viewed himself as an honest broker who saw to it that all views were presented to the president. This had to be apparent to cabinet members and the rest of the White House staff in order to prevent them from trying to establish back channels to the president in order to get their own views heard. "It is important that the rest of the troops feel that we will honestly present their position to the president."[39]

Cheney felt that establishing a chief of staff in the White House entailed some risks, but that they were worth it.

It's really a matter of trade-offs. There is no question that to the extent that you involve a number of people in the consultative process before you make a decision, you raise the level of noise in the system. You enhance the possibility of premature disclosures and leaks. You also take more time, cut down in efficiency. On the other side, by encouraging different viewpoints you make sure that the President's got a wide variety of options so he won't be blindsided. But it's a very risky business to classify an open system with a lot of consultation as all good, and a very tightly run system with little consultation as all bad.[40]

Cheney concluded from his experience in the White House that the Roosevelt and Kennedy system would no longer work: "Somebody has to be in charge."[41]

At a White House staff party Cheney was presented with a bicycle wheel mounted on a large board with all of the spokes of the wheel mangled and tangled except for one that was all that held the structure together. A plaque mounted on the board read: "The spokes of the wheel: a rare form of management artistry as conceived by Don Rumsfeld and modified by Dick Cheney." When the Ford administration left office on January 20, 1977, Cheney left the present on his desk and appended a note reading "Dear Ham, beware the spokes of the wheel."[42]

Jimmy Carter did not heed Cheney's warning. Carter, like Ford, was reacting to Watergate and the Nixon presidency and promised "no all-powerful palace guard in my White House, no anonymous aides, unelected, unknown to the public, and unconfirmed by the Senate, wielding vast power from the White House basement."[43] Carter also started out with nine advisers reporting to him, and he intended to be his own chief of staff. This came naturally for Carter, who prided himself on being a good manager and who enjoyed (or was obsessed with) the details of policy and management. As a result, it was difficult sometimes to determine who was in charge short of the president. And minor issues tended to be elevated to the presidential level.

The situation was aggravated by the transition conflict between the Watson and Jordan staffs. Valuable time was lost waiting for the dispute to be resolved; and while Jordan was unquestionably the winner, Carter refused to give him unambiguous authority over the White House staff. This was in part because the White House was dominated by a small band of Georgians, and Carter was unwilling to choose one to put first. But also Jordan did not want the title of chief of staff, because he did not enjoy the routine duties of administration as much as the formulation of political strategies.

In retrospect, Jack Watson concluded that the spokes-of-the wheel organization model is "a fatal mistake" in the White House. The Carter attempt resulted in "lack of cohesion" and coordination of decision making. Watson felt that appointing a chief of staff earlier in the administration might have ameliorated the administration's problems with Congress and lack of clarity about who was speaking for the president.[44]

Carter tolerated the lack of any formal chief of staff until July 1979, when he went up to Camp David to consult with various prominent people from throughout the country and made his speech about the crisis of confidence he felt in the country. He then demanded the resignations of his White House staff and cabinet and accepted those of five cabinet members: Michael Blumenthal, Joseph Califano, James Schlesinger, and Brock Adams, as well as Griffin Bell. At this time Carter finally admitted the obvious need for a chief of staff to run the White House and officially appointed Jordan to the post. Later, when Jordan moved to work on the 1980 campaign, Jack Watson took over the title. After his four years as domestic policy adviser to President Carter, Stuart Eizenstat concluded: "It is critical to have one person in charge."[45]

THE REAGAN WHITE HOUSE

The Reagan administration came to office with the conscious intention of avoiding the mistakes they thought that President Carter had made. Edwin Meese, who had overseen the transition, was put in charge of policy, the cabinet, and national security. But Meese was not the president's only top staff aide. He shared his primacy with Michael Deaver and James Baker. Thus Reagan's White House was organized in a modified spokes-of-the-wheel and chief of staff system.[46]

Meese and Deaver had been with Reagan when he was governor of California and were longtime, trusted associates. Baker was brought in after the election; his choice, since he had worked for George Bush, showed that President Reagan was not threatened by advisers who were not old-time Reagan loyalists. It can be argued that the early Reagan successes were due to his willingness to bring in old Washington hands, like Baker, Richard Darman, Max Friedersdorf, Kenneth Duberstein, and David Stockman; and not limit his immediate advisers to those who had been personally loyal to him over the decades of his political career.

Initially Baker was given the functions of "administration" and implementation with the title of chief of staff. Meese took control of "policy," the cabinet, and national security. Michael Deaver, who was closest to the president, handled scheduling, travel, support services, and the First Lady's office. Deaver was not particularly interested in issues or policy, but saw himself as steward of the presidential image and protector of the president's time.[47]

On November 17, 1980, Meese and Baker came to an agreement on the division of duties between them and, as befits two lawyers, wrote it down in a memorandum that was initialed by each. Meese would have cabinet rank while

Baker would not. Meese would coordinate the work of the Domestic Policy staff and the National Security Council staff. Baker got the traditional office of the chief of staff and control of the paper flow to the president and hiring and firing authority in the White House staff.[48]

This division of labor, though it was not immediately obvious, was loaded in favor of Baker. Meese would have responsibility for the long-term Reagan agenda, and Baker would dominate day-to-day operations. It is a predictable rule that in the White House day-to-day firefighting drives out longer-range (six months or longer) planning. Baker's control of operations, paper flow, and personnel would give him the upper hand.

Baker brought in Richard Darman as his aide. On February 17 Darman was named as the "contact person" to coordinate and plan activities related to the economic recovery program and was named secretary to the Budget Review Group. Darman wrote a memo on February 21 arguing for the need to coordinate legislative strategy in order to achieve a "planned string of successes" to develop momentum in Congress. From this memo grew the Legislative Strategy Group that met in Baker's office and included only the highest-level officials in the White House. It played the crucial role in directing the administration's relations with Congress during the budget victories in its first year in office. Darman was secretary to the Legislative Strategy Group.[49]

During the first year of the administration, Meese, Baker, and Deaver ran the White House by "troika" and met each morning for breakfast. But control of policy gradually flowed to Baker through his domination of the budget and legislative strategy of the administration and his control of day-to-day operations.[50]

Ideologically Baker was seen as a "moderate" or "pragmatist" and was viewed as anathema by the right wing of the Republican party. But his pragmatic abilities to get things done in Washington may have been an important reason that he came to be such a strong chief of staff. Despite his longtime loyalty to Reagan, Deaver was also seen as a pragmatist, and he was instrumental in getting Reagan to bring Baker on board. Ideological conservatives on the right saw only Meese among the three as the protector of the "real Reagan" of ideological purity. They were also displeased when William Clark, who had come to the White House as national security adviser and was seen as a true Reaganite, left to be secretary of the interior when James Watt was fired.

The White House organization dominated by the troika (or quadrumvirate when Clark was there) seemed to work quite well for the first part of the administration. The first year's victories seemed to be engineered quite well by the functional separation of duties among the three top advisers. They all had direct access to the president, and they coordinated their work with daily meetings and a minimum of friction. In late 1983, however, reports began to surface that some of the traditional problems of lack of monocratic hierarchy (each person having only one boss) were being felt.

The problems stemmed from the fact that no one staff member was clearly in charge, and the president was not closely enough engaged in policy making and administration to settle disputes quickly. One White House official who had served other presidents said: "I've never worked in an organization like this. There is no one person to give orders, except the President. This lends itself to jockeying for position and not letting anyone else get too far ahead."[51] Another administration official said that the early collective management team approach no longer was operating and that top aides acted as "individual lords, each possessing his own fiefdom, with middle-level people often brandishing the swords."[52] A former White House official put it this way: "It's hell to work in that kind of situation. It's not natural. I think it's because the President doesn't lay down the law. He wants to stay out of the whole thing. It kind of goes against his nature, so he lets a few people he trusts just fight it out."[53]

The beginning of President Reagan's second term was marked by major personnel and organizational charges. At the invitation of Donald Regan, James Baker agreed to swap positions with him in the administration. The change put Baker in charge of the Treasury Department and Regan in charge of the White House staff. At the same time Edwin Meese left the White House to become attorney general and Michael Deaver left to establish a public relations firm. Thus the triumvirate was no longer in charge at the White House, and Donald Regan moved to establish his dominance.

The chief of staff's power might have been undercut by the dual roles played by Meese and Baker. Each was to head a White House policy council as well as his cabinet department. Meese would be in charge of a council on domestic policy, and Baker would head one on economic policy, which were to replace the seven cabinet councils of the first term. The two hats worn by Baker and Meese had the potential to give them powerful policy-making roles, but Regan fought that, and Regan prevailed. Baker and Meese continued to be able to pursue successfully their personal policy initiatives. But this was due to their personal stature and access to the president and not to their roles as heads of cabinet councils.

Regan began to establish his preeminence with important changes in White House personnel. David Stockman, who resigned as OMB director in the summer of 1985, was replaced by James Miller, who was agreeable to Regan. Robert McFarlane, the national security adviser, left the administration in December, in part because of conflicts with Regan. In addition, other members of Reagan's first-term team were leaving the White House, including Max Friedersdorf, Edward Rollins, and Kenneth Duberstein. These White House aides were replaced with people who were acceptable to Regan.

A former marine major and chairman of Merrill Lynch, Regan moved to establish control through a tight hierarchy in the White House. "He considers the Executive Branch to be like a corporation," said one of his aides. "Cabinet members are vice presidents, the President is the chairman of the board, the chief of staff is the chief operating officer."[54] He personally approved virtually everything concerning the president: speeches, schedule, paper flow, appointments, and phone calls.[55] Some thought that his control of the Reagan White House was even more complete than Sherman Adams's was over the Eisenhower White House, in part because Adams did not have jurisdiction over foreign policy; Regan did. "Regan often sits alone with the President and talks quite a bit. No one knows what he says," said one Reagan White House official.[56]

Regan's approach to control contrasted sharply with the politically smooth style of James Baker, though Regan gradually became more accustomed to the fragmented power of American government. "When I was chief executive [at Merrill Lynch] and I said, 'Jump,' people asked, 'How high?' As Secretary of the Treasury, when I said, 'Jump,' people said, "What do you mean by jump? What do you mean by high?' But having entered this milieu, I think I have learned to live in it."[57] Regan considered the crowning achievement of his first few months in office to be the elimination of the collective management system of president Reagan's first term.[58]

Regan saw his duty as chief of staff to take some of the heat for controversial decisions for the president. "One of the reasons I've gained so much prominence is because of the blame coming my way. It's kind of nice for the President to be able to lay the blame off and say: 'I didn't do it, it was somebody down the line.' "[59] At times, however, he chafed at the role of lightning rod for the president. "If someone gets a cold in this town, I get blamed."[60] In 1986 Regan characterized his role as leader of the "shovel brigade" that follows the circus through town. He saw himself as director of political damage control after others had made blunders.

Regan's tight control of access to the president solved the first-term problem characterized by one aide as "nobody knows who's in charge of what, and people . . . slip in the back door and get policy changed at odd hours without anybody realizing what's happened."[61] But the other side of the better coordination coin is the perception of less access to the president for other White House staff members. This was the reason for the departure of some White House aides after Regan took over.[62]

David Stockman criticized Regan for operating on the "echo principle" by reinforcing President Reagan's optimism about the economy and firm opposition against any tax increase to narrow the deficit gap. To Stockman this was preventing White House aides from presenting the full fiscal policy picture to the president. To Regan this was merely carrying out the policy preference of the president and "letting Reagan be Reagan."[63] "I'm not interested in how I can influence policy. I'm interested in how Reagan's plans and policies get developed and actually become part of American life."[64]

In 1986 Regan's performance as chief of staff came under attack when it was disclosed that White House staffers had arranged for shipments of arms to be made to Iran for the purpose of freeing U.S. hostages and attempting to influence "moderates" in the Iran government. Many critics of the administration argued that the policy amounted to appeasing terrorists and that it would encourage the taking of future hostages. They also claimed that our credibility with our allies may have been seriously undermined by the U.S. government's sending arms to the radical Iran government while at the same time strongly urging our allies not to sell arms to Iran.

Even more damaging to the administration was the revelation that proceeds from the sale of the arms to Iran were diverted into Swiss bank accounts and destined to aid the Contra rebels in Nicaragua. This happened at a time that the "Boland Amendment" was in effect which prohibited any direct or indirect U.S. aid to the Contras. Thus it seemed that the administration was trying to achieve its policy goals of aiding the Contras by secret means in spite of laws to the contrary. This raised questions of circumventing the constitutional prerogatives of Congress as well as possible violations of laws by the administration.

Major issues were thus raised about the procedures set up to advise the president on foreign policy. With regard to sales of arms to Iran, the president did consult with Secretary of State George Shultz and Secretary of Defense Caspar Weinberger, both of whom advised against the sales. The attempted rapprochement with Iran, regardless of its wisdom, was probably within the president's prerogatives as head of state and commander in chief. The delivery of arms to Iran, a terrorist state, without notifying Congress may have been a violation of the Arms Export Control Act. But the president said that he had no knowledge of the diversion of funds to the Contras. An NSC staffer, Lieutenant Colonel Oliver North, was said to have carried out the operations without knowledge of Don Regan or the president.

The question was raised: Could a lieutenant colonel on the National Security Council staff have carried out such a complex operation without the knowledge of the White House chief of staff? The irony is that Donald Regan had prided himself on being in charge of every aspect of the White House. His style was one of tight control, and he told his subordinates that he did not like surprises. His purview included foreign policy and national security issues to a broader extent than other presidential chiefs of staff.

So Regan was caught in a dilemma: either he knew about the diversion of funds and was thus potentially guilty of serious breaches of the law, or he did not know about it and therefore was not in control of important actions of the White House staff that affected U.S. foreign policy and national security.

Several issues were raised by these matters regarding the strong chief of staff system of the second Reagan term. What is the proper role of the NSC staff? At its creation in 1947, its role was not intended to be operational. It was created as a staff agency to coordinate national security policy. Operations are normally carried out by the State Department in diplomatic matters, by the Defense Department in military matters, and by the CIA in clandestine matters. These agencies have strong institutional capabilities and professional personnel to carry out their missions. In the important matters of the arms to Iran and aid to the Contras, these professional agencies were bypassed (except in minor matters) by the NSC apparatus.

The other issue is whether the exceptionally strong management control over the White House exercised by Don Regan and the exceptionally detached style of President Reagan contributed to the developments. It is doubtful that the diversion of funds of the Contras would have happened if the policy had been vetted with the members of the White House triumvirate of the first Reagan term (Baker, Meese, and Deaver) or if the secretaries of state and defense had been consulted. So, insofar as Regan's operating style and procedures encouraged excluding the president's normal advisers, the system may have allowed the scandal to occur when it should have been nipped in the bud.[65]

It was the Iran-Contra scandal that proved to be Regan's downfall. According to the report of the commission headed by former senator John Tower: "More than almost any chief of staff of recent memory, [Donald T. Regan] asserted personal control over the White House staff and sought to extend this control to the national security adviser. . . . He must bear primary responsibility for the chaos that descended upon the White House." The day after the report was released in February of 1987, President Reagan decided to replace Regan as chief of staff with former senator Howard Baker. Baker's experience in politics and in Congress provided a sharp contrast with the background and style of Donald Regan. According to one former Reagan White House official,

> Don never realized that while Wall Street runs one way; Pennsylvania Avenue is a two-way street. He never realized there is a difference between being an elected and appointed official. He never realized the distinction between being a staff person and the chief executive officer. He never realized that the White House demands talent throughout, rather than talent derived. He never realized his job was to compensate for the perceived strengths and weaknesses of others, rather than to dominate those weaknesses.[66]

In this case the detached and passive leadership style of the president combined with the rigid and controlling approach of his chief of staff resulted in disaster.

This scandal, however, ought not to lead future presidents or the Congress to overreact. The president needs to have a chief of staff to organize the White House to suit the president's management style. Congressional meddling with the president's personal staff will not solve the problem. Future presidents should be aware of the potential for problems of operational units in the White House and the potential dangers of a chief of staff who tries to shut out all others. But they should also remember the Ford and Carter administrations if they are tempted to try a spokes-of-the-wheel advisory system.

WHAT HAVE WE LEARNED?

No one questions that the modern presidency needs an active White House staff. Cabinet members may complain, and staffers may abuse their power, but the president cannot operate without a staff to protect his political interests and keep the administration focused on the central agenda. Departments and agencies, as Stuart Eizenstat argues, are inherently incapable of coordinating themselves. "Agencies simply do not trust each other. . . . This lack of trust means that, when we have to deal with cross-cutting, conflicting, complex issues of the day that involve more than one agency, it is very difficult, if not impossible, to entrust to one agency the responsibility to coordinate the development of policy that affects several agencies. . . . Without a centralized, strong, and effective White House staff, it is simply impossible to assure the neutrality of the policymaking process."[67]

There is also a developing consensus that in the White House staff someone must unequivocally be in charge. In the words of one Kennedy aide: "Everybody believes in democracy until he gets to the White House and then you begin to believe in dictatorship, because it's so hard to get things done."[68] On this issue we have the informed opinions of presidential chiefs of staff H. R. Haldeman, Donald Rumsfeld, Richard Cheney, and Jack Watson. Each of them has concluded that if the president does not designate someone to control White House rivalries and competition, chaos will result.

Even Richard Neustadt, who had urged Presidents Kennedy and Carter to be their own chiefs of staff, concluded that "letting the president be his own administrative coordinator was probably unrealistic in 1976."[69] Reagan's first term, with its troika of differentiated jurisdictions, has brought into question whether access to the president must be controlled by only one person. Three staffers had regular access to Reagan, but James Baker was clearly chief of staff with control of White House personnel and paper flow to the president. The second-term Reagan White House, however, reverted to a domineering chief of staff. The special personal chemistry of the first-term Reagan White House troika was an unusual occurrence.

It is still possible that a president may be elected with the skills and intelligence of a Franklin Roosevelt or a John Kennedy, who can act as the hub of the wheel and be his own chief of staff. But the increased size of the White House staff, the enhanced technological capabilities of the White House, its increased centralization, and the experience of recent presidencies has brought into question whether we can return to the less formal days of the 1930s or even the 1960s. The consequences of attempting a spokes-of-the-wheel model of White House organization and failing, as Presidents Ford and Carter discovered, are apparent and present a serious risk for any president who tries it.

Several major functions must be performed by the White House chief of staff:

1. The chief of staff must organize the information flow to the president to ensure that issues are "staffed out" and coordinated. All important options and every relevant side of an issue must be presented to the president for his consideration. For instance, if the president gives a speech, all of the substantive issues touched upon must be cleared through the cabinet secretaries affected by them. Secretaries should not, of course, have any final power over content, but the president must have confidence that each relevant person has considered the issue and has raised any reservations to the president.

The chief of staff must be, and be perceived to be, an "honest broker" in ensuring that the views of all concerned administration officials are presented to the president. If this is not done, cabinet members will do their utmost to establish "back channels" to the president. The chief of staff must assure that the president's time is not dominated by one person or point of view and that dissenting opinions have a chance to be presented.

One of the most important coordinative functions of the chief of staff, and the one that causes much trouble with members of the cabinet, is the necessity to prevent "Oh, by the way" decisions. That is, if a member of the cabinet catches the president after a meeting or in a social situation and tries to get a decision on a policy issue, there is the danger of a hasty or poorly planned decision. The president may not be immediately aware of the full ramifications of the decision. It is the chief of staff's duty to delay the decision until it can be "roundtabled" and input can be gained from all the relevant administration officials.

2. Another indispensable function of the White House chief of staff is to take heat for the president. Presidents must inevitably make unpopular decisions and difficult personnel choices. If these unpopular actions can be perceived to be the doing of the chief of staff, the president can be spared some of the negative fallout, though not the responsibility, for them. When a high-level administration official must be fired, it is the president's decision, but "somebody has to do it . . . if there's a dirty deed to be done, it's the chief of staff who's got to do it. The president gets credit for what works, and you get the blame for what doesn't work."[70]

3. The chief of staff must be the person who negotiates with cabinet members over budgets and personnel for their departments. There is no one else, short of the president, who has the clout to arbitrate among members of the cabinet. The president does not have time to do it, and so the chief of staff must massage the "giant egos" and decide when a little "presidential stroking" is needed. "I can't count the number of times I would get a phone call, probably once a month, and it would be a situation in which Pat Moynihan [ambassador to the United Nations] was calling threatening to resign or Henry Kissinger [secretary of state] was threatening to resign because they didn't like each other," recalls Richard Cheney.[71]

Other functions that must be performed by the White House staff, according to Bradley Patterson, who spent fourteen years on the White House staff, include

(1) the interrogation/orchestration/moderator function on crosscutting policy issues; (2) the personal policy development function on issues especially sensitive to the president; (3) the ferret task: of receiving and judging informal, anticipatory information on problems about which cabinet officers are embarrassed or reluctant; and (4) selective intervention where policy changes or crises make necessary a White House monitorship even of operational details. Patterson argues that these are functions unique to a White House staff and that no cabinet officer would be able to perform these functions along with those of heading a cabinet agency.[72]

The presence of a strong White House staff is not without its dangers. There will inevitably by complaints from the cabinet and others that the White House staff is isolating the president and limiting their access to him. These perceptions will persist even though it will often be the president's personal decision not to see a cabinet member. Criticisms of the White House staff will often be intended for the president. The danger is that these complaints will be well founded and that the president may come to depend too heavily on his staff and limit his sources of information.

Presidents must depend heavily on their immediate staffs, but they must maintain a delicate balance between unconditionally supporting them and undermining their decisions. The danger of giving too much rein to White House staffers is that they may claim to be speaking for the president when they are merely pushing their own agendas. This, of course, is what cabinet members often suspect of the White House staff, but it is often too risky for a cabinet secretary to have a showdown to settle the issue. But the danger of a president regularly undercutting the decisions of senior staff is that pretty soon the staff person is seen as a cipher, and all decisions are appealed to the president.

Presidents are also faced with the danger that the chief of staff may take a domineering approach to the job, as did Sherman Adams, H. R. Haldeman, Donald Regan, and John Sununu. Each of these chiefs of staff abused his power while alienating members of Congress, the press, and his own colleagues, and each ended up harming his president. Each of them also resigned in disgrace.[73] Thus every president must appoint a chief of staff who can firmly control the White House staff and operations, but if that person takes a domineering approach to the job, the president will be ill served. Don Rumsfeld, Dick Cheney, Jack Watson, and James Baker have demonstrated that the job can be done with restrained firmness. The conduct of the chief of staff office in the Bush and Clinton administrations will be taken up in Chapters 7 and 8.

2
The Holy Grail of "True" Cabinet Government

During the transition it is important for presidents to set ground rules for the cabinet members' role and the relationship between the White House staff and the cabinet. If it is not clear what is delegated *before* secretaries get settled in their departments, authority may be assumed that is very difficult to call back into the White House. Presidents Nixon and Carter both felt that they had delegated too much to their cabinet secretaries early in their administrations, particularly regarding subcabinet personnel selection. In both cases this proved to be an expensive mistake, when they finally resorted to replacing several cabinet members, as Nixon did after the 1972 elections and Carter did in the summer of 1979.

Every president from Lyndon Johnson to Ronald Reagan came to office promising to give his cabinet a large voice in the running of the government. Nixon began by giving his department secretaries broad leeway in personnel and policy, but ended up drawing tight control into the White House. Ford promised to abandon the domination by a strong White House staff and guaranteed personal access to his cabinet secretaries. Carter promised true cabinet government, but in the end felt he had given away too much power to the cabinet and tried to take it back in the summer of 1979. Reagan promised cabinet government and instituted a system of cabinet councils that worked partially in his first term and was abandoned in his second. George Bush made no promises, yet gave his cabinet secretaries more leeway than his immediate predecessors. Bill Clinton continued the centralizing trend, and conducted most of his administration's initiatives from the White House.

The president's cabinet in the United States has no formal authority or constitutional mandate. The use of his department heads as an advisory "cabinet" was initiated by George Washington and used by his successors to varying degrees as a sounding board or for advice. The term *cabinet government* in the United States means, in general, delegating significant authority to cabinet mem-

34

bers and consulting the cabinet regularly on policy issues. It is not the equivalent of cabinet government in a parliamentary system, in which cabinet members are also members of the legislature and constitute the executive power of the government, subject only to parliamentary votes of "no confidence."[1]

In every administration there is a major tug-of-war over control of administration policy between the cabinet secretaries and the White House staff. John Ehrlichman has observed that presidents begin their terms with strong cabinets and end them with dominant White House staffs. This was certainly true of the Nixon and Carter administrations, but the Eisenhower and Reagan presidencies also began with strong White House staffs. There is no way to avoid a strong White House staff in the modern presidency; the challenge is to see that it does not overwhelm the legitimate prerogatives of the cabinet.

Presidents-elect feel pressure to name their cabinet designates within a month or two of their election. These early appointments are seen as clues to the direction of the new administration. This chapter will examine the uses to which recent presidents have put their cabinets. The emphasis will be on the contrast between the rhetoric of cabinet government and the reality of White House domination. The question of how much "loyalty" to the president can be expected of cabinet secretaries will be examined.

CABINET SECRETARIES: CAUGHT IN THE MIDDLE

Cabinet selection processes and criteria guarantee that members will not be chosen only for their personal and ideological loyalty to the president. Other factors tend to dominate cabinet choices, such as partisan concerns, symbolic statements, policy expertise, management experience, and clientele concerns. A president may want to unify the party or the country after a divisive election campaign and appoint someone from the opposite wing of the party or from the opposition party. He may want to appoint a woman or black, a Jew or Catholic, to demonstrate his commitment to a broadly based administration. Whoever is chosen, the traditional constituency of the department often has a strong say in the nomination or can exercise a veto. James Watt, President Reagan's secretary of interior, was a highly visible exception to this rule. Presidents must also be concerned with the internal management of the departments. An appointee will have difficulties if he or she does not fit into the bureaucratic culture of the agency and is not perceived by its career personnel as a legitimate leader. An appointee with no management experience or skills will also likely have trouble.[2]

Thus the way members of a cabinet are chosen leads us to expect that they will not always see eye to eye with the White House. Once in office, moreover, the cabinet secretary is pulled away from the president by strong centrifugal forces. The duty to carry out the laws and to be responsive to Congress is accentuated by the dependency of cabinet members on the career bureaucracies and the clientele groups of their agencies. Even if a cabinet secretary is an expert in the field of his appointment, only the career staff has the hands-on, nitty-gritty expertise necessary to run the programs. In addition, they have the institutional memory crucial to the new secretary. Thus new departmental secretaries must win over the goodwill of the people whom they will be leading. If they do not, the danger comes not from bureaucratic sabotage, but from the mediocrity of "maintenance management" and the merely carrying out of orders without positive action to support the new secretary.

The support of the career bureaucracy is won by seeming to listen to their collective wisdom whether or not their advice is taken. But it is also won by being seen as a strong advocate of the programs of the department. This advocacy may sometimes be in conflict with the priorities of the White House, and when it is, the cabinet member is caught in a difficult dilemma. He must act in the president's best interests while at the same time convincing his career subordinates that he is sticking up for them. Ironically, a presidential appointee may have to resist the president in the short run to be more effective in the long run. "The paradox is that a president ultimately may be best served by an agency head who is willing to risk occasional presidential displeasure to defend his agency's territory and vital interests. Once he has established his credibility within his agency, he can be much more effective in achieving his own goals and mobilizing support for the president's program."[3]

There is also a natural division between the interests of the president and those of his cabinet appointees because of the nature of their jobs. They are chosen to head departments because they believe in the importance of the department's mission. They thus have a stake in the organizational means to accomplish its mission, that is, their organizational and jurisdictional turf. In order to do their jobs well they must defend their turf against threats, even if the threats sometimes come from the White House. In these squabbles the White House is part of "them," not "us."

This problem came up when the Nixon administration moved to place loyalists in the departments in order to assure White House control. One of those responsible for the placements said: "For the guy to be worth controlling, he has to know what is going on in his department. If he knows what's going on there, he's less likely to be amenable to central control."[4] For a person to be able to be of use to the White House, he must also be trusted and accepted as a defender of the values represented by the agency and its mission. Because the White House must sometimes make decisions affecting the division of missions with other agencies, it is sometimes seen as a threat to the agency.

This is part of the origin of the distrust of the White House found in departments and agencies. John Ehrlichman tells the story of going over to the Commerce Department for a meeting. Arriving a half hour early, he decided to chat with some of the employees in order to get a feel for their jobs and opinions and to introduce himself. After five or ten minutes the undersecretary came rushing in and said: "You can't do this, you've got the whole place terrified. If you need anything from this department, come to my office. I'll get it for you."[5] Of course, any direct intervention by the White House in any department below the secretary level undermines the authority of the secretary and is considered a threat by the department.

Executive branch agencies depend on clientele groups to make their cases before Congress in support of authority and appropriations, and interest groups see agencies as advocates in the government. Cabinet officers consider it part of their duty to maintain friendly liaison with major interest groups so that they can be mobilized to support presidential initiatives when needed. But at the same time they feel that they need to keep some distance. One cabinet officer put it this way: "It may be too strong a statement to say that they regarded us as their advocate. They regarded us as their door. . . . I would say we were the doorway in rather than the real advocate; if persuaded we would be the advocate."[6]

The point of all of this is that managing the cabinet in the U.S. system is a particularly thorny problem for the presidency. On the one hand cabinet members owe their allegiance to the president who appointed them and who can remove them at his pleasure. On the other hand, cabinet members have constitutional duties to the law and to Congress as well as dependencies on the career bureaucracy and their clientele groups. These nonpresidential demands are legitimate claims on the allegiance of cabinet members. Presidents expect loyalty from their cabinet members; but to expect rigid, literal obedience is asking too much from the American separation-of-powers system.

THE EISENHOWER CABINET MODEL

Eisenhower came to office with strong ideas about the way it should be organized that stemmed from his military experience and previous contact with the White House. "For years I had been in frequent contact in the executive office of the White House, and I had certain ideas about the system, or lack of system, under which it operated. With my training in problems involving organization it was inconceivable to me that the work of the White House could not be better systemized than had been the case in the years I observed it."[7] He was also critical of the use to which previous presidents put their cabinet meetings. He told his newly designated cabinet in January 1953: "I have gone there as a specialist to talk about the European problem or a military problem of some kind. Sometimes I have had to sit while the Cabinet, so-called, went through its gyrations, and there is certainly no more charitable word that you could use with respect to what I have seen."[8] So Eisenhower resolved to organize his presidency much more formally than had his two immediate predecessors. He did this through his formal staff system and through the use of his cabinet and the cabinet secretariat.

One factor in Eisenhower's ability to use his cabinet effectively was his choice of personnel, who were mostly successful businessmen ("eight million-aires and a plumber").[9] He felt that the interpersonal aspects of teamwork were important: "In organizing teams, personality is equally important with abil-ity. . . . Leadership is as vital in conference as it is in battle."[10] His initial con-cerns with putting together the right combination of personalities resulted in a cabinet with relatively little of the backbiting, conflicts, or leaks that have marked more recent administrations. Eisenhower used his cabinet by delegating as much as possible to his cabinet secretaries and by using the collective cabinet as a deliberative, though not a decision-making, body.

Eisenhower felt that many decisions were not presidential, and he wanted as many of these as possible made by cabinet members and not brought into the White House. This insulated the president from the details of managing the gov-ernment and may have contributed to the public image that he was detached from his administration. Much of this was deliberate and the result of a con-scious effort to create buffer zones around the president.[11] The main buffer was Sherman Adams, who carefully screened all business going to the Oval Office, including most cabinet members' access to the president. Adams also spent much time trying to get cabinet members to settle interagency disputes before issues went to the president. "I always tried to resolve specific differences on a variety of problems before the issue had to be submitted to the President. Some-times several meetings were necessary before an agreement was reached. But with a few exceptions I was successful." Sometimes he would have to "point out, with emphasis, that a resourceful department head should be able to find an answer himself without expecting the President to find it for him."[12] Eisenhower was careful to preserve as much as possible the public image of the chief of state who was not involved in the seamier aspects of politics or details of man-aging the government.[13] When Press Secretary James Hagerty complained that he would "get hell" from the press if he gave them a certain story, Eisenhower retorted, "My boy, better you than me."[14]

While Eisenhower delegated as much as possible to his cabinet secretaries individually, he wanted to use the cabinet collectively as a deliberative body. As he told his newly selected cabinet before he took office, "My hope will be to make this a policy body, to bring before you and for you to bring up subjects that are worthy of this body as a whole."[15] But he did not intend for the cabinet to be a decision-making body, and Eisenhower did not take votes on issues. In fact many issues had already been decided by the time they were brought before the cabinet.[16]

The cabinet thus served several important functions, though policy making was not one of them. He used it to bring his administration together, to instill the values of teamwork, to sound out his ideas, and to get the administration line out to the troops. In addition the cabinet functioned as a co-opting mechanism. Cabinet members would be more committed to a policy if they had been consulted on it in advance and could feel that their opinions had been considered. They also could think of themselves as statesmen in being asked to consider issues broader than their individual jurisdictions, and they could better defend the position of the administration in more than their own policy areas.[17] On the other hand, the high purposes of cabinet meetings were not always met in practice. Douglas Dillon remembered one meeting: "We sat around looking at the plans for Dulles Airport. They had a model and everything, and we would say why don't you put a door there, and they would explain why they didn't."[18]

Cabinet meetings were relatively formal, with fixed agendas and focused discussions and follow-through. Much of the organization of the cabinet meetings was due to Eisenhower's introduction of the cabinet secretariat in 1954. The function of the cabinet secretariat, as described by Bradley Patterson, who was a member of it, was to circulate cabinet papers prepared by the departments so that they could be considered by members before the meetings and to assure that important matters were included on the agenda. This was not always easy because cabinet members did not necessarily want to air their problems in front of the whole cabinet. "The Cabinet Secretary had to dig, wheedle, persuade and finesse Cabinet members to bring to the common table what were clearly common matters, but which the department heads, in their century-and-a-half-long tradition, would much prefer to bring privately to the Oval Office. It was only because they knew that Eisenhower wanted it this way and no other that they reluctantly acceded to the Cabinet Secretary's or Sherman Adams' agenda-planning."[19]

At the end of each meeting the secretary to the cabinet would make a record of decisions made by the president and would follow up with the departments that were to take any action. Also the secretary to the cabinet would hold a meeting of the cabinet members' designated assistants from the departments to go over the issues and decisions covered at the cabinet meeting. These meetings would be used for follow-through on presidential decisions.

The Eisenhower model of cabinet government is the standard against which future presidents would measure their intentions for the presidency. Kennedy and Johnson consciously reacted against what they thought was too rigid a system. Nixon and Carter, however, both promised delegation and consultation with their cabinets, but were unable to avoid major conflicts between their cabinets and White House staffs. Reagan promised cabinet government and experimented with a system of cabinet councils, an alternative to the Eisenhower model.

THE KENNEDY REACTION

Just as President Kennedy rejected the Sherman Adams model of White House organization, so he also rejected the Eisenhower model of cabinet organization.

Both of these moves were urged on Kennedy by Clark Clifford early after the election.[20] Clifford advised Kennedy to reject the Eisenhower model and characterized it with a bit of overstatement: "Apparently President Eisenhower considered the Cabinet to be in the nature of a corporate Board of Directors. Decisions would be made by the Cabinet and he would carry them out. This is contrary to every basic concept of the Presidency and should be junked. Cabinet meetings were attended by 30 to 40 persons, and as a result were sterile and time consuming."[21]

Richard Neustadt argued against the Eisenhower practice of delegation to cabinet secretaries. In an early transition memorandum he argued that Kennedy ought to ensure that disagreements within the administration be brought to the presidential level for decision by appointing strong cabinet members with conflicting views on public policy. "If the President-elect wants both 'conservative' and 'liberal' advice on economic management, for example, and wants the competition to come out where he can see it and judge it, he needs to choose strong-minded competitors and *he needs to put them in positions of roughly equal institutional power,* so that neither wins the contest at a bureaucratic level too far down for the President to judge it."[22]

While Eisenhower used organizational channels to delegate and keep decisions out of the White House, Kennedy followed Neustadt's advice and drew matters into the White House so that he and his staff could be actively involved in governmental decisdions.[23] He said the presidency ought to be "the vital center of action in our whole scheme of government . . . the President *must* place himself in the very thick of the fight."[24]

Part of this was due to Kennedy's suspicion that the permanent government was not flexible or venturesome enough to be trusted with his New Frontier initiatives. The White House was to be the center of action in his administration. So he did not follow Eisenhower's model in delegating, nor did he follow strictly the chain of command. Instead, he adopted a style of management more similar to that of Franklin Roosevelt. He would ignore the organization chart and deal directly with officials at the subcabinet level. When asked about personal calls to the State Department he replied, "I still do that when I can, because I think there is a great tendency in government to have papers stay on desks too long. . . . After all, the President can't administer a department, but at least he can be a stimulant."[25] According to Sorensen, Kennedy seldom did this, but the few times he did was enough to keep people on their toes.[26]

In line with Kennedy's desire to be personally in charge of the government rather than presiding over the institutions of government, he held few cabinet meetings, preferring to deal with his departmental secretaries one at a time. Kennedy felt "Cabinet meetings are simply useless. Why should the Postmaster General sit there and listen to a discussion of the problems of Laos?"[27] His postmaster general, J. Edward Day, was not quite as enthusiastic about this approach: "For the domestic Cabinet, personal meetings with the President became fewer and farther between, and more than one member grew increasingly unhappy because it was so difficult to see the President."[28] "President Kennedy did not in his campaign promise to do anything with the Cabinet," according to Theodore Sorensen, "and he made good on that promise. He didn't do anything with it. He regarded the Cabinet largely as an anachronism. . . . So he called Cabinet meetings as infrequently as possible . . . and only because he was expected by custom to call them."[29]

Lyndon Johnson, like Kennedy, ran the government from the White House, relying on his White House staff. He held cabinet meetings more regularly than Kennedy but used them as briefing forums rather than as consultative mechanisms. Toward the end of his administration he relied increasingly on those involved with his national security decision-making process, and became distrustful of those outside his immediate circle. He told President-elect Nixon when they met at the White House in December 1968: "Let me tell you, Dick, I would have been a damn fool to have discussed major decisions with the full Cabinet present, because I knew that if I said something in the morning, you could sure as hell bet it would appear in the afternoon papers."[30]

NIXON'S DISILLUSIONMENT

Richard Nixon began his administration with the intention of reversing the personalized White House control of the government that had developed in the Kennedy-Johnson years and returning to a cabinet-centered government. He intended to concentrate his efforts as president on foreign affairs and delegate domestic policy to his cabinet. "I've always thought this country could run itself domestically without a President. All you need is a competent cabinet to run the country at home. You need a President for foreign policy."[31]

At a meeting of his newly designated cabinet members the day after he presented them on television, he exhorted them to seize control of their departments and not cave in to the bureaucrats. It sounded as if he intended to let them run their departments with a minimum of White House interference.[32] At one of the first cabinet meetings in 1969 he delegated to his cabinet secretaries authority to choose their own subordinates based on the criteria of ability first and loyalty second.[33] In the beginning he had the general notion that the cabinet would serve a collegial and advisory function, but soon changed to view secretaries primarily as managers of their departments.[34]

According to John Ehrlichman, Nixon was either quite optimistic or naive. But disillusionment soon set in. Nixon believed "all these wonderful guys would help him and all he would do is take the 'big plays.' But it doesn't work that way. The news summary comes in and Wally Hickel has been putting his foot in his mouth. You can't give these guys carte blanche."[35] After only a few weeks into the administration, Nixon began to reverse his earlier stance on delegation and give orders to his cabinet secretaries through his White House staff. For instance, Nixon would mark up his daily news summary and have Ehrlichman call up Robert Finch at HEW to give him his marching orders. According to Ehrlichman, they would be quite specific orders: "Bob you can't do this. Do this. You can't do this anymore. Stand up. Sit down."[36]

The main driving force behind Nixon's concern with his cabinet's behavior was his reelection. "As time passed, it appeared that whenever discretion was granted to the Secretaries they failed to do things the way Richard Nixon wanted them done. Since Nixon was the one who had to go back to the people after four years, to explain why things had gone as they did, he reacted to their 'failures' by retaining almost all of the discretion. . . . If he had to pay the political price for his Cabinet Secretaries' mistakes, then he, by God, had the right and obligation to correct those mistakes."[37] Nixon came to view cabinet meetings as virtually useless. At one White House meeting he said: "We'll have no more unstructured Cabinet meetings. There'll be no hair-down political talk with those people. . . . We'll have a one-hour Cabinet meeting every two weeks, at which I intend to say less."[38] Nixon's view of cabinet meetings was mirrored by some of his cabinet members. Elliot Richardson recalled that "in the Nixon Cabinet, as a special treat, Vice President Spiro T. Agnew would occasionally give us a travelogue."[39]

If Nixon was disappointed in his cabinet, the feeling was often mutual. Members of the cabinet often felt that they did not have enough direct access to the president and that he was overly insulated by his White House staff. Some of them complained, even publicly, of their lack of access, including John Volpe, Walter Hickel, and Budget Director Robert Mayo. According to Jeb Stuart Magruder, they were not all wrong.

> From our perspective in the White House, the cabinet officials were useful spokesmen when we wanted to push a particular line—on Cambodia, on Carswell, or whatever. From their perspective, however, it was often a rude awakening to have Jeb Magruder or Chuck Colson calling up and announcing, "Mr. Secretary, we're sending over this speech that we'd like you to deliver." But that was how it was. Virtually all the cabinet members had to accept that they lacked access to the president and that their dealings would be with Haldeman and his various minions.[40]

Because of this there was constant friction between cabinet members and the White House staff. According to John Ehrlichman, "He kept reminding us that he was the one who had to run for reelection. Eventually the Cabinet became show-and-tell sessions, and we set up working groups which dealt with the White House staff."[41]

Nixon took three steps to deal with the unacceptable situation: he relied more heavily on his White House staff, particularly H. R. Haldeman; he juggled his cabinet to appoint members with greater loyalty to himself; and he attempted to reorganize the executive branch in order to make it more responsive to the president.

The day after his landslide victory over George McGovern, Nixon convened a meeting of his senior staff. After a few words about the mandate from the voters, he left the room, turning the meeting over to H. R. Haldeman. Haldeman told the group:

> As the president has indicated, some things are going to change around here. . . . Now, the President and I are meeting with the cabinet shortly. We are going to direct them to obtain letters of resignation from all appointed sub-Cabinet officers in the government and submit them along with their own resignations. And the President has directed that everyone in this room also hand in a letter of resignation. This doesn't mean that you won't be asked to stay on, of course. We will review each situation individually. We just want to show we mean business.[42]

Several of the resignations were accepted and the cabinet was redesigned. Political scientist Nelson Polsby has observed that Nixon's first cabinet was made up of men who were politically diverse and who enjoyed independent political status of their own. In contrast, his second cabinet was dominated by those "with no independent public standing and no constituencies of their own."[43] The purpose, of course, was to make the cabinet more responsive to the White House and less responsive to the deparments' constituencies and to Congress.

In addition to personnel changes, Nixon wanted to reorganize the executive branch in a major way. Based on a report by the Ash Commission, he intended to replace the constituency-oriented Departments of Agriculture, Labor, Commerce, and Transportation with four goal-oriented departments: Community Development, Natural Resources, Human Resources, and Economic Affairs.[44] In addition, he wanted to limit access to the president to five assistants and have three counselors (for Human Resources, Natural Resources, and Community Development) report to them. The result would give the White House staff effective control over the whole government and limit the cabinet secretaries to a ministerial role with no direct access to the president. By this time, however, the Watergate revelations were beginning to break, and the plan was abandoned.

Nixon was thwarted in his early intentions to use his cabinet as a collegial body and to delegate much of the management of the government to them while he reserved himself for the "big plays." Failing to achieve his domestic agenda and frustrated by a Democratic Congress, he resorted to the tools of the administrative presidency to achieve his goals.[45] He impounded unprecedented amounts of funds that had been provided for domestic programs by law.[46] He took military actions in Southeast Asia without consulting or informing Congress. He tried to undermine the Civil Service system by using political clearances and placing Nixon loyalists throughout the career bureaucracy.[47] And he tried to reorganize the executive branch by making its upper levels subordinate to a super-cabinet of White House aides as described above.

How did Nixon arrive at these solutions to many of the same frustrations that plague most presidents? Richard Neustadt argues that the Nixon administration response resulted from the lack of constitutional tradition among his aides. They thought the president had the sole right and duty to run the government. "Nixon's aides sought only to preserve his interests as they understood them. Knowing nothing of Rooseveltian distinctions—how could they—these men perceived no difference between White House and Executive Office or, indeed, between their President and the Executive branch. . . . They thought the Constitution's 'take-care' clause made him a general manager as though ours were a unitary government with powers hierarchical, not shared."[48] While presidents expect loyalty from their appointees in the executive branch, compelling pressures from clientele groups and the career bureaucracy are inevitable. In addition, Congress is jealous of its constitutional duty to set governmental policy.

PRESIDENT FORD'S OPEN PRESIDENCY

President Ford, who took office with the intention of ridding the country of the Watergate specter, organized his administration to provide a sharp contrast with the Nixon administration. His transition team recommended that Ford return to a larger cabinet role in presidential decision making and reject the Nixon pattern of gathering power in the White House, with its staff acting as intermediaries between the president and cabinet secretaries."[49]

While President Ford was not successful in running the White House without a chief of staff, he was able to return collegiality to the cabinet. He was always accessible to cabinet members. According to Richard Cheney, "Nobody ever screens out a cabinet member. The president will always be told so and so wants to see him."[50] Unlimited accessibility, however, is not an unmixed blessing. According to one Nixon holdover, "Ford sees everyone in sight. One of the difficulties we encountered during the transition was that there were so many players."[51] Ford was also quite accessible to members of Congress, his recent colleagues. Too many of them thought of him as "good old Jerry" and felt comfortable giving him the benefit of their own wisdom.

Ford began to use the cabinet as a collegial forum and presided over monthly meetings. As with previous presidents, Ford did not use his cabinet as a decision-making body, but as a forum for exchanging information and deliberating about issues. According to Richard Cheney:

Nixon was not one who liked extensive policy debates with large numbers of people. He liked to work off paper. He liked to consult with one or two individuals but never with a group. . . . Under President Ford, it is a very different situation. When there is a major decision to make, he likes to get everyone in the room so you may end up with 15 or 20 people sitting around the cabinet table.[52]

Despite Ford's accessibility and his reactivation of the cabinet as a delibera-tive body, his administration did experience conflict between the cabinet and his White House staff. But the problems were not as great as the ones that plagued the Nixon or the Carter presidencies. According to Richard Cheney, "By the end we hardly ever met with the Cabinet as a group."[53]

The Ford administration created the Economic Policy Board, a cabinet and White House staff standing committee that operated as the central forum for the administration's foreign and domestic economic policy. It met over 500 times during the Ford administration and was one of the most systematic advisory structures created in the White House to advise the president in a broad area of domestic policy. The EPB was to serve as a model for the cabinet council system developed by the Reagan administration, and its executive secretary, Roger Porter, was brought into the Reagan administration to help install it.[54]

JIMMY CARTER'S CABINET GOVERNMENT

Jimmy Carter's vision for his presidency was formed in reaction against what he saw as the abuses of the Nixon administration. Carter would have no chief of staff, and he would rely heavily on his cabinet and remain accessible to them. In meetings with his newly designated cabinet members in Georgia during the Christmas holidays in 1976, Carter explained that he wanted to "restore the Cabi-net to its proper role as the President's first circle of advisers."[55] Carter wanted to be his own chief of staff on the Kennedy and Roosevelt model and refused to designate a chief of staff. He would be the hub at the center of the wheel, and all White House staff members would report to him.

His cabinet would advise him and have access to him. "I believe in Cabinet administration of our government. There will never be an instance while I am President when the members of the White House staff dominate or act in a supe-rior position to the members of our Cabinet."[56] Like Nixon before him, he initially intended to delegate much domestic policy making to his cabinet. Hamilton Jor-dan, his principal adviser, said: "The problem is too many presidents have tried to deal with all of the problems of the country from the White House. The first line of offense or defense is the Cabinet. That's where the problems should be dealt with, in the departments and agencies. You can't do it all from the White House."[57]

Thus Carter let his cabinet appointees choose their own subordinates on the theory that they should be able to put together their own management teams. While this pleased cabinet members, it was objected to by some of his White House staff, and particularly by members of Congress who wanted to have patronage appointments made. They had supported Carter during the campaign and the transition and were owed some favors. But when they called the White House they were told to talk to the departmental secretaries upon whom they had much less claim.

Carter's early cabinet meetings were useful as an introduction of the new members to each other and as a means of getting information out. Each secretary would be asked to report on the past week and what would likely come up the next week in their areas of responsibility. But after a year or so of this type of meeting, often without an agenda, attendees began to tire of them. Hamilton Jordan said they were a "waste of time."[58] Secretary of Commerce Juanita Kreps said: "The Cabinet meetings are fairly useless."[59]

Cabinet meetings were not used for decision making, and tough problems were discussed in smaller meetings with the president.[60] According to Carter a collegial approach to problem solving is more useful with a small number of people who are directly concerned with the problem at hand. "A President's time is too precious to waste on many bull sessions among those who have little to contribute."[61] Stuart Eizenstat reports that because of this, "At first Carter held Cabinet sessions every week, then every two weeks, then they tended to disintegrate into show-and-tell sessions."[62]

Well into the second year of the administration, the cabinet meetings began to decrease in number and signs of tension between the cabinet and White House staff began to arise. Some White House staff members thought the experiment with cabinet government was ill-advised. According to one, "It was one of his biggest mistakes. Carter was naive about how the government works. He really believes all this stuff. He is an optimist and an idealist when it comes to working with people. He doesn't think people are evil or capable of disloyalty. In effect, he trusts people too much." Another said: "All of our problems are aggravated by the so-called 'cabinet government' efforts. . . . People took it too literally—including the White House staff. But you can't run a government that way—from 10 different locations."[63] White House staff members thought that cabinet members were disloyal in advocating policies at variance with White House wishes. Joseph Califano opposed creation of the Department of Education. Michael Blumenthal felt tax reform should be more limited than White House proposals. Other cabinet members felt their own programs were more important than the president's promise of a balanced budget. Friction between White House staff and in cabinet increased.

Cabinet members, as might be expected, had a different perspective on the administration's problems. They felt their own authority was undermined by leaks from the White House and reports that the president was displeased with their performance. They complained that White House staff members seldom returned their phone calls.[64] Patricia Harris argued that it was not disloyalty to disagree with the White House staff before a final decision had been made by the president on what the policy of the administration was to be. Communicating with the White House staff, she said, could be improved by "putting phones in the White House staff offices and the staff using them."[65]

The friction between the Carter White House and cabinet came to a head in the spring and summer of 1979 when Carter decided that something had to be done. The White House staff felt there was no discipline in the administration and that Carter had to take charge forcefully. The experiment with cabinet government and spokes-of-the-wheel organization had not worked. According to Jack Watson, the president was not feared enough in his administration. Robert Bergland, Carter's secretary of agriculture, said, "The time has come to crack some political heads. You're not breaking enough arms."[66]

To respond to these concerns, Carter went to Camp David in July 1979 to consult with advisers and prominent people from around the country. When he came back he had decided to name Hamilton Jordan to be chief of staff. He announced to the cabinet at a meeting that he was told that they were not working for him but for themselves and that he was going to make some changes. He demanded written resignations from each member of the cabinet. Despite objections that this would seem too much like President Nixon's demand for resignations in 1972, he went forward with it and told them he wanted them to fill out evaluation forms on their immediate subordinates to evaluate their loyalty to the administration.

The resignations were dutifully turned in and Carter accepted five of them. When accepting Califano's Carter explained it was due to friction with the White House staff. "Your performance as Secretary has been outstanding. . . . You've been the best Secretary of HEW. The Department has never been better managed. . . . The problem is the friction with the White House staff. The same qualities and drive and managerial ability that make you such a superb Secretary create problems with the White House staff."[67]

REAGAN'S CABINET COUNCILS

Ronald Reagan came to office with a remarkably coherent agenda and set of policy priorities. His priorities to increase defense spending significantly and cut spending on virtually all domestic policy areas lent themselves to a narrow focus and simple set of values for his administration. This set of priorities was a litmus test in recruiting personnel for the administration. Personal and ideological loyally were the primary criteria for appointees.[68] The coherence of values led to an administration with much more unity than has marked recent administrations with more disparate policy agendas and more varied personnel.

Reagan also came to office with the notion that he wanted his administration to employ some form of cabinet government. Delegating significant authority to the cabinet fit well into his style of leadership and consciously departed from President Carter's tendency to become embroiled in the details of decisions. What Reagan did *not* intend, however, was to delegate to cabinet secretaries authority over their budgets or selection of personnel.

Initial budget decisions were made by the White House staff and David Stockman. Except for Defense, most agencies' budgets included significant cuts, and newly designated cabinet members were brought into the White House to sign off on them. In a meeting with Stockman, the president, and several White House aides, they were given a chance to react to the proposed cuts, but it was difficult because "they're in the position of having to argue against the group line. And the group line is cut, cut, cut," according to David Stockman's account.[69] The newly designated secretaries were at an added disadvantage because they did not have their management teams together and had not yet had a chance to know their career executives. "We had brow-beaten the cabinet, one by one, into accepting the cuts. It was divide-and-conquer, not roundtabling."[70]

The Reagan White House felt that Carter and Nixon had lost the personnel battle to their cabinet secretaries and worked hard to keep tight control of sub-cabinet appointments in the White House. They were successful, and the Reagan administration kept closer control of personnel than any other recent administration. The slowness of the appointment process resulted in many delays in appointing the subcabinet. This early lack of personnel put the new secretaries at an added disadvantage in challenging the White House staff, if they had wanted to.

Given this tight White House control of the budget, personnel, and the legislative agenda, how could the Reagan system be considered cabinet government? Edwin Meese explained that the "cabinet concept" intended that cabinet members would be the president's principal advisers and that they would not be undercut by other members of the White House staff. He further explained that President Reagan had an eighteen-member cabinet: the heads of major departments as well as Meese as counselor to the president, the directors of OMB and Central Intelligence, the U.S. Trade Representative, and the U.S. representative to the United Nations.[71] "The President . . . has direct access to, and depends upon, his Cabinet as his principal policy advisers, rather than his staff," according to Meese.[72]

Meese explained that no major administration decision was made without at least one member of the cabinet present, and this ensured that the president would have input from the cabinet. This is an expansive concept of cabinet government that corresponded with Reagan's expanded cabinet membership. But the tight Reagan White House control of administration policy and its legislative agenda was a far cry from previous attempts at cabinet government, whether Eisenhower's, Nixon's (first term), or Carter's.

The new White House staff very consciously and systematically used the transition period to impress on the administration the importance of the central agenda. According to one participant:

> In the early days—December '80 and January '81—what we did was we had a group of people which consisted of Ed Meese, Jim Baker, Marty Anderson and Dave Stockman. We sat these four at one end of the table. We had the cabinet-appointees-to-be paraded in with whomever they wanted to bring and put them at the other side of the table. And we handed them a list of things we wanted to do and suggested that they give at the office. That was a process where every item was fought out line by line. They had not seen their natives yet. And we were extraordinarily successful in our track record.[73]

In addition, the administration's early agenda was dominated by the economic priorities of the budget and tax cuts, which were engineered by David Stockman and OMB. According to one participant: "So, the early cabinet meetings were Stockman, on behalf of the president, and the other presidential advisers just laying out, 'Here's what we're going to do fellows, and I expect you to support it'. . . . The Cabinet met often . . . but just to receive their marching orders and to hype each other up."[74]

During the transition period and early days of the administration, Alexander Haig began to suspect signs of White House domination of the cabinet. When the cabinet designates met on January 7, 1981, Ed Meese dominated the meeting, giving a primer on the president's ideas, procedures, and priorities, while Reagan sat passively.[75] This feeling was later reinforced when Meese did not give to the president Haig's carefully negotiated delineation of roles in the foreign policy field put into writing as NSDD1. Haig recalls that he had "the distinct feeling that Ed Meese and his colleagues perceived their rank in the Administration as being superior to that of any member of the cabinet."[76] At the first cabinet meeting Meese and Baker were sitting at the cabinet table in sharp contrast with previous practice. Haig wrote in his notes of that meeting: "Government by Cabinet or troika?"[77]

Initially Meese had intended to structure White House cabinet relations as Reagan had in California with a small "super cabinet" that would preside over the administration. It would include the "inner Cabinet" secretaries of state, defense, treasury, and justice and four top White House staff members. This body would act as a board of directors that would operate with the president as chairman.[78]

This idea, however, was rejected by James Baker and others as unworkable in the national government, and the structure of cabinet councils was agreed upon. The idea was based on President Ford's experience with the Economic Policy Board, the first effective standing cabinet committee in the domestic area.

Porter, who had written a book on his experience with the EPB entitled *Presidential Decision Making,*[79] was brought in from the Treasury Department to help put together the cabinet council system and to be executive secretary of the Cabinet Council on Economic Affairs.[80]

The creation of five cabinet councils was announced by the White House on February 26, 1981: Economic Affairs (CCEA), Commerce and Trade (CCCT), Human Resources (CCHR), Natural Resources and Environment (CCNRE), and Food and Agriculture (CCFA). The following year the Cabinet Council on Legal Policy (CCLP) and the Cabinet Council on Management and Administration (CCMA) were added. The purpose of the councils according to the White House was to act as a "means for deliberate consideration of major policy issues which affect the interests of more than one department or agency."[81]

The aim of the cabinet councils was to provide forums for cabinet participation and deliberation on issues that cut across the cabinet departments while excluding secretaries whose jurisdictions had nothing to do with the policies being considered. They also were to provide for interaction and integration of cabinet views with those of the White House staff and to avoid the strains that had marked so many earlier administrations. The system would also allow second-level policy issues to be dealt with below the presidential level and would help keep the focus of the administration on the central Reagan agenda. The cabinet councils were to be the focus of a policy network that integrated both cabinet and White House resources and input.

The cabinet councils were all formally chaired by the president with a designated cabinet-level chairman pro tempore and six to eleven members, with meetings open to all cabinet members. Council activities were coordinated by the Office of Policy Development and the Office of Cabinet Affairs. They were supported by executive secretaries, and functioned with interdepartmental working groups.

The most active was the CCEA, which met 271 times in the first term, with the next busiest being the CCCT with 91 meetings and CCNR with 66. The least active was the CCLP, which met only 15 times.[82] The president attended about 15 percent of the meetings, and the councils often initiated issues to consider, not waiting for presidential initiation.[83] The meetings were held in the Roosevelt Room, across from the Oval Office.

During Reagan's first term the cabinet council system worked well as a means of getting cabinet and White House input and developing issue analysis in an orderly way, though as has been pointed out, the councils themselves enjoyed varying success. Such a system entails certain prerequisites for it to accomplish its coordinating goals.[84] First of all, there has to be a commitment by the White House and the cabinet to play by the rule, the main rule being that issues are not to be brought up to the president on a bilateral basis, but that all issues are to be "roundtabled" by discussing them at a cabinet council meeting.

Each cabinet member's policy proposals are to be subjected to the scrutiny and criticism of cabinet peers and White House staff members.

Thus the White House staff might have to guard the president from being lobbied unilaterally by a cabinet member. Of course, this will be perceived by the cabinet member as the White House staff barring the cabinet from access to the president. Secondly, the president must reject attempts by cabinet members to induce him to make decisions outside of the structure. If all members of the cabinet have confidence in the integrity of the process, they will be less likely to try to end-run it by going to the president privately. As one member of the Reagan administration said:

> As long as they know that the president doesn't want to hear from them or their colleagues independently or in private sessions, they know they've got to play this game and do what they might otherwise resist. That is, expose themselves to arguments against their point of view from their colleagues . . . we just don't make time on his schedule for people to come in and privately review matters with him or lobby him on some issues. . . . If they happen to do it, during a photo opportunity or some other thing . . . he's not at all reluctant to turn to me and say, "We've got to get this on the agenda." At that point the integrity of the process is protected, the cabinet officer is satisfied that he's raised the issue, and we have a forum for dealing with it.[85]

This type of process will only work in an atmosphere of reasonable mutual trust, which seemed to mark the first-term Reagan cabinet (with the exception of Alexander Haig). It is hard to imagine how it could have worked in other administrations that suffered from backbiting and competition among cabinet members and the White House staff.

But the system is not without its problems. The system can be finessed by cabinet members in several ways. The "lead agency" in a policy area can go charging head on its own without submitting issues to the process, claiming it has jurisdiction and exemption from bringing it through the council system. Or an agency can use the excuse of confidentiality or national security and argue that roundtabling the issues poses too great a danger of leaks. While these tactics will always be used, the success of the system depends on keeping their use within commonly accepted limits. One other problem with the system is that it can suppress conflict by putting the norm of cordiality above the need for thorough criticism of ideas. Also, the presence of the president at a council meeting can sharply cut criticism; whichever department has its issue on the agenda can escape tough challenges to its position.[86]

Alexander Haig criticized the system, arguing that it led to domination by the White House staff. It was not clear, he contends, whether an issue was brought up for council consideration at presidential initiation or at the whim of a staffer. He says there was no guarantee that the president would see the results of a council deliberation. He was also disturbed that the secretary of state was not included on the Food and Agriculture Council inasmuch as the grain embargo and other agricultural issues had important foreign policy implications. "In practice, the chairmanship went to the Cabinet officer with the strongest vested interest in the subject at hand, an efficient method for setting the fox among the chickens and producing solutions that were politically loaded in favor of the major domestic vested interest concerned."[87]

These comments on the cabinet council system reflected Haig's criticisms of Reagan White House relations with the cabinet. Haig felt that he was denied access to the president by the White House staff, who had too much anonymous and unscrutinized power.

> But to me the White House was as mysterious as a ghost ship; you heard the creak of the rigging and the groan of the timbers and sometimes even glimpsed the crew on deck. But which of the crew had the helm? Was it Meese, was it Baker, was it someone else? It was impossible to know for sure.[88]

In President Reagan's second term there were major changes of personnel and structure. Virtually the full cabinet changed hands, and many of the top White House staff positions turned over. The structure of White House organization shifted from the troika to a tight hierarchy headed by Donald Regan. The elaborate cabinet council system with its support system collapsed of its own weight. In theory, the seven councils were to be replaced by two major policy councils: the Domestic Policy Council, headed by Attorney General Edwin Meese; and the Economic Policy Council, headed by Treasury Secretary James Baker.

The dual roles of Meese and Baker had the potential to give them major influence across the full range of domestic policy development, but Regan's domination of the White House policy apparatus and personnel did not allow that to happen. The Domestic Policy Council met only once in the first six months of the second term and had no executive secretary in the White House. The Economic Policy Council met five times in the first six months, but was not used as the vehicle for some key policy deliberations, such as early development of the administration's tax reform proposals.[89]

As in the first term, many of the most important decisions were not made through the cabinet council apparatus. In the first term major administration strategy was set by the Legislative Strategy Group dominated by Baker, Darman, and Stockman, who often ignored cabinet council decisions.

A similar pattern continued during the second term with the cabinet councils on economic and domestic policy continuing to operate, but ignored at important decision points. Baker resisted council involvement in his initiatives involving tax reform, international debt, and international exchange rates. Edwin Meese avoided the cabinet council system in seeking changes in the affirmative action requirements for federal contractors.[90] Donald Regan maintained tight control of other policy matters and of access to the president.

So the Cabinet councils fulfilled the useful functions of allowing for interaction among cabinet members concerned with the same policy areas and for the development of many policies up to a certain point. But some important policies continued to elude the council system, and major presidential aides could ignore or end-run the system.

WHAT HAVE WE LEARNED?

Presidential experience over the past several decades has taught us several lessons about cabinet government in the United States. We know that there will inevitably be conflicts between the cabinet and the White House staff; it is inherent in their differing functions. The challenge is to foster a dynamic tension rather than letting things degenerate into a destructive hostility. This can be done if each side recognizes the legitimate functions of the other side. It is particularly important that White House aides recognize that the legitimate, constitutional roles of cabinet members, along with profound political pressures, give them perspectives not always in line with those of the White House. As the Carter presidency taught us, legitimate pressures must be used to extract loyalty and coherence from the cabinet. But as the Nixon presidency demonstrated, expecting a rigid discipline and subordination to the White House is unrealistic and harmful.

It is important to move quickly with the major priorities of the administration. One of Nixon's top policy aides argued:

> Everything depends on what you do in program formulation during the first six or seven months. I have watched three presidencies and I am increasingly convinced of that. Time goes by so fast. During the first six months or so, the White House staff is not hated by the cabinet, there is a period of friendship and cooperation and excitement. . . . After that, after priorities are set, and after a president finds he doesn't have to talk with cabinet members, that's when the problems set in, and the White House aides close off access to cabinet members and others.[91]

Early cabinet meetings are important so that members can get acquainted with each other and take each other's measure. They are useful for distributing information and letting people know what the party line is and for developing a team spirit. They are particularly important for keeping the focus on the central agenda and encouraging new cabinet members to keep the White House perspective in mind. Thus it is useful to have cabinet meetings often early in the administration. Later it is harder to keep people's attention, and they feel they have too many important things to do to listen to issues that are of secondary importance to their own duties.

A newly elected president can take certain steps to establish cordial relations between the cabinet and White House staff. They have to do with personnel, early actions and meetings, and organizational structures. The president-elect can recruit cabinet members who can get along with each other and will not be threatened by the White House staff. Eisenhower consciously tried to do this and largely succeeded. In most presidencies, however, cabinet choices are based upon many factors, with personal compatibility often a minor consideration.

The president does exert control over the agenda of the initial days of his transition and administration. One of the lessons learned is that it helps to set the ground rules early. Bowman Cutter, who played important roles in the Carter and Clinton administrations, argues that the president should have a "set speech" to give to every new cabinet member. This speech should spell out the role that cabinet members are expected to play with respect to the White House staff, OMB, and any important issues the administration is expected to be faced with. He argues that this is hard because after the election victory everyone is in a state of euphoria and any critical thinking about organization is apt to be lost. Lack of clarity of role and jurisdiction leads to turf battles that are wasteful and divisive.[92] John Ehrlichman argues that ground rules must be set before the cabinet member gets settled in the new post, because trying to get power back once it is perceived to be delegated is "like pulling teeth." It is also crucial that the president sit in on the meetings personally to let the cabinet members know it is coming from him and not merely the White House staff.[93]

The Reagan administration learned this lesson well from their predecessors and clearly set out the expectations of the White House for cabinet members with respect to budget and personnel matters. This was one of the reasons that the Reagan administration was less troubled by cabinet conflicts than were the Nixon and Carter administrations.

Another thing new administrations can do is to set up some kind of structure to facilitate the implementation of the president's agenda without causing a rift between cabinet and White House staff. There are several precedents here. The first is the Eisenhower model of using cabinet meetings as deliberative sessions, but few presidents since then have been successful to the extent that he was in this. A second approach, also established by Eisenhower, is the establishment of a cabinet secretariat that ensures that all issues are staffed out with input from any department that has a legitimate stake in the issue. The secretariat can also be used to ensure that any presidential decisions are implemented.

The cabinet council system is another structure for managing relations and trying to prevent a gap from growing between the cabinet and the staff. President Reagan's experiment with the cabinet council system was only partially successful. Seven separate councils are probably just too many for the system to bear. The three-council system of Reagan's second term—National Security, Economic Policy, Domestic Policy—seemed to be a more manageable structure.

The lesson of the Reagan experience with the cabinet council system may be that no policy apparatus can process all important issues. Those individuals in the White House or cabinet who are determined, persuasive, and skillful will be able to achieve their goals in spite of any system.[94] This does not mean that policy development systems are futile or irrelevant. It merely means that no single system can contain all of the policy situations and personalities likely to be present in the White House.

In order for a White House to operate well, there must be an intermediate level of structure that imposes some discipline and process on the development of policy. But if it is to be successful, such a system cannot create so rigid a hierarchy that the special claims of major White House and cabinet members are ignored. If it does, it will quickly become irrelevant. On the other hand, the lack of any policy development structure at all will result in chaos and will leave the president at the mercy of entrepreneurial members of the administration.[95]

3
Personnel Control: Staffing the Administration

"Every time I make an appointment I create nine enemies and one ingrate," lamented President Taft. President Lincoln continually felt hounded by office seekers, and President Garfield was assassinated by one. Presidential appointment politics are still marked by such pressures, but the volume and complexity of the task have increased greatly in the modern presidency. According to Pendleton James, President Reagan's director of personnel recruiting, "The appointment process is a mine field that I tiptoed through daily, and sometimes, I stepped on one of the mines. . . . There's no way my job wins friends and influences people."[1] According to John Ehrlichman, "There isn't any good way to handle the job."[2]

THE INITIAL ONSLAUGHT

On the surface, making the personnel appointments for a new administration would seem to be a dream job. The president-elect's personnel staff is fresh from the flush of victory and is charged with the job of dividing up the spoils of victory. There are many plums to hand out and a chance to help mold the president's team. But as each new administration learns the hard way, the task is often a thankless one, and sometimes it seems impossible. One political appointee characterized the process: "We telescope what in a rational world would be a month's if not year-long process for how you would staff up a business half of one percent the size of the Federal Government. We just throw people at it."[3]

The need to move quickly is made impossible by the staggering number of appointments that have to be made. While in England and France, with their parliamentary governments, a newly elected government may change 50 to 500 positions, the U.S. government has more than 5,000 positions that can be filled with political appointees.[4] The volume of applicants for the positions is daunting; in recent administrations 1,500 résumés and recommendations poured in every day.[5]

Each incoming administration has the authority to appoint a number of officials who are responsible for formulating, directing, and advancing administration policies, or who serve in a confidential relationship to policy makers. These appointees are members of the "excepted service" in that they serve at the pleasure of the president and are not subject to the merit system requirements of the Civil Service. The top cabinet and subcabinet positions (including independent agencies and regulatory commissions) number over 650. The president also appoints about 165 ambassadors, 187 U.S. attorneys and marshals, and more than 400 people who work in the White House.[6]

Ten percent of the Senior Executive Service, about 700 of 7,000, are non-career members, that is, political appointees. The option is also available to appoint a number of "limited term" or "limited emergency" Senior Executives. Finally, there are Schedule C positions, about 1,700 in number, at the GS (General Schedule) 15 level and below. Schedule C duties include policy-determining responsibilities or a confidential relationship to key officials. All of the above officials supervise the career Civil Service, both the General Schedule (GS 1–15) and career SES members.

Each election year the House Committee on Post Office and Civil Service publishes *Policy and Supporting Positions*. It is known as the "Plum Book" because its cover was once plum colored, but more to the point, because it lists all of the "political plums" available to the incoming administration. It lists by agency each administration incumbent by name, position, and salary. During every transition there is a scramble for this publication because it identifies those positions the new administration can fill and the names of the political appointees who must leave.[7]

More imposing than the number of positions that must be filled is the volume of demands that pour into the administration soon after the election: "That avalanche, that onslaught at the beginning, that tidal-wave of people coming from all over the country, who've been with a candidate for years, and who have been waiting for this chance to come in and help."[8] There is no quality control on the incoming flood of applicants for jobs, and presidents need to recruit their administrations from a much broader pool than this self-selected lot. While many national politicians feel they know enough people throughout the country to fill many positions, no one person can handle this volume. John Kennedy recognized this when he faced the task of filling his administration. "I thought I knew everybody and it turned out I only knew a few politicians."[9] His problem as he saw it was: "I must make the appointments now; a year hence I will know who I really want to appoint."[10]

Cooperation between the incoming and outgoing administrations is strained when there is a party turnover of the presidency, and those who have just won the election usually do not take advantage of the experience of the previous administration. Dan Fenn recalls ironically, "We were a little bit hubristic—our impression was that there wasn't an awful lot that they could do for us that we couldn't do for ourselves. . . . To us, at least, it was perfectly clear that presidents over two hundred years of American history had screwed everything up. The last thing we wanted to do was to pay the least bit of attention to the terrible Eisenhower administration."[11] The lack of institutional memory and the unwillingness to learn from one's predecessors have not been mitigated until recently by careful preparation for the personnel task by presidential candidates.

The importance of the timeliness of appointments to the success of a presidency should not be underestimated. During a transition of the presidency the permanent career bureaucracy continues to operate the government. But the governmental machinery is in neutral gear. Routine operation will go on without many problems, but new directions in policy making will not be undertaken. Leadership is required that can only be provided by the appointees of a new president. The longer the bureaucracy drifts, the longer it will be before the new president's priorities and policies can be implemented.

But the necessity for speed must not dilute the need for quality of appointees, for the character of an administration and its success depend upon the quality of its officials. In addition, mistakes in other areas can be mitigated by the quality of appointees. According to Theodore Sorensen, personnel is "clearly the highest priority. You can't spend too much time on personnel . . . the key is getting the right people in office. That will overcome many errors in organization and getting to know the Congress."[12]

HEADHUNTERS AND RECRUITMENT SYSTEMS

Dan Fenn, who was hired to run John Kennedy's personnel operation in 1961, observed that the traditional system of recruitment for executives in presidential administrations is "BOGSAT": "a bunch of guys sitting around a table saying, 'whom do you know?' "[13] Early in the administration the Kennedy people had created what was called the "talent hunt," which was divided into two distinct functions. The political side, headed by Larry O'Brien, was concerned with finding jobs in the administration for those people who had supported the candidate during the election. The other side tried to identify the positions that could be filled by the new administration and then find candidates who would be appropriate to fill them.

Under Fenn, the Kennedy administration set up the beginnings of a White House personnel system that was much more systematic than it had been in the past. When Fenn joined the Kennedy administration in June of 1961 he decided that "we were going to be in the recruiting business and not in the screening business. We were not going to be just going through the junk that was coming in over the transom."[14] His process tried to assure that the White House would have the final authority for all major presidential appointments throughout the administration. It also tried to set up a capacity for active outreach and recruiting of qualified candidates who were not personal acquaintances of administration members.[15]

Lyndon Johnson also had a two-tier personnel process. The first was a formal executive recruitment system run by John Macy. Macy was at the same time the chairman of the Civil Service Commission, which had the responsibility of staffing the executive branch with career personnel on merit principles. His approach to recruiting political appointees began with identifying a position to be filled and then searching for a person with the right qualifications to fill it. The second tier was "based on a shifting constellation of personal relationships among Johnson, his White House aides, and his numerous confidants outside the executive branch and often outside the government as well."[16] Despite the importance of the second tier, the Johnson personnel operation was a much more formal process than Kennedy's had been, and Johnson made primary use of Macy's process.

What marked the Johnson personnel operation, in contrast to those of President Eisenhower and Nixon, was the personal involvement of the president. According to John Macy, Johnson "was deeply involved in a large number of appointments. He had a fantastic memory, and he could recall some detail on a summary that we would send him, months and months afterwards, and would frequently enjoy challenging me on whether I could remember as well as he could what those particular details were."[17]

Though the Nixon campaign had not done much preparation for taking office, shortly after the election a large personnel recruitment operation was set up under Harry S. Flemming. In line with Nixon's intention to hire the best people from the broadest possible pool, Flemming sent out a mailing to those listed in *Who's Who in America* soliciting names of candidates for jobs in the Nixon administration. The mailing resulted in an avalanche of paper of dubious quality that inundated Flemming's personnel operation. John Ehrlichman recalls: "I can remember going down to see Flemming's operation, and I worked my way through a room with boxes and boxes of paper, and there was Harry—beleaguered."[18] After the inauguration the personnel operation was taken over by Peter Flanigan, who had about fifteen people in the operation that eventually employed sixty people.

In 1970 Frederick Malek was brought in to tighten up the personnel selection process. Malek recommended the centralization of all administration personnel operations in the White House Personnel Operation. When he took over the personnel office he felt that "the shop that they had there was more a political screening shop as opposed to a recruiting shop. . . . The first thing I felt we needed to do was to go way beyond the screening. They had no outreach capability."[19] Under Malek's direction the WHPO developed a recruitment capability and a systematic way to continue personnel replacement throughout the administration.

Unfortunately, the WHPO also tried to control appointments in the career Civil Service through a political clearance process. "During the period 1969 to 1973 political considerations assumed prime importance in connection with providing preferential treatment to certain candidates for career positions. Political influence was exerted principally from the White House Personnel Operation through a network of centrally controlled 'Special Referral Units' operated in various executive departments and agencies completely outside the normal personnel channels."[20] While other administrations had committed similar abuses in placing political pressures on the career system, this effort was much more systematic, and included the active involvement of the Civil Service Commission.[21]

Jimmy Carter's personnel operation began in the summer of 1976 in Atlanta, Georgia, when Jule Sugarman and Jack Watson formed the Policy Planning Group and began to plan the Carter administration transition into office. The personnel portion of the operation was known as the "Talent Inventory Program," or TIP. The TIP operation in Atlanta collected thousands of résumés from around the country and began to match them with appropriate positions in the new administration.[22] It was a delicate situation that had to keep an extremely low profile in order not to make Carter seem presumptuous of victory or to alienate factions of the party that might think they were being ignored.[23]

The TIP search covered the gamut of positions for the new administration, including the cabinet secretaries. Candidate files ranged from the sublime to the ridiculous, which was one of the problems with the personnel operation. A lot of time was spent on cabinet positions, but cabinet appointments include important political and symbolic considerations that can only be judged by the president-elect and his closest advisers. A transition group can compile lists of candidates for subcabinet positions, but only the president-elect can make the trade-offs that must be weighed in selecting the cabinet.

The Policy Planning Group's personnel operation ran into trouble when a rift developed between the transition planners and the campaigners. The campaigners, headed by Hamilton Jordan, were spending their time winning the election while the transition team, headed by Watson, was planning the takeover of the government. There was little contact or coordination between the two groups, both because it was not built into the organizational apparatus and because the campaign had its hands full trying to win. As a result friction developed between Watson's and Jordan's staff members; each began to see the other group as "them" instead of as part of "us." Watson said he saw the rift unfolding as a "Greek tragedy," but the pressure of the campaign did not allow a reconciliation before the election.[24]

After the election Jordan began to set up his own personnel selection process with the conviction that the Watson effort did not pay enough attention to practical politics.[25] As a result of the rift, a lot of time was lost immediately after the election as Jordan asserted his primacy; the parallel personnel systems also resulted in lost time and effort. In the end the TIP files were used, and many of the eventual appointees had been included, though it is not clear that they were appointed as a result of the TIP operation.

Jack Watson concluded in retrospect that the operation involved a lot of "wheel spinning," and that if he were to do it again he would scale down the numbers and focus on fewer positions. "We spent an enormous amount of time on that; it was not productive time."[26] Harrison Wellford, who worked for Watson, felt that real screening of candidates is not possible before the election because it creates too many jealousies, but that you can do background research and do "tiering of appointments."[27]

The Reagan administration "undertook transition personnel selection with more forethought, with a larger commitment of resources, and with more systematic attention to detail than any administration in the post-war period, perhaps more than any administration ever."[28] Pendleton James was asked by Edwin Meese in April 1980 to set up a personnel operation for the Reagan administration. The administration demonstrated the importance it placed on staffing the Reagan presidency when James was appointed to an Executive Level II position in the White House, and the personnel operation was headquartered in the West Wing, both firsts in the postwar presidency.[29]

President Reagan's cabinet selections were made in consultation with his "kitchen cabinet," a group of Reagan's close friends and political associates. James worked with the kitchen cabinet on the cabinet appointments, but took over most of the work on the subcabinet appointments. The Reagan administration resolved that it would not make the mistakes of earlier presidencies and lose control of its personnel appointments, but that close control of all appointments at all levels would come from the White House.

In order to do this they set up an elaborate clearance procedure to be followed in appointing personnel. Each nomination had to run a formidable gauntlet running from the cabinet secretary and the personnel office to Lyn Nofziger (political clearance), to White House counsel Fred Fielding (conflict of interest), to either Martin Anderson (domestic) or Richard Allen (national security), to the triad (James Baker, Michael Deaver, Edwin Meese), to the congressional liaison office, and finally to the president himself.[30]

This screening process assured that each candidate would be thoroughly examined and that all important officials would have a chance to exercise a veto. But because of the clearance process and ideological battles over candidates, there were delays in staffing the administration.[31] Complaints came from the Hill that officials who should have been available to testify on administration programs were not yet appointed. There were complaints from the administration that the few top officials on board were spending all of their time testifying on the Hill. And there were complaints from the career bureaucracy that essential program leadership was missing, resulting in policy drift and inefficiency.

Pendleton James continued to deny that the pace of appointments was particularly slow and maintained that quality of personnel was more important than speed. Despite administration claims that it was making major appointments faster than Presidents Carter and Kennedy, the *National Journal* reported that after ten weeks Reagan had submitted to the Senate 95, as opposed to Carter's 142, nominations.[32] *Time* magazine calculated that, as of the first week in May, of the top 400 officials only 55 percent had been announced, 35 percent formally nominated, and 21 percent actually confirmed.[33] The Reagan administration was distinguished by the carefulness of its clearance processes and the percentage of its appointees to which that clearance process applied. Even lower-level Schedule C appointments, customarily left to the discretion of agency heads, had to be cleared through the White House.

Although the slow pace of appointments was disruptive in many ways, some administration officials saw the silver lining, or found virtue in necessity. They argued that the lack of appointees made it very difficult for agencies to resist the severe budget cuts that the White House was advocating.[34] While the slowness of appointments may have helped the President's budget program, it did little to facilitate the transition in the administration of the executive branch.

The major focus of the president's personnel office should not be on the seekers but on the sought. As important as it is to stay on top of the flood of job applicants and recommendations and to respond to requests from the Hill, the president's programs and reputation will depend on the quality of the top-level managers who will administer the government. The White House personnel office must actively go out and get the best candidates that it can. If a system to do this is not in place immediately after the election, the new administration may find itself burdened with appointees of poor quality who will be difficult to fire. The problem is that the best people are not always bringing themselves to the attention to the White House.

The institutional capability of the White House personnel office to conduct active recruitment and outreach has developed greatly since the early 1960s. The recruiting that Dan Fenn was doing with three people, Frederick Malek was doing with twenty-five to thirty, and William Walker with thirty-seven or thirty-eight. In 1981 Pendleton James had 100 people on his staff to recruit for the Reagan administration.[35] The rank and access of the president's chief personnel person has also increased, with James holding the title of assistant to the president (Executive Level II) and having an office in the West Wing of the White House. But the professionalism and competence of the White House personnel office can only be put to good use if it has the support of the president. Presidential leadership is important because the president's priorities in personnel selection need to be accurately communicated to the recruiters.

CRITERIA FOR SELECTION: WHAT KIND OF LOYALTY?

There is no formula for choosing the best person for any given job in an administration. Loyalty, of course, is a prerequisite, but there are different types of loyalty: personal, ideological, partisan. Competence is important, but there are different indicators of competence. Previous experience may be an indicator, but should it be government experience or private-sector work? Does it have to be in line management, or will staff experience do? Expertise can come from a variety of sources: trade groups, the legal profession, academia, business, or nonprofit organizations.

One of the surest sources of loyalty to the president-elect is the presidential campaign. Every candidate will have a few senior aides who are professionals with political and governmental experience. But these people are expensive, and only a few will be able to leave their careers for a risky political campaign. So much of the campaign will be staffed with loyal though inexperienced people. Stuart Eizenstat argued that "there are an inordinate number of incompetent people in any campaign; who can take two years off for a campaign?"[36] The answer is: people just starting their careers who do not have family responsibilities. These people make dedicated campaign workers, but may not have the maturity or experience to perform well in high-level government positions.

All presidents rightfully insist on loyalty in their senior staff and lower levels in their administrations. But loyalty comes in different shades, in different degrees, and the criteria may change during the course of an administration. Lyndon Johnson defined loyalty in a personalized way: "I don't want loyalty. I want *loyalty*. I want him to kiss my ass in Macy's window at high noon and tell me it smells like roses. I want his pecker in my pocket."[37] But Johnson's definition of loyalty changed as his administration developed. After his election, he perceived loyalty as commitment to the Great Society programs, but as opposition to the Vietnam War grew in intensity the definition shifted to mean those who backed Johnson over his critics. During the latter phase of his presidency the Macy personnel operation with its emphasis on professional competence came to be overshadowed by Marvin Watson, who recruited people loyal to the president's Vietnam policies.[38] Similarly, toward the end of the Nixon administration when concerns about Watergate began to dominate, personnel selection shifted more toward patronage concerns, particularly those who might help on Capitol Hill.[39]

One obvious measure of loyalty is active membership in the political party to which the president belongs. While it is true that presidents fill most of the positions in their administrations with the party faithful, some presidents are more stringent than others about partisan loyalty. Nixon, for instance, mindful of his narrow election victory, tried to bring several prominent Democrats into his administration: Hubert Humphrey and Henry Jackson, as well as John Connelly and Patrick Moynihan, who did join the administration.[40] John Kennedy appointed Republican Douglas Dillon to head the Treasury. Usually at the sub-cabinet level there are professional experts from the other party that cabinet members want for certain posts because of their expertise. They usually have to fight presidential aides who are worrying about patronage and reactions from party stalwarts on the Hill. The Reagan administration was very strict in not allowing Democrats to carry over from the Carter administration. They also included career civil servants in their definition of those to be "thrust out" of policy positions.

One indicator of competence is previous experience in the government. Experience in large organizations in the private sector can also be valuable in being able to step into a high administration post and get up to speed quickly. However, experience in the private sector, while providing a valuable source of new ideas and management expertise, does not necessarily provide experience directly related to heading a large governmental agency. President Nixon's OMB Director Roy Ash, who had formerly been the head of Litton Industries, observed that the public sector was difficult for private-sector executives to adjust to: "It's not like going from the minor leagues to the major leagues in baseball. It's like going from softball to ice hockey.[41]

Pendleton James, with his experience as head of a private-sector "headhunting" (executive search) firm, sought out candidates for positions who had proven track records who would be loyal to the administration. "We had five criteria all along—compatibility with the President's philosophy, integrity, toughness, competence, and being a team player."[42] James, who had worked in the personnel operations of the Nixon and Ford administrations, naturally found many competent people among those who had served in previous Republican administrations. The problem with them, from the perspective of the Republican right wing, was that some of them had not supported Ronald Reagan soon enough. Eisenhower, in contrast, did not even bother to check whether a prospective employee had supported him at the Republican Convention in 1952.[43]

In late January and February 1981 conservative right-wing supporters of Reagan's candidacy began to complain vociferously that Reagan campaigners were being systematically excluded from the personnel selection process. John Lofton, in the February issue of the *Conservative Digest,* claimed that the Reagan administration was being filled with "retreads" from the Ford and Nixon administrations and called for James to be fired. Declared Lofton: "There will be no Reaganism without Reaganites."[44]

The person carrying the conservative banner on the inside was Lyn Nofziger, who ran White House political operations. He met regularly with conservative groups, and in March 1981 told the president that conservatives were being frozen out of his administration. His criteria for administration personnel differed significantly from those of James. He felt the personnel process should root out not only Democrats, but also Republicans who in the past had supported other candidates than Reagan. "I have problems with them. This, damn it, is a

Reagan Administration."[45] Notziger's conception of competence also differed somewhat from that of James: "We have told members of the Cabinet we expect them to help us place people who are competent. . . . As far as I'm concerned, anyone who supported Reagan is competent."[46] He also had a list of six criteria for appointments in the administration. Number 6 was: "6. Are you the best qualified person for the job? But that's only Number 6."[47]

Due to Nofziger's efforts and pressure from conservative groups, the appointments process took a turn to the right in February 1981, at least enough to mollify right-wing critics.[48] James's deputy was replaced by John S. Herrington, who was more acceptable to the right-wing interest groups. It is important to note that President Reagan staffed the top levels of his White House with competent and politically experienced people; notable among whom was James Baker, who had headed George Bush's campaign in 1980. It was over subcabinet appointments that most of the ideological battles within the White House took place. The overall result of Reagan's personnel selection process was an administration staffed with officials selected more systematically for their ideological loyalty to the president than any other recent administration.

It is inevitable in all administrations that there will be friction between those concerned with the president's political interests and those primarily concerned with managing programs. In the real world, each candidate must be matched with each position on an ad hoc basis, and seldom can both loyalty and competence be maximized in one person. There is no formula for combining the several qualities included in competence and loyalty. John Macy gives a sense of the trade-offs involved:

> If there was a vacancy as Assistant Secretary of Commerce [for example] it wasn't enough to see whether or not there was some kind of statutory prescription for that particular job. It was a matter of having that and then looking at the job in the context of that particular department at that particular time. What did the chemistry need to be with the secretary? What was important in that particular position? Was it effectiveness in dealing with Congress on legislation? Was it effectiveness in answering interrogation about a particular problem that has come up? Was it a matter of gaining support among interest groups? Was it the need for a high degree of professional specialization in a particular field? Was it need for someone who had a strong administrative background?[49]

APPOINTING THE SUBCABINET: WHO DECIDES?

In every administration there will be friction between the White House and cabinet departments and agencies over whose wishes will prevail in naming the immediate subordinates of the secretary or agency head. While the appointments are clearly the legal prerogatives of the president, the agency head has a legitimate claim on them as well. On the one hand, it is the president's administration, and he has to live with the consequences of his appointments in the departments and agencies. But on the other hand, if agency heads are to be held responsible for managing their own organizations, they ought to have some discretion in putting together their own management teams.

Many people with White House experience tend to believe that subcabinet appointees should owe their primary allegiance to the president and not to the cabinet member for whom they directly work. They see a danger that appointees will become more responsive to their own bureaucracies, interest groups, and Congress than to the White House; a process John Ehrlichman called "marrying the natives." They feel the White House should, at the very least, clear the nominees, hold a veto prerogative, and name the nominee in cases of importance to the president. Some White House staffers, however, are less adamant than others. Jack Watson, President Carter's chief of staff, felt that the president must have "considerable control," but "you cannot dictate to people like Cyrus Vance; it would not work, and if it did, it would be counterproductive."[50] Theodore Sorensen recommended that "superiors should always be selected before, and consulted on, their subordinates," though President Kennedy did not always follow this dictum."[51]

The perspective of people who have worked in the departments and agencies, as might be expected, is often different. They recognize the legitimate interest of the White House in staffing the administration, but they are suspicious of the motives of the White House staff; they suspect that the president's personnel office may be more interested in placing people with powerful sponsors than in placing people with the management expertise to run the agency. The questions of building a management team and interpersonal chemistry are also of direct concern to agency heads, but of less concern to the White House.

Frank Carlucci, after a long career as a presidential appointee and career bureaucrat, advises: "Spend most of your time at the outset focusing on the personnel system. Get your appointees in place, have your own political personnel person, because the first clash you will have is with the White House personnel office. And I don't care whether it is a Republican or a Democrat. And if you don't get your own people in place, you are going to end up being a one-armed paper hanger."[52]

Being able to select your own management team is crucial to doing a good job, according to Graham Claytor, deputy secretary of defense for President Carter: "We had an absolutely first-class team, every one of whom was picked by Harold Brown, Charlie Duncan and me jointly. Had it been done in the way Reagan did it, or the way that Carter would have done it after he got organized, we would have had a lousy team. We would have had a bunch of stooges who represented some constituency that some politico thought important. That's the way it's usually done and that's a disaster."[53] John Gardner, secretary of HEW from 1965 to 1968, said that President Johnson gave him virtually carte blanche in his choice of subordinates. On the other hand, when he appointed somebody the president was not enthusiastic about, Johnson would chide Gardner: "John here thinks I'm smart enough to pick him for Secretary but not smart enough to pick any of his people."[54]

In a study of assistant secretary appointments in the Truman, Eisenhower, and Kennedy administration, Dean Mann concluded that the selection of assistant secretaries was "a highly decentralized and personalized process revolving around the respective department and agency heads."[55] The study reported that the president was relatively inactive in the assistant secretary appointments and that the selections were dominated by department heads. "Where the secretary and White House staff conflicted over an appointment, the secretary generally won."[56] While the normal amount of internal administration friction between White House and cabinet priorities went on during these administrations, these presidents did not express major reservations about delegating many of their subcabinet selections to their cabinet appointees.

The same cannot be said of Presidents Nixon and Carter, both of whom felt that they gave too much discretion to their department heads in personnel matters at the outset of their administrations. President Nixon, at an early cabinet meeting, announced that appointment authority would be vested in the cabinet. Immediately after making his announcement he turned to an aide and said: "I just made a big mistake."[57] H. R. Haldeman wanted to control the appointments process more closely, but was not able to stay on top of it. "It just happened by inertia; we just had too much to do. Flemming was not strong enough to control it."[58] But Harry Flemming had a tough job since the president had already given away the authority. Once the authority is perceived to be delegated to the departments, getting it back is "like pulling teeth," according to John Ehrlichman.[59]

Jimmy Carter's version of cabinet government entailed delegating most subcabinet appointments to cabinet secretaries. When Carter gave Joseph Califano at HEW discretion to choose his whole management team, Staurt Eizenstat concluded, "That's the whole ballgame."[60] The president had intended to have a system of mutual veto, but the White House seldom exercised its side of the veto.[61] When Arnie Miller took over the personnel operation for President Carter in 1978 he observed: "The President had given away the store for the first two years. He thought that appointments were appropriately the responsibility of cabinet members. He then realized that this was a mistake and asked us to come in and try to take that power back."[62]

The Reagan administration decided that the Carter and Nixon delegations of appointment authority to cabinet members were mistakes that it would not repeat. "Nixon, like Carter, lost the appointments process," declared Pendleton James.[63] This time it would be different, "The president has to decide right off the bat," said Edwin Meese, "that there will be one central control point. And that while you encourage department heads to develop names, the ultimate approval is to be that of the president."[64]

It was inevitable that such an approach would cause some friction. At the highest levels of power the stakes are high and some egos are fragile. Those secretaries that were strongest had the best chance to win the disputed cases. Alexander Haig got his choices (with the exception of the White House choice of William Clark for his deputy) through the White House personnel process, if not through the Senate, with dispatch.[65] Defense Secretary Caspar Weinberger is reported to have prompted the resignation of a White House personnel staffer by saying "I will not accept any more recommendations from the White House, so don't bother sending them."[66] But these were exceptions in the Reagan administration.

In addition to the immediate subcabinet appointments, assistant secretary and above, there are many lower-level appointments at the discretion of an administration. These include the 700 noncareer Senior Executive Service positions and 1,700 Schedule C positions. Several issues are involved in deciding how much control the White House should exert on these positions, although SES and Schedule C appointments are technically agency head, rather than presidential appointments. One question is *should* the White House attempt to control these appointments rather than delegate them to the officials who are closer to the needs of the agency? The other question is *can* the White House make these appointments effectively, or are the numbers of appointments just too large for the White House to handle?

Dan Fenn explained that the Kennedy White House did not control any appointments under the assistant secretary level, and they did not do Schedule Cs.[67] As a matter of management principle he felt that the agencies and departments ought to be able to choose the lower levels of their noncareer appointees. Pendleton James stated the Reagan administration principle: "We handled all the appointments: boards, commissions, Schedule C's, ambassadorships, judgeships . . . we made a concerted effort in the planning stages at the very beginning before we became an administration, that if you are going to run the government, you've got to control the people that come into it."[68] Frederick Malek felt that there were dangers of going as far as the Reagan administration in White House control of appointments: "I think I leaned more in the direction of Dan's [Fenn] philosophy. . . . If you try to do everything, I'm not so sure you can succeed . . . if you try to do too much, you may be diluted to the point where you're not as effective."[69]

The Reagan administration represents the polar extreme in the direction of complete White House control of appointments at all levels. This was the culmination of a four-decade trend of deeper penetration by the White House of departmental noncareer appointments. Elliot Richardson is critical of the deep level of White House control over appointments. "There didn't used to be anything like the degree of control exercised by the White House over presidential appointments. . . . I think this [the Reagan] administration has tried to cut too deep into the system by turning jobs traditionally held by career people over to appointees. The price paid is I think significant . . . the lower the level job the less attractive it may appear to one coming from the outside. . . . This administration is full of turkeys who have undercut the quality of public service in their areas."[70]

While there is no "correct" level of White House personnel control, a modus vivendi must be worked out between the White House and the departments and agencies. It might be a mutual veto system. What is important is that the White House clearly set out the ground rules at the beginning of an administration about which appointments it will make, which are a matter of negotiation, and which it will delegate to departments.

CREATIVE PATRONAGE

On November 22, 1963, a man from Dallas sent a letter to Lyndon Johnson. The letter began: "My dear Mr. Vice-President: In a very short while, you will become the President of the United States. I am hurrying to direct this letter to you before you assume the duties of that illustrious office. My Private Secretary, [name], has been desirous of working for you for many months—even years." The letter concluded: "I think he would make the President of the United States the kind of personal secretary he should have. I urge your consideration of his qualifications."[71] One might think that the assassination of a president would slow the pressure for patronage, but apparently it did not in this case. The letter was clearly dictated in the short time between President Kennedy's death and the swearing-in of Lyndon Johnson.

After every election there are tremendous pressures for patronage (sometimes referred to as "jobs for slobs"), that is, rewarding the party faithful with government positions. The purpose is not only to reward people for previous work, but also to ensure that the government is staffed with advocates of the new president's priorities. The whole presidential appointment system is based on the premise that a new president is entitled to have his own choice of people to run the government at its top levels. The usual connotation of patronage, and the one being used here, is the appointment of people for political, rather than management, reasons. Such people are sometimes referred to pejoratively as "political hacks."

From the perspective of a new president's personnel operations, pressures for patronage can be very frustrating. Everybody, it seems, wants to ride the president's coattails into office; and recommendations for specific placements come from all sides: the campaign, the political party, self-initiated job seekers, and most powerfully, from Congress. If a president-elect's transition operation does not have in place a system to handle this deluge the day after the election, it will be swamped with demands and will be at risk of losing control of the appointments process. The demands for patronage can never be completely satisfied. The trick is to use patronage in legitimate ways for political gain and to deflect patronage pressures when they threaten to undermine your ability to manage the government.

The pressures for patronage begin in earnest immediately after the election. According to Pendleton James, "The House and State Republicans just start cramming people down your throat. Then the [White House] political office wants to find places for all the campaign workers. The collision is sometimes horrendous to behold."[72] After the election of President Nixon, Senator Robert Dole complained that the administration was not making enough room for congressionally backed candidates for positions. He sarcastically proposed that congressional Republicans include the line in letters of recommendation to the White House: "Even though Zilch is a Republican, he's highly qualified for the job."[73]

President Carter also was criticized for not appointing enough Democratic campaign workers in 1977. Loud complaints came from Congress, and the Democratic National Committee even passed a resolution chiding Carter for not consulting enough with state officials about administration appointments.[74] Carter described the pressure for appointments: "The constant press of making lesser appointments was a real headache. Even more than for Cabinet posts, I would be inundated with recommendations from every conceivable source. Cabinet officers, members of Congress, governors and other officials, my key political supporters around the nation, my own staff, family and friends, would all rush forward with proposals and fight to the last minute for their candidates."[75]

Not all pressures for patronage are illegitimate; but they are inevitable, and new administrations must be prepared to deal with them. There are several ways to deflect these pressures when confronted with candidates you do not want to hire. According to Frederick Malek, the best defense is a good offense. If the White House has a capable personnel system, there will be explicit job qualifications for each position. This may immediately eliminate Senator X's favorite nephew. Even better insurance is to have ready a list of candidates eminently qualified for the position.[76] Another way to deflect undue pressure from the Hill is to put a congressional ally in charge of coordinating all requests for appointments from Congress to help absorb some of the disappointment that is sure to result from candidates not being appointed.

One of the major functions of the White House personnel recruitment operation is to buffer the president from patronage pressures. When an important politician makes a personal request of the president to consider a favorite candidate for a position, the president can say that all requests are being handled through the personnel system. Lyndon Johnson used John Macy's political personnel operation in this way. When he was pressured for patronage appointments, he would say, "I am doing this through the merit route." And when someone was displeased with a particular appointment he would say, "Don't blame me. It's that goddamn Macy—he insists on merit."[77] Of course, in order to do this, the president must consistently back his personnel operation, because if he lets it be bypassed too often, it will soon lose much of its usefulness to him.

Often pressures for patronage can be deflected in a low-key, but proper, manner. John Ehrlichman argued that many demands for patronage from Congress could be handled by letting them know that you were giving the nominee a fair shake and were seriously considering their candidate. "Most congressmen don't expect you to appoint their guy. They expect to be protected so they can say he was seriously considered." This demands a personnel and liaison system that can respond quickly and appropriately to inquiries from the Hill. But Frederick Malek argued that it's not always that easy: "You've got to get back to those ten members of Congress and explain to them why their candidate didn't get it. You can't just say, 'Sorry Charlie.'"[78] The problem, then, is separating the serious "musts" from the courtesy calls. John Macy argued, "It's important to have a face-to-face discussion with the alleged sponsor. I frequently found he wasn't the sponsor at all. It was somebody using his name"[79]

Another path to follow if the proffered candidate is someone that should be placed, but there is no obvious program or management slot, is to have the person named to an honorary commission or committee. Transition teams can also be used for this purpose, though this is likely to create expectations that a more permanent job will be forthcoming after the inauguration, whether the person is qualified or not.

Finally, Schedule C positions, which are generally thought of as traditional patronage slots, can be used for "must" placements. Schedule C positions were created after President Eisenhower was elected, because he felt that he would have a difficult time gaining full support for his policies from a bureaucracy that had spent the past two decades under Democratic administrations.[80] The slots are supposed to be confidential or involve advocacy of administration policy, and they can be filled at the discretion of the agency head. In January 1977 the Civil Service Commission approved a rule allowing agencies to increase their allotted Schedule C positions by 25 percent for 120 days "in order to facilitate the orderly transition of duties as a consequence of a change in Presidential Administration."[81] On June 16, 1981, Donald Devine, director of the Office of Personnel Management, authorized extension of the period for another 120 days for the Reagan administration, "since a number of key political officials have not yet been appointed to federal agencies, thereby continuing the transition period for the new Administration."[82] Thus there is precedent for keeping on these additional patronage appointees for the first eight months of a new administration. At the Senior Executive Service level administrations can use Limited Term or Limited Emergency appointments for those they feel they must appoint, but do not want to appoint to permanent positions with the administration.

WHAT HAVE WE LEARNED?

Experience with the presidential appointments process has taught us some lessons. First of all, a quick start is desirable, and this means some work has to be done before the election. This work must be low-key and discreet. It should be concerned with compiling lists of candidates for subcabinet positions and should not waste time on recommendations for members of the cabinet. This transition operation must be coordinated with the campaign organization, and the presidential candidate should assure that rivalries do not impair the transition into office.

Tensions between the White House staff and cabinet secretaries over naming subcabinet members is to be expected. The White House should be sympathetic to the team-building needs of department heads, and cabinet members should be sensitive to the political needs of the president. The president should establish early in the transition that the White House has primacy in choosing the subcabinet, but it should exercise this prerogative sparingly. The mutual veto ideal is a useful target for cooperation.

A new administration must expect that patronage pressures will be fierce. It should use patronage to its political advantage, and deflect those demands it does not want to accommodate. The best defense is an effective recruitment system that has job qualifications and prospective candidates ready. A member of Congress as a patronage coordinator is a useful buffer, and all requests from important politicians should be handled appropriately and with dispatch.

The best way to ensure that the personnel operation accurately reflects the president-elect's values is active involvement on the part of the president. Because of other transition pressures, the president cannot be involved in most appointments, but he should set the tone for the operation and make his criteria for appointments clear to the personnel office. Its director, in order to be effective, must have the confidence of, and access to, the president.[83]

Finally, although loyalty to the president is the sine qua non of presidential appointments, that loyalty should not be construed too narrowly. A president will be remembered in history more by the accomplishments of his administration than by the ideological purity of his appointments. Expertise, experience, and competence should be given appropriate weight in the selection of personnel. There is a dynamic balance, for which there is no formula, between management and politics. "Attention only to personnel management is bad politics; attention only to politics is bad management."[84]

4
Presidential Control of the Bureaucracy

Most presidents take office with an abiding distrust of the bureaucracy that constitutes the executive branch of government they will be heading. They may even have come to believe the antibureaucrat and antigovernment rhetoric that helped them get elected. Such attacks play well in Peoria because they strike a popular chord; everyone has a bureaucratic horror story and has been slighted by some minor bureaucrat. Combine this with many insecure people's need to believe that some faceless "them" controls their fate, and you have a potent political appeal.

This potent political tactic, however, may become a liability when the candidate has actually won the election and becomes the leader of all those "faceless bureaucrats." Expectations tend to become self-fulfilling prophesies; distrust and suspicion toward the career bureaucracy are mirrored back toward the administration. But the president is now dependent on the bureaucracy to implement his campaign promises, even if those promises include cutting back the bureaucracy.

Despite the conventional wisdom that "the bureaucracy" wields unchallenged power in Washington and will undermine a new administration, the frustration of presidential desires is more often due to opposition from interest groups, Congress, and the president's own appointees than from the career bureaucracy. Further, the same political appointees who are so suspicious at the beginning of an administration experience a "cycle of accommodation" with career appointees and gradually come to appreciate their essential contribution to managing the government.

Any delay in the takeover of the executive branch bureaucracy will necessarily result in delays in the implementation of policies and programs. The focus of this chapter will be on how a new administration can gain control of the administrative apparatus as quickly as possible and avoid some of the many pitfalls and land mines of bureaucratic Washington.

RECENT PRESIDENTS: SUSPICION AND HOSTILITY

When Dwight Eisenhower came to office after two decades of Democratic rule, there was a feeling that the bureaucracy was filled with civil servants committed to New Deal policies and that the president needed more of his own appointees than merely those at the top of departments and agencies. Thus Schedule C positions were created to let him put his own people in positions below the GS 16 level. These positions were to be confidential or policy-making in nature, made at agency head discretion, and not subject to the usual Civil Service requirements.

John Kennedy campaigned on the promise to get the country moving again. He thought the career bureaucracy might be too committed to slow, bureaucratic routines and wondered if it was vigorous enough for the New Frontier. This view led Kennedy to draw policy making into the White House and act through temporary task forces that could move quickly and ignore bureaucratic rules and red tape. He wanted to draw decision making into the White House and not have bureaucratic disputes settled before he had a chance to make his decision. Kennedy, according to Theodore Sorensen, "paid little attention to organization charts and chains of command which diluted and distributed his authority. . . . He relied instead on informal meetings and direct contacts—on personal White House staff, the Budget Bureau and *ad hoc* task forces . . ."[1]

Richard Nixon came to office with a legendary distrust of and hostility toward the bureaucracy. "One of our most important tasks would be to place our stamp on the federal bureaucracy as quickly and as firmly as we possibly could."[2] To Nixon, the bureaucracy consisted of "dug-in establishmentarians fighting for the status quo." "I think it is repugnant to the American system that only the bureaucratic elite at the top of the heap in Washington [believes it] knows what is best for the people."[3]

The primary example of bureaucratic sabotage cited by Nixon and Haldeman is the failure of the IRS to audit the tax returns of prominent Democrats. Haldeman wrote: "By 1971 Nixon had realized he was virtually powerless to deal with the bureaucracy in every department of the government. It was no contest. Nixon could rave and rant. Civil servants, almost all liberal Democrats, would thumb their noses at him. . . . As far as civil servants are concerned, every Republican administration is a transient phenomenon of no lasting importance."[4] He believed that the Eisenhower administration had not been thorough enough in throwing out the Democrats and did not want to make the same mistake.[5]

"If there was any campaign advantage to incumbency," Nixon argued, "it had to be access to government information on one's opponents. . . . Even now it frustrates me to think that our efforts to gain whatever political advantage we could from being in power were so tentative and feeble and amateurish in comparison to the Democrats'. . . . It is ironic that when we were out of office they really used to crucify us—now that we are in office they still do, due to the fact that the bureaucrats at the lower level are all with them."[6]

After repeated attempts to get the IRS to check up on George McGovern's key staff and campaign contributors, the White House drew a blank.[7] Ironically, the person who put his foot down on using the IRS to audit the political enemies of the president was George Shultz, Nixon's secretary of the treasury, who earned the White House epithet of "candy-ass" for his scruples. Shultz backed the professional judgment of the career employees of the IRS that such White House demands were improper. When asked for more examples of bureaucratic sabotage or foot dragging, H. R. Haldeman replied: "I really can't give you specific examples. I can simply assure you they are countless. It happened every day."[8] As a result of this initial distrust, the Nixon administration never worked very closely with the career bureaucracy, and the administration was marked by a mutual distrust.[9]

Because of its frustration in trying to get its initial legislative proposals through the Democratic Congress, the Nixon administration decided to adopt an administrative strategy.[10] Part of this strategy was to set up a "counterbureaucracy" in the White House centered around the Domestic Council and the National Security Council.[11] Subcabinet working groups were set up in the White House to deal with policy initiatives, sometimes with the exclusion of cabinet secretaries.[12] Impoundment of funds was used systematically to achieve what the congressional budget process would not yield.[13] A fundamental reorganization of the executive branch was proposed, and the Civil Service Commission was manipulated to place Nixon loyalists in career positions.[14]

Jimmy Carter, running for the presidency as a self-avowed outsider, was very critical of the Washington establishment. In a statement to the Democratic Platform Committee he said: "Our government in Washington now is a horrible bureaucratic mess. . . . We must give top priority to a drastic and thorough reorganization of the Federal bureaucracy."[15] He argued that his experience as governor of Georgia would enable him to deal with the Congress, and he promised to reorganize the bureaucracy and install zero-based budgeting as he had done in Georgia. In a statement that his staff came to regret, he promised to reduce the number of agencies in the government from 1,900 to 200.

Many in the Carter campaign reflected the morally superior attitude of their president and saw the career bureaucracy as symptomatic of the old-style establishmentarian politics that bred the imperial presidency and Watergate. While Carter's cabinet included some of the same establishment figures that had been criticized in the campaign, the second- and third-level appointments included those who were contemptuous of the career service.

One highly respected career executive with experience in OMB and other agencies told of one of the Carter appointees coming into a meeting early in the administration and saying, "We hate you guys." These Carter appointees came to do battle with the bureaucratic behemoth. The senior executive said that later in the administration, after working with the bureaucracy for several years, the political appointee came back and apologized to him for his earlier statement.[16] James Sundquist illustrates this attitude with another example: "The top career person in one large bureau tells of entering the office of the bureau chief—a small-business man from a southern state, new in town—and being greeted with, 'I hate it every time I see you walk through that door because you represent everything I despise most—the bureaucracy.' "[17]

Candidate Reagan was even more of an outsider than Carter had been. He had a long record of harsh criticism of the federal government and promised that if he were elected there would be no more "business as usual." Government, he said, was part of the problem, not the solution. he promised to "get the government off of our backs" and severely cut back domestic programs and agencies.

In addition to strict White House control of political personnel, the Reagan administration imposed a highly visible hiring freeze upon career employees immediately after inauguration and later made it retroactive to the election. This freeze, combined with reductions in force and lowered personnel ceilings, reduced domestic employees in the government by 92,000 between 1981 and 1983, though domestic cuts were offset by increases in defense personnel.[18]

The Reagan administration took other steps to assert its control over the bureaucracy. The president fired all of the inspectors general whose positions were created by statute in 1976 and 1978. There was considerable doubt that Congress intended that the IGs were to serve at the pleasure of the president, but the Reagan administration asserted its prerogative to fire them, though it ended up reappointing some of the same persons to their positions. The Federal Aviation Agency fired air traffic controllers who had voted to go on strike in August of 1981 and effectively broke their union, the Professional Air Traffic Controllers Association (PATCO). The administration also took early budgetary measures to cut spending and eliminated the Community Services Administration.

THE POLITICS/ADMINISTRATION DICHOTOMY

In its simple form the politics/administration dichotomy holds that there is a distinction between policy and administration, and that political leaders make decisions about what policy should be and those in the bureaucracy merely carry out policy and follow orders from their political superiors. Those who have argued for the strict separation of politics from administration have based their reasoning on Woodrow Wilson and Max Weber.

Wilson argued: "Administration lies outside the proper sphere of politics. Administrative questions are not political questions."[19] Weber characterized the contrasting roles of the politician and the bureaucrat: "To take a stand, to be passionate . . . is the politician's element . . . indeed, exactly the opposite, principle of responsibility from that of the civil servant. The honor of the civil servant is vested in his ability to execute conscientiously the order of the superior authorities. . . . Without this moral discipline and self-denial, in the highest sense, the whole apparatus would fall to pieces."[20]

But in the modern, industrialized, technocratic state these simple distinctions break down. Just as a legislature cannot specify all of the details of complex programs, neither can political appointees give precise and complete orders about how their policy decisions must be implemented. They cannot because they do not have the time, but more importantly they do not have the expertise. Career civil servants have made their careers managing the details of programs, and may even have helped write the legislation that established them. They have the information upon which programmatic decisions must be made. In addition, they are experts at applying bureaucratic rules and regulations to particular programs: oiling the budget, personnel, and paper flow parts of the machine.[21] This simple version of the politics/administration dichotomy "assumes a degree of hierarchy of authority, of simplicity of decision, and of effective political supremacy that now seems unrealistic to students of modern government."[22] As a practical matter this type of division of labor is impossible.

Because of this many social scientists have declared the politics/administration dichotomy to be hopelessly naive.[23] But despite the impossibility of a simplistic dichotomy between politics and administration, it remains a very important normative ideal. It is from Weber's normative sense, rather than from Wilson's empirical claim, that we should derive the contemporary meaning of the politics/administration dichotomy. "Modern critics have scored points by mistaking social science theory for what was actually a normative political doctrine," Hugh Heclo argues.[24]

This theory stresses that the legitimate authority for administration policy making derives from the president and is delegated to his appointees in the government. Despite the fact that career bureaucrats are, of necessity, involved in policy decisions, they ought not to lose sight of the democratic imperative that presidential appointees are the legitimate locus of decision making in the executive branch. The appropriate posture of the civil servant is to carry out faithfully legitimate policy decisions, despite personal preferences. Without this chain of legitimacy, the democratic linkage between the electorate and the government would become unacceptably attenuated.[25]

In addition to these normative distinctions, there are differences of style and values between bureaucrats and politicians, each set of officials making different contributions to the formulation of public policy. Appointees' political skills are needed to identify goals and to mobilize support for them. The strength of civil servants, on the other hand, lies in designing programs to implement those goals.[26] These different styles reflect different roles and are rooted in institutional positions. Political appointees are in-and-outers. That is, they are recruited to serve a particular president and rarely stay longer than the president does, usually much less. The average tenure of a political appointee in a position is about two years. This rapid turnover is often motivated by the desire of presidential appointees to make their mark quickly and to move on, either to a higher position in the government or back to the private sector to make more money. Much of the appointee's agenda is driven by the mandate to reelect the president, or to leave a good record for the partisan heir apparent to run on.

Career executives, in contrast, have a longer-term perspective. They will still be operating programs and administering agencies after the political birds of passage have left. This causes them to pay attention to the health of institutions and to the integrity of the processes that are intended to assure nonpartisan implementation of the laws. The rules and regulations designed to do this can also be used to insulate and protect civil servants from either legitimate or illegitimate political control. This perspective makes them less willing to upset long-established practices quickly. But "bureaucratic inertia" is not a sufficiently subtle description of this type of behavior. Hugh Heclo describes the elements of bureaucratic dispositions as gradualism, indirection, political caution, and a concern for maintaining relationships.[27] Bureaucrats are concerned about the institutions they manage as well as the current policies of those institutions. Politicians tend to see organizations as convenient tools to achieve their policy objectives.[28]

The basic dilemma that underlies modern democratic government in the United States is that the government must be responsive to the current president, yet it must maintain the necessary professionalism in its career managers to accomplish missions effectively and efficiently. The different strengths of political appointees and career bureaucrats must thus be merged in an appropriate balance if the U.S. government is to be both responsive and effective.

THE CYCLE OF ACCOMMODATION

Despite their initial distrust of career executives, political appointees usually develop over time a trust for the career executives who work for them. This is a predictable cycle that has operated in all recent presidential administrations, even if not in all political appointees. The cycle is characterized by initial suspicion and hostility, which is followed by two or three years of learning to work together. This results in a more sophisticated appreciation of the contribution of the career service and a mutual respect and trust.

To take an extreme case, John Ehrlichman, who had characterized relations with the bureaucracy as "guerrilla warfare," later felt that it was a "big mistake" for the Nixon administration to exclude career executives from policy deliberations, both because of their expertise and because of their ability to develop support for the administration's programs. "I did not encounter devastating problems with the bureaucracy." You have to remember that the career service is not a "faceless, formless enemy."[29]

Other high-level White House officials have come to similar conclusions about the career service. Theodore Sorensen recalled his White House experience with the bureaucracy: "The career services are a vastly underused resource, particularly by new presidents who come in suspicious of the career services and confident that they can run everything themselves with their political hired hands. That's a mistake. I don't think that a president needs to have a vast number of political appointees going well down into the agencies. I believe the career services will respond to a president who has some confidence and trust in them, and who knows how to tap their expertise."[30]

After serving in the Carter White House for four years, Jack Watson had strong feelings about the career bureaucracy: "I honestly believe that the career bureaucracy for the most part are professionals, civil servants in the positive sense, who want to serve the new administration. . . . I never experienced some sinister counter force out there seeking to undermine and sabotage our administration. A president should go into office with an operating assumption, a rebuttable presumption, that the people of the government are there to serve him and to help him succeed."[31] Harrison Wellford, Carter's top management person at OMB, says "one good careerist is worth ten campaigners."[32]

Craig Fuller of the Reagan White House said, "My experience in the four years that I've been here is that . . . the relationship between the political appointee and the career people in the departments is very much a partnership. . . . I don't come at this with some notion that we have some norm of behavior among the career staff that is totally at odds or variance with the ideals of the political appointee."[33]

These attitudes of White House aides are shared by most experienced presidential appointees in recent administrations. In a survey sent to all presidential appointees between 1964 and 1984, each appointee was asked to characterize how *responsive* and *competent* the career employees of their agencies were. Those who responded that career employees were "responsive" or very responsive" (4 or 5 on a 5-point scale) were as follows:[34]

Administration	Competent	Responsive
Johnson	92%	89%
Nixon	88	84
Ford	80	82
Carter	81	86
Reagan	77	78

Thus the evidence is overwhelming that experienced political appointees, regardless of administration, party, or ideology, believe that career executives are both competent and responsive. The unanimity across administrations is striking, particularly since the Reagan administration respondents had not had as long to experience the cycle of accommodation as had appointees of other administrations.

More personal reflections of presidential appointees from different administrations reinforce these statistical data.[35]

The Johnson administration—John Gardner, secretary of health, education, and welfare:

> I would strong urge any incoming top official to come in with the recognition that he has a lot of potential allies around him. . . . People who would be glad to help if they got the chance. One of the great mistakes people make in coming in is developing a we/they attitude toward their own staff. . . . Big mistake. There are a lot of potential teammates out there, and you have to find them. And the faster you do the better. . . . So that I fairly soon found the people who could keep me out of the beartraps and could advise me . . . and I found that immensely helpful, and I think any newcomer will.

The Nixon administration—Elliot Richardson, secretary of commerce, defense, HEW, and attorney general:

> I did find them easy to work with. I did find them competent . . . they saw their own roles in a manner that virtually required political leadership. They didn't want to have to make the choices on competing claims that are the function of the political process. . . . People who have devoted a lifetime or significant part of it to expertise in their field are entitled to be listened to with respect . . . many presidential appointees make the gross mistake of not sufficiently respecting the people they are dealing with . . . and get themselves into trouble as a result.

The Carter administration—Walter McDonald, assistant secretary of treasury:

> Without exception I never found an administration as it was leaving office that had anything but praise for the career service in general, and respect. . . . I think a learning process takes place. I think politicals learn after they're burned a few times that careerists are really there to serve them. They're not wedded to any party. . . . And it's very hard for the politicals to understand that . . . and it takes four years to convince them of this. How you do this, God, I don't know.

The Reagan administration—Richard Lyng, secretary of agriculture:

> In every case, I found career people that were absolutely splendid. Their

experience was absolutely invaluable. I needed them, it was essential. The career people kept me from shooting myself in the foot. . . . The way you get them [career bureaucrats] with you is to treat them like equals, point out I need you to help me. These people want the job done right. I never cared if a fellow was a Democrat or a Republican, because . . . all of them are non-partisan. . . . A presidential appointee who doesn't work with the career people will not make it.

Scholar Robert Maranto has done important new research on the relationship between political appointees and career executives during the Reagan, Bush, and Clinton administrations. He found that in the Reagan administration there was little conflict but rather general goal congruence between the two groups in the Defense Department; both career and political appointees favored increased defense spending. Relationships between the two groups were more conflictual in domestic agencies, as would be expected. In the Clinton administration he found some tensions at the beginning in both DOD and domestic agencies, with some skepticism about the proposed cuts promised by the proposed administrative reform, the NPR. Maranto's overall conclusion was: "By the time an incoming administration gets its act sufficiently together to politicize the bureaucracy, the politicians have realized that most bureaucrats just want to do a good job no matter what the partisan make-up of the administration. (And when this is not the case, the bureaucrats are likely to have the support of outside power sources which demand respect.) Over the course of an administration bureaucrats make themselves indispensable, and are then safe from retaliation."[36]

CAREER EXECUTIVES AND POLITICAL MANAGEMENT

The ways in which career executives are crucial to the success of their political superiors are many. They are highly educated and they know the intricacies of the laws and regulations governing programs they implement. They are the repositories of organizational memory. They remember who were allies and enemies in past turf battles. They know who to go to for help in OMB, OPM, GAO, or the Hill. Their personal intelligence and communications networks have been built up over many years dealing with the same organizations, people, and issues. One political appointee described the importance of the memory of career executives: "Those same people keep you out of trouble. You get a decision, someone recommends this and some special interest group comes in and says 'do this,' or some agency in the government or the White House. You bring in the staff and say, what if we do this? They'll say well, if you do that, this is what will happen, and these guys will get mad. Or they'll say, yeah, that was tried in 1931 and again in 1938 and here's what happened. You've got to have those guys with you."[37] To ignore this source of advice and expertise is shortsighted and self-defeating.

Not only are career executives responsive, but they perform functions that are essential to the proper operation of the government and to the success of the political appointees for whom they work. While we expect career executives to be responsive to political leadership, at the same time we expect them to resist illegal or unethical direction from above. For instance, we would expect career bureaucrats to resist any orders to allocate grants based on illegal or political criteria at variance with the established laws and regulations governing the grant process. We would also expect them to blow the whistle rather than to cover up illegal activities by their colleagues or political superiors. One example of appropriate bureaucratic resistance was the refusal of the IRS to audit McGovern aides' tax returns at the order of the White House. Thus we expect bureaucrats to be responsive, but not *too* responsive.

Essential Functions

In legitimate matters career executives should be expected to do more than passively carry out orders. A "Yes, boss" attitude is not merely inadequate, it may be downright dangerous. One career executive remembers warning his newly appointed political boss that a sole source contract granted to the boss's former colleagues "would not pass the smell test" in Washington. His boss did not grant the contract and later thanked him for the warning.[38] In contrast, one "responsive" bureaucrat followed orders without questions and "left my ass in one of the biggest slings in town by letting me redecorate the office," according to one political appointee.[39] These contrasting examples illustrate the types of responsiveness that may make or break a new political appointee.

True neutral competence is "loyalty that argues back," argues Hugh Heclo.[40] One appointee of President Reagan described his relations with career civil servants: "They were responsive to clear, rational guidance. They wouldn't always agree, I would have been concerned had they always agreed with me; but I was always the boss, that was never in doubt."[41] Having "my own person" in the job is not enough; that person must have the requisite knowledge and skills to make the bureaucratic machine work and the good judgment to warn the boss about impending trouble.

The usefulness of the career service has also been documented in responses to the NAPA survey of political appointees. When asked "To what extent were senior career employees helpful to you" in the following areas, those replying "helpful" or "very helpful" were as follows:[42]

	Career executives were *"Helpful" or "Very Helpful"*
Mastering substantive details	81%
Day-to-day management tasks	80
Technical analysis	80
Liaison with the bureaucracy	76
Liaison with Congress	42
Anticipating political problems	34

It is not surprising that career executives were considered to be very help-ful with the first four issues, because these are traditional areas of bureaucratic expertise. But it is significant that more than a third of the presidential ap-pointees found careerists to be helpful in dealing with Congress and anticipat-ing political problems.

Motivations

The career executive corps on the whole is a highly professionalized and care-fully selected group. Career bureaucrats will cooperate with a new administra-tion for two main reasons: their role perception and their own self-interest.[43] First, they realize that a new president was elected by the voters and has a legit-imate mandate to implement his programs and priorities. A study of the 1980–1981 transition found no evidence of a desire to resist the policies of the new Reagan administration on the part of SES members. As one said: "Of course there will be changes around here—there's been an election, and nobody elected me."[44] Also the full range of mainstream political values is represented in the career service, from liberal interventionist values to conservative doubts about the government's ability to solve certain social problems. An agency head who wants to put together a team of careerists sympathetic to any particular administration will have no trouble doing so.

Secondly, most career executives see themselves as professionals and neu-tral (nonpartisan) experts. They take pride in their craft and satisfaction in accomplishing the mission of their agency. This partisan neutrality does not rule out agency and programmatic turf values, but these are often shared by political appointees as well.

If the above, somewhat idealistic, motives attributed to career executives do not seem sufficiently convincing, there are the more basic motivations of self-interest. First of all, career executives are ambitious, or they would not have achieved their executive status. They value the professional recognition, pres-tige, power, and status that come with their jobs. They have chosen the bureau-cratic arena and intend to succeed in it. They are not going to undermine their careers by lightly opposing a presidential administration.

But they cannot fulfill their professional roles if they are not part of the action. They want to be part of the management team that runs their agency and its policies. Their jobs are challenging and fulfilling only if they can exercise their skills, and they cannot do that without being asked by their political superiors. They also want their contributions to be recognized and valued by their superiors. This professional and psychological need to be included on the part of career executives is not compatible with foot dragging, sabotage of administration policies, or merely adequate performance of duties.

Finally, at the most basic level, career bureaucrats want to keep their jobs and paychecks. They realize that if they are found to be undermining administration policies in any important way, they can be fired, demoted, moved geographically, or given a job with no function. This fear of losing one's job will keep bureaucrats from undermining policies, but it will not motivate them to do more than a merely adequate level of work; for positive motivation, trust and responsibility are necessary.[45]

The dedication of the career bureaucracy was demonstrated in particularly trying circumstances early in the Reagan administration. President Reagan had decided to "zero out" (in David Stockman's term) the Community Services Agency that was the descendant of President Johnson's Office of Economic Opportunity. Dwight Ink, a career professional who had served many administrations, was given the job. Ink made it clear that he would tolerate no opposition from within the agency and that he would use career professionals, rather than political appointees, to do the job. Through several difficult months the CSA career executives worked themselves out of their jobs. Even the employee union, once it was clear that Congress was going to back the president, participated in trying to make the closedown as smooth as possible.[46]

Several studies have measured the opinions of career executives in the Nixon administration and concluded that President Nixon was correct in believing that many career members of the executive branch were not entirely sympathetic with his political values.[47] But measures of opinion and political party affiliation miss an important point.[48] What counts is how these officials behave in the context of their jobs; personal political values are appropriately reflected in the voting booth. In the Community Services Administration of 1981 there is little doubt that most career executives did not share the president's evaluation of the agency or its mission; nevertheless, they shut it down in a professional manner.

This argument that members of the career service are unlikely to resist legitimate direction from political appointees does not imply that there will be no resistance to presidential policies. There will be; it is inevitable and inherent in the nature of the U.S. political system. Bureaucratic warfare and turf battles will always plague administrations, but the cleavages will run along agency and programmatic lines, with political appointees and bureaucrats on the same sides of the barricades. Incidents like end runs to Congress and leaks to the press will surface in any administration, but as likely as not they will be instigated by the president's own political appointees.

Bureaucratic resistance to presidential interests and directives is inevitable, but it is important to keep in mind that this resistance is due to the self-interest of members of Congress, interest groups, and executive branch agencies. Career bureaucrats may be a part of these opposing forces, but they are not the primary instigators or even the most influential participants. Using the career service as a scapegoat for all resistance to presidential desires may be comforting, but it does not represent an accurate analysis of power in Washington.

The argument here is that most career executives will willingly support a new administration and not resist its legitimate policy initiatives. If there is resistance to political leadership of an administration, heads of departments and agencies have many tools to help them enforce their desires. While they do not have quite the hiring and firing discretion that most private-sector managers have, they are not helpless. They do make policy; they set priorities; they control the timing of issues; and they determine promotions and assignments. Even if career executives cannot be fired without a battle, much can be accomplished with this impressive array of managerial tools. But potentially the most powerful set of tools an administration has to control the executive branch is provided in the SES provisions of the 1978 Civil Service Reform Act.

THE SENIOR EXECUTIVE SERVICE

The SES provisions of the Civil Service Reform Act (CSRA) of 1978 provide each new administration with a broad set of managerial tools that it can use to control the bureaucracy and achieve its policy goals. The SES was created to deal with problems and rigidities in the Civil Service system's provisions for supergrades (the highest levels of career officials). Prior to 1978 a new administration could appoint its own supergrade executives (GSA 16–18), but they could only be placed in positions that were designated for political appointees. The new agency head could transfer career executives, but only to a position of equal rank and status. If the move involved a promotion or demotion it had to be reviewed by the Civil Service Commission. The backers of CSRA felt that career supergrades' loyalties were too much oriented to their own programs and agencies, and that they were too insulated from legitimate political control by their superiors.

The framers of the 1978 CSRA believed that it was time to restore to executives more control over their personnel systems. If political executives were to be held accountable for accomplishing the missions of their organizations, they ought to have the authority to put together their own management teams to do the job. They also felt that political executives should have the management tools to be able to motivate their subordinate managers. The new flexibilities include the ability to assign either career or noncareer executives to most SES positions, the authority to establish and fill SES positions by the agency head, and the authority to reassign SES members within an agency.

A new administration can fill up to 10 percent of the SES with its own political appointees. These executives can be placed in any general SES position. About 40 percent of SES positions are designated "career reserved" because of their sensitive nature. The general positions are not classified as either career or noncareer and can be filled by either a career or a political appointee. Agency heads can now create SES positions in their agencies and fill them as they see fit. The Office of Personnel Management merely oversees the process and sets overall allocations of SES positions among agencies.

Most importantly, agency heads now can reassign career senior executives to any SES position within their agency. SES positions are not graded, so transfers do not constitute demotions or adverse actions. Thus agency heads can rearrange the whole top leadership in an agency, placing their chosen political appointees in whatever general position they choose, and moving career executives to positions chosen by the agency head. Agency heads can now put together their own management teams.

Reassignments are facilitated by the establishment of a rank-in-person corps, as in military systems. In the past, people's rank depended on the particular position they held. If moved to another position, they received the rank of the usual incumbent of that position. Now an executive's rank in the SES (which is officially a gradeless system) is guaranteed no matter what assignment he or she may receive.

In addition, agency heads have the ability to motivate senior executives in positive and negative ways. it is much easier now to demote career executives. They may be removed from the SES if they receive an unsatisfactory evaluation. And they must be removed from the service if they receive two unsatisfactory performance ratings within three years or two less than satisfactory ratings within a five-year period. Although SES members have fallback rights to the GS 15 level, they cannot appeal a management evaluation unless they claim it is based on a prohibited personnel practice. The positive incentives set up by the CSRA include bonuses and rank awards.

As a safeguard, career executives cannot be reassigned against their wishes or evaluated within 120 days of a new president taking office or a new agency head being appointed. This stems from experience with the general cycle of accommodation that has been described. Voluntary reassignments, however, are permitted during the 120-day waiting period.

REORGANIZATION AS AN ADMINISTRATIVE STRATEGY

"Reorganization has become almost a religion in Washington. . . . Reorganization is deemed synonymous with reform and reform with progress. . . . The myth persists that we can resolve deep-seated and intractable issues of substance by reorganization," observes Harold Seidman, an astute student of government and longtime official of OMB.[49] Reorganizations can be sweeping or narrowly limited, and they can be undertaken for a variety of purposes. Some of the reasons for reorganizations include saving money, shaking up the bureaucracy to show who is in charge, narrowing the president's span of control and placing similar functions in the same agency, better management control, and making symbolic statements of priorities to the public.

Richard Nixon's grand plan to reorganize the executive branch was part of his strategy for control of the government that he undertook after he had failed to achieve his policy goals through legislative means. Nixon's approach to reorganization was to attempt what Ronald Moe has characterized as the "architectonic strategy" recommended by the Ash Council. Nixon felt the major cause of ineffectiveness in the government was "principally a matter of machinery." He called his plan "the most comprehensive and carefully planned . . . reorganization since the executive was first constituted in George Washington's administration 183 years ago."[50] The proposal was to abolish the departments of Agriculture, Commerce, Labor, and Transportation, which were clientele oriented, and replace them with four superdepartments that were goal oriented: Community Development, Economic Affairs, Human Resources, and Natural Resources.

According to H. R. Haldeman, the purpose of the reorganization was to delegate policy implementation in order to get it out to the departments and agencies "where it belongs." The tendency since 1960 to bring policy formulation and also problems into the White House was certainly present in the Nixon administration. Haldeman argues that policy making should be done in the White House, but implementation ought to be delegated: "You don't want the janitor coming in and saying 'should I use Comet or Ajax?' You want him to make that decision himself. Theoretically he can make a better decision than the president can."[51] This, he argued, was the real purpose of the reorganization plan.

The logical and orderly vision of the Ash Council, however, was never to get by Congress because Watergate intervened. But it is doubtful if the Nixon plan would have been passed by Congress even without Watergate. It would have threatened the clientele of many bureaus and agencies and the jurisdictions of congressional committees who are much more interested in political power than administrative symmetry.

Jimmy Carter was a believer in the orthodox view that reorganization could cure many, if not all, administrative ills affecting the national government. When he announced his campaign for the presidency in 1974 he promised a major reorganization effort: "This is no job for the faint-hearted. It will be met with violent opposition from those who enjoy a special privilege, those who prefer to work in the dark, or those whose private fiefdoms are threatened." He wanted to address the problem of the federal bureaucracy's "complexity," "remoteness," and "intrusiveness" through reorganization as he had done in the state of Georgia.[52] He felt that his advocacy of reorganization was one of the reasons he was elected.[53]

He argues in his memoirs that his record on reorganization was quite good. Ten of the eleven reorganization plans submitted to Congress went into effect, which he compares favorably with Lyndon Johnson's less than one-third success record.[54] Some of his major successes were the creation of the Departments of Energy and Education and the Civil Service Reform Act. He was not, however, successful in reducing the number of federal agencies from 1,900 to 200 as he promised in his campaign. It is not clear how he came up with 1,900; Harold Seidman speculates that it included 1,189 advisory committees.[55]

Carter's reorganization efforts seemed to have no principle or organizing theme. Carter dealt with organization as if it were an end in itself divorced from program and policy rather than flowing from the president's goals and priorities. Seidman concludes that the results were disproportionate to Carter's "huge investment of political capital, time, and staff resources."[56] Carter's senior aides were sensitive to this squandering of resources and resisted his impulse to cast so wide a net. They succeeded in limiting reorganizations to those made necessary by campaign promises or congressional pressure.[57] One of the Carter advisers who resisted was Vice President Mondale, who said: "Organizing the government is very much like cutting the Federal budget. Everyone is for it in principle, but the difficulties and controversies arise when you get specific."[58]

Reorganization can be undertaken for a number of purposes. Some of the most often cited reasons are the following:

Economy and efficiency. Most presidents feel a need to pay obeisance to the orthodox view that all reorganizations must save the taxpayers money. But most studies have concluded that money is seldom saved. Only four of ninety-two reorganization plans submitted to Congress from 1949 to 1973 claimed to save a specific number of dollars.[59] Franklin Roosevelt said, "We have got to get over the notion that the purpose of reorganization is economy. . . . The reason for reorganization is good management. . . . It is awfully erroneous to assume that it is in the reorganization of Departments and Bureaus that you save money. This is a very easy fallacy to fall into. Where you save money is by lopping off debts and lopping off employees and stopping the spending of money"[60]

Shaking up the bureaucracy. "Periodic reorganizations are prescribed if for no other purpose than to purify the bureaucratic blood and to prevent stagnation."[61]

The problem is that there are important political reasons for the organizational structure of the executive branch. Much of the real power of the bureaucracy lies at the bureau level and their relationships with the Congress. Reordering the bureaus in a more coherent fashion will not break these ties between bureaus and congressional committees.

It must also be borne in mind that reorganizations exact a high price from the agency and its employees. During reorganizations, as during transitions, uncertainty is high and mission accomplishment is set aside while people worry about their careers and scramble to protect their jobs. Undertaking a reorganization immediately after a transition can prolong the period of uncertainty so that it could be a year or more before the agency can get down to work seriously on the president's program.

Reorganization is much more like gardening than it is like architecture or engineering, Peter Szanton argued. The hard work (overcoming bureaucratic, congressional, and interest group opposition) comes immediately; while the rewards will appear only later after the new arrangements have shaken down, and may accrue only to one's successors. Reorganization is not a useful tactic for those with short time horizons.[62]

Placing similar functions together. This approach fits with the accepted orthodoxy and may also serve to limit the president's span of control. In addition to having fewer people reporting to the president, the intention is that vexing questions of bureaucratic turf can be settled lower in the hierarchy without bringing them into the White House. This was part of the reason for the creation of the Department of Defense in 1948 and for President Nixon's grand scheme. President Carter also had this in mind when he argued that it would be best to consolidate the forty-one federal sewer programs, and the ten agencies promoting business in local areas.[63]

Lyndon Johnson was defeated in his attempt to consolidate the Departments of Labor and Commerce into a Department of Economic Affairs in 1967. Jimmy Carter also was unsuccessful in establishing a Department of Natural Resources from the Interior Department, the Forest Service from Agriculture, and NOAA (National Oceanic and Atmospheric Administration) from Commerce.[64] Each separate constituency wants its own organizational representative and will fight for it. Richard Cheney, President's Ford chief of staff and later a member of Congress, argued that it is foolish to waste a lot of time on trying to straighten out the federal executive branch. You can try to design the perfect system, but you will end up with a bunch of political compromises, which is the way it was designed in the first place. "Of course it's chaos; you've got to work around it."[65]

Management control. This is a good reason for reorganization, but it is effective only on a relatively small scale. Nixon's Reorganization Plan Number 2 of

1970, which created the Office of Management and Budget, is a good example of this. It separated budget and management functions, created the Domestic Council, and placed political appointees (program assistant directors) at lower levels in the administrative structure than in the old Bureau of the Budget. Whatever one thinks of the wisdom of these changes, they did give the president more control.

President Carter's Civil Service Reform Act also was useful for this purpose. The personnel reforms gave the president's administration much more control of the career bureaucracy. The organizational change creating the Office of Personnel Management and having its director (Executive Level II) report to the president gave the president closer management control of the federal personnel system.

Symbolizing presidential priorities. One of the important uses of reorganization is to show the country that the president is vitally interested in a certain public policy area. Thus the creation of the Departments of HEW (Health, Education, and Welfare) in 1953, HUD (Housing and Urban Development) in 1965, and the Environmental Protection Agency in 1973 showed that the federal government would play a more important role in welfare, housing, and environmental policy. In pushing for the creation of a Department of Energy, President Carter wanted to show the country the importance of energy to the security and self-sufficiency of the country in addition to consolidating agencies scattered throughout the government. The Department of Education was created to symbolize the importance of education in the country as well as to fulfill a campaign promise. It is noteworthy that in 1983, after the reports of several national commissions decrying the state of primary and secondary education in the United States, the Reagan administration did not push for the abolishment of the department it had promised to eliminate. The symbols would have worked the wrong way, even though the president had not changed his mind about the proper role of the federal government in education.

Real power as well as symbolism resides in organizational location, and reorganization here can make an important difference. Kennedy placed the Peace Corps in the Executive Office of the President to give it a chance to establish itself. Johnson put the Office of Economic Opportunity in the EOP as well, to protect it and symbolize the importance of the War on Poverty. Kennedy decided not to put the Arms Control and Disarmament Agency in the Department of Defense to assure it some independence. The Forest Service is still in the Department of Agriculture, which was more sympathetic to its mission than was the Interior Department when the decision was made to place it there. The importance of symbolism also explains why the Council on Environmental Quality fought so tenaciously (and successfully) to keep its place in the Executive Office of the President and not be banished to the outer reaches of the Department of the Interior by the Carter administration's transition plans.

In conclusion, the problems associated with large-scale reorganization exact a high cost in terms of presidential energy, political capital, and goodwill. They take up valuable time and must be traded off against other policy priorities. Turf battles must be fought with Congress, the bureaucracy, and interest groups who are all jealous of whatever power they have and will not give it up without a fight. In addition, even members of the president's administration may resist. Joseph Califano related his experience when he worked for President Johnson: "The president needs some help from his own cabinet and agency heads, which is rarely forthcoming." With few exceptions "the cabinet officer or agency head destined to lose a program in a reorganization opposed the plan . . . the cabinet officer or agency head who was gaining jurisdiction through a reorganization favored it."[66] "Where one stands on the issue of executive reorganization is determined by . . . where one has sat in the executive branch."[67] His insight was borne out in his opposition to the creation of the Department of Education when he was secretary of HEW during the Carter administration: "All of my experience in government . . . leads me to urge, in the most forceful way I can, that you reject the narrowly based separate department on the merits as inimical to the President's policy-making, managerial, and budgetary interests."[68]

Reorganizations can be compared to garbage cans in the sense that they are receptacles for whatever combination of people, opportunities, problems, or solutions happen to be present when they occur. They are subject to "the happenstance of short-run political attention, over which reorganization groups typically have little control."[69] Any reorganization will be considered an opportunity by some and a threat by others, and it is difficult to control the outcomes as these political forces work themselves out.

The Reagan administration wisely avoided battles over the Departments of Energy and Education, which it had promised to abolish when it came to office. It decided that its economic priorities were too important to jeopardize them by side battles with Congress and interest groups over reorganization. It did, however, fight the much smaller battle and accomplished the abolishment of the Community Service Administration. Other reorganizations went on at the department level, where they had direct management payoffs.

The question must be asked: Are there better ways to accomplish the same goal as a reorganization? Can the problem be solved with shifted budgetary allocations, personnel increases or transfers, new legislative authority, or changing decision-making processes? If the answer is yes, it is probably safer and will expend less energy to take the less disruptive route of administrative actions short of reorganization. In its management reform initiative, the National Performance Review (NPR), the Clinton administration did not attempt major structural reorganizations but focused on changing organizational culture and processes.[70]

TEMPTATIONS TO OVERMANAGE

While presidents naturally want the most effective control over the bureaucracy that can be achieved, the most effective kind of control for policy implementation is not necessarily the tightest control. That is, some degree of delegation of authority is necessary, and the most effective control is to appoint good, loyal managers, and let them manage their departments and agencies. Policy direction must come from the White House, but management details in most cases ought to be left to the managers closest to the program.

Overcontrol

Most administrations are tempted to establish tight control systems and centralize decision making for understandable reasons. Some controls are responses to abuses of discretion or scandals that have political repercussions. But the same controls that help prevent scandals are also counterproductive to good management because they reduce management flexibility and inhibit creativity.[71] Another reason for centralized control is to assure fairness, equity, and merit in federal operations. Merit system principles and equal opportunity have made the U.S. Civil Service system one of the best in the world, but these same concerns have also made the personnel process slow and cumbersome.

Besides preventing scandals and ensuring equity, central control systems are created in order to prevent poor management decisions. The temptation is to set up reporting and oversight systems so that decisions are either controlled by a system of centralized procedures or they get passed up the hierarchy so that top management can make the decision itself. This approach takes decisions away from the manager closest to the situation and bucks them up to higher levels in the organization that may not be familiar with the situational demands. It also tends to overload higher levels with too many decisions.[72]

In sum, the cumulative impact of centralized controls is counterproductive to good management. Delegation of authority does, however, entail some risks. Poor decisions will be made and abuses will occur, but management is an inherently risky business. Russell Stout argued: "Management functions arise in organizational situations that are important precisely because they are not under control. . . . Despite popular understanding, there is an inverse relationship between the ability to control and the necessity to manage."[73] The argument is not that central controls are always wrong, but that the right balance between control and delegation has to be struck.

Management Fads

Presidents who are concerned with the management of the federal government are vulnerable to management fads that periodically flash across the governmental landscape. Lyndon Johnson was impressed with the way that Robert Mc-

Namara used the planning-programming-budgeting system to control the Department of Defense. He was so impressed that he made PPBS the coin of the realm and declared that *all* agencies must formulate their budgets using PPBS techniques, concepts, and formats. The problem was the PPBS was not appropriate for many of the programs run by the federal government, and a lot of time and energy was wasted while this was discovered. President Nixon dropped the PPBS requirement in 1971.

Richard Nixon had his own management technique to try, Management by Objectives was meant to establish in each agency clear, measurable objectives for each manager.[74] This would make agency goals explicit and give managers an objective means of measuring their subordinates' performance. While MBO looked good in theory and led to some management improvements, in time it became a paper exercise and was abandoned.

Governor Jimmy Carter read an article about zero-based budgeting and had it implemented in the state of Georgia. He liked it so much that he brought it to Washington and had it instituted throughout the federal government. In contrast to PPBS, ZBB was relatively easily implemented in the federal government. It fit well into traditional budgetary practices. The corollary of this is that it did not change much in the way the government spends money. Few priorities were reordered or programs abolished as a result of ZBB.[75] ZBB procedures were abandoned by the Reagan administration.

The common thread throughout all of these reforms is that each president saw successful examples of a management technique and decided it was so good that *everyone* should use it. In each case, however, a new president came in and dropped the requirement for using his predecessor's technique. The conclusion to be drawn is not that management systems are useless, but that they have a short half-life. Despite the abandonment of PPBS, ZBB, and MBO, elements of these systems are still being used where they are appropriate. Valuable lessons were learned. The point is not to avoid all management systems, but rather to not expect final solutions to broad-ranging management problems, and to beware of inappropriate standardization.[76]

WHAT HAVE WE LEARNED?

Presidential control of the executive branch will always be incomplete, but new presidents can act to maximize their opportunities for successful policy implementation. Much might be accomplished by trying to shorten the cycle of accommodation experienced by each administration. This can be done by tempering antibureaucratic campaign rhetoric and by encouraging presidential appointees to work with, rather than against, career executives. The Senior Executive Service can be used to mold management teams for the new administration. Large-scale reorganizations consume much time and political capital, and are likely to be more trouble than they are worth.

5
Taking over the Budget

Each new administration is faced with the challenge of putting its own stamp on the federal budget. This is crucial to a new president for two reasons. The budget is a symbolic statement of the priorities of the country. Overall trends, as well as cuts or increases in specific programs, communicate to the country and the world what the new administration stands for. But the budget also provides specific dollar amounts for programs. The ability to implement a program effectively depends on resources such as spending authority and personnel that are determined by the federal budget. Gaining control of the institutions and processes of the federal budget quickly is imperative to a new president.

A new administration, however, is faced with formidable obstacles to overcome. When it takes office it faces two budgets: the budget for the current fiscal year and the proposal for the next one. Presidents can make some changes in the current budget, usually by proposing supplemental appropriations. But the real challenge is making changes in the lame-duck budget that has just been sent to Congress by the outgoing administration. If a major effort is not made to affect this budget before Congress acts on it, the new president will not have a real chance to change budget priorities until midway through his first term. The lame-duck budget is the proposal for the fiscal year beginning in October; and the next fiscal year will begin twelve months later, or twenty months after the president is inaugurated.

So the lame-duck budget must be changed, but the task is monumental because the work involved is prodigious. The outgoing president's budget is the product of the previous year's work of the Office of Management and Budget. Throughout the year, OMB planned and negotiated with agencies in an iterative process that resulted in the lame-duck budget. Trade-offs, compromises, and promises were made. The budget document is the result of a process rather than a discrete set of decisions. This process cannot easily be redone in a few weeks.

Second, the time pressure is great. Since the 1974 Budget Act reformed the congressional budget process, Congress needs the president's proposals so that legislative committees can report spending plans to the budget committees by March 15. This means the president has to act within his first month to six weeks in office, at the same time that personnel and administrative pressures on the new administration are also greatest.

Even if a new administration succeeds in mastering OMB as the president's tool in budget control, two major constraints still face an administration. Any change in budget priorities will be limited by the rigidity of budget composition. Three-quarters of total expenditures are "uncontrollable" in the short run. That is, they can only be affected by changes in laws that will have an impact in future years. So spending priorities cannot easily be changed to reflect a new administration's values.

In addition to spending priorities, presidents also want to affect the U.S. economy through fiscal policy, that is, total governmental spending, revenues, and the deficit (or surplus). Every president from Lyndon Johnson to Ronald Reagan promised to balance the budget, but none was able to deliver on his promise. Presidents Bush and Clinton each made serious attempts to reduce the deficit, but neither was successful in substantially moving the budget toward balance. The reason is that the budget is heavily influenced by the performance of the economy, and presidents cannot substantially control the economy, despite their promises. Campaign promises for major economic changes are usually overstated.

ACCESS TO OMB

In gaining control of the budget, "The single most important thing is access to budget materials," according to Stuart Eizenstat, domestic policy adviser to President Carter.[1] The only place that has authoritative budget materials is the Office of Management and Budget in the Executive Office of the President. This section will examine the role of OMB in transition and how it must be used by a new president to put his own stamp on the budget. But first it must be noted that recent presidents have prepared themselves and their administrations much more thoroughly than have previous presidents.

At the end of the Eisenhower and Johnson administrations, the Bureau of the Budget played the major institutional role in preparing for the coming transitions (neither incumbent was running). The preparation included budget as well as other aspects of the coming transition. Kennedy came to office with conventional budget and economic values and made minor changes in the Eisenhower lame-duck budget. Although Nixon favored cutbacks in domestic programs, he did not come to office with detailed budget plans. The Nixon campaign did little advance planning because of the old superstition of not counting your chickens before they are hatched.[2]

Carter was the first presidential candidate to prepare in any detailed way for taking over the government. The Carter-Mondale Policy Planning Group in Atlanta devoted most of its resources to personnel and budget issues. As a result of this, Carter staff people were very well prepared to take over the budget immediately upon taking office. Candidate Reagan four years later also set up an elaborate bureaucracy to run his transition, and they were successful in moving quickly on budget matters.

Much of the detailed work the Carter people did prior to the election on budget issues was not useful. Bowman Cutter, who worked on Carter's transition staff and became executive associate director of OMB, said their efforts were necessarily incomplete because of lack of access to most governmental budget sources. He argued that budget and economic priorities have to be developed in conjunction with the president's campaign. Detailed policy analysis done prior to the election is "useless" to the candidate, who must focus on general priorities and not the details of policy implementation. After the election, congressional and some executive branch sources become more available to the transition organization.[3]

Another aspect of moving quickly on the budget is the preparation and experience of key budget personnel. There is not time for on-the-job training. Designations for budget positions should be made soon after the election so budget staffers can begin to prepare themselves and the administration's budget without spending their time jockeying for appointments. In preparation for his job in OMB, Bowman Cutter (executive associate director of OMB in the Carter administration) talked with every previous director of the Budget Bureau. By inauguration day he was well prepared to take over responsibility for the budget.[4] David Stockman was named soon after the election to be head of OMB for President Reagan. His experience as a congressman and his previous interest in budget policy made him as well prepared as anyone to take over budget duties.

To prepare the budget realistically, access to OMB staff is essential. OMB staffers are the ones who have put together the lame-duck budget, and they know what changes are technically and legally possible. When there is a party turnover, however, cooperation with the new administration is a delicate question. The outgoing president is in the process of preparing his last budget, and quite rightly believes he is responsible for the government and its budget until noon of January 20. The budget director needs to protect the integrity of the president's budget and needs to keep the OMB staff working for the president, not the president-elect.

After an election in recent administrations, there has usually been a spirit of cooperation, despite the animosities from the campaign. The government must go on, and budget directors want to be helpful, up to a point. The career staff is more inclined to be helpful because of OMB's traditional role in maintaining continuity as well as wanting to assist the person who will be their boss in several weeks. A traditional story at OMB is that if the Martians landed and took over the earth, the

OMB staff would remain in their offices to assist in the transition. Sometimes the career staff takes the lead in seeking permission to talk with the incoming administration.[5]

There is a tradition of BOB/OMB cooperation with incoming administrations. Joseph Dodge, Eisenhower's designee, was allowed to sit in on BOB budget meetings after the election of 1952.[6] Kennedy's first budget director, David Bell, was allowed to talk with BOB staff but did not get to sit in on budget meetings.[7] Alan Greenspan, representing Richard Nixon's transition office in New York, talked with BOB staffers, but the Nixon budget preparations before he took office were not thorough.[8]

The Carter transition efforts in budget preparation were more thorough by far than those of any of his predecessors. On the request of Carter, the OMB staff of Dale McOmber, assistant director for budget review, prepared a schedule showing how fast the Carter administration would have to move in order to make significant changes in President Ford's FY1978 budget. Cutter had the report on December 1, 1976.[9] On December 15 Cutter met with McOmber and his staff to discuss the schedule. The next day the Carter budget staff met with the House and Senate Appropriations Committees.[10] After the election, congressional staffs and CBO are more willing to provide budget information and analysis to an incoming administration.

During the Reagan transition, similar contacts took place with the incoming budget staffers. Stockman's staff met with OMB career staff during the last week of the Carter administration, and McOmber's staff was asked to react to Stockman's "Black Book" of proposed budget changes to see if they were technically feasible and legal.[11] Much of the Reagan budget success was due to the advance planning of Stockman. The groundwork for specific budget cuts was laid by Stockman in his two terms in the House. His systematic criticisms of the "social pork barrel" laid a philosophical justification for cuts that he would attempt during Reagan's first year in office. A major advantage of the Reagan administration was that they knew fairly specifically what they wanted to do with the budget.

UNCONTROLLABLES: THE EFFECT OF THE ECONOMY ON THE BUDGET

The state of federal finances has always provoked the concern of citizens, but since the 1960s the health of the economy and the federal budget have become major campaign issues. Presidential candidates attack the incumbent of the other party as fiscally irresponsible and promise to turn things around as soon as they are elected. The temptation to overpromise is great; voters want to hear that all of our budget problems can be solved easily. When the economy is doing poorly, challengers to incumbents have a great advantage. Candidates Carter and Reagan both ran against the economic record of their opponents. They argued that as outsiders they would not be beholden to establishment interests, and they both promised to balance the federal budget by the end of their first term.

Voters are ambivalent about federal spending. Consistent majorities in public opinion polls favor reductions in government spending. Americans believe that government is too big and spends too much money. On the other hand, when asked which activities of the federal government should be cut, only foreign aid, space exploration, and welfare are losers—not a large portion of federal expenditures. In other areas respondents feel that federal spending is about right or not enough.[12] So, as much as there is a mandate to cut federal spending in general, there are specific mandates to maintain or increase spending in most policy areas. A president wishing to cut spending in any of these areas in the name of the general good will face focused and concerted pressure from beneficiaries of that government spending.[13]

Presidential candidates also assume that the federal government is infested with waste, fraud, and abuse. This is a convenient belief, because they can claim that billions could be saved by tightening up federal management. But as presidents they are bound to be disappointed when their appointees face the reality of managing organizations as large as those of the federal government. David Stockman realized this in 1981 when he complained that he had to educate the people in the White House about the realities of budget cutting: If you want to produce significant savings, you have to cut programs. "They [in the White House] really thought you could find $144 billion worth of waste, fraud, and abuse."[14]

Slashing "waste, fraud, and abuse" will not lead to large savings for several reasons. First, while organizational slack and inefficiency do exist in all large organizations, rooting them out takes good management at the micro level. Management improvements leading spending reductions at this level are desirable and possible, but do not lead to large-scale savings. This is not a promising way to reduce the deficit. Second, many allegations of waste are really assertions that the government ought not to be engaged in certain activities; that is, they are disagreements about public policy priorities. This kind of waste is eliminated only by cutting programs that some people want and some do not. By 1984 David Stockman felt there was little opportunity left to save money through eliminating waste: "Some still think there are vast pockets of fraud, waste, and abuse out there. In fact, nearly every stone has been turned over."[15]

Presidents cannot easily control the federal budget or eliminate deficits because of "uncontrollables," commitments of the government that cannot be reduced merely by cutting appropriations. Other laws and policies must also be changed. One category of uncontrollables is contracts from previous years. Such obligations constitute legal claims against the government and amount to over 10 percent of total budget outlays. Interest on the national debt is a fixed cost that must be paid. It has been growing rapidly and amounts to 15 percent of outlays.

The largest category of uncontrollables, however, is payments to individuals, which now amount to almost 50 percent of all federal outlays each year.[16] These payments have grown from 3.7 percent of the gross national product in 1955 to 11.2 percent in 1984.[17] Such payments cannot be easily controlled because they are "entitlements"; that is, anyone who is eligible to receive them has a legal right to payment. The state of the economy and demographic changes influence the costs of these programs, many of which are linked to the consumer price index (inflation). If a president wants to cut costs here, eligibility rules must be changed. When inflation increases, so do payments to individuals; and when the economy falters, more entitlement payments must be made. Before 1962 entitlement programs were not indexed in any formal way, but by 1980, 30 percent of total federal outlays were indexed, including Social Security, military and civilian retirement programs, and other nonmeans-tested programs.[18]

The main causes of the growth in expenditures for these programs have been inflation, demographic changes, and expanded benefits. Expenditures for Social Security and civilian and military retirement have been growing because the age of the U.S. population is increasing, and people are retiring earlier with pay levels that are higher than previous retirees. They are thus on benefit rolls for longer periods and out of the tax base earlier. Although Medicare and Medicaid are not formally indexed, the cost of health care has actually risen much faster than the increase in inflation.

The costs of these programs are closely tied to the health of the economy. The rates of inflation, unemployment, interest, and GNP growth have a great, and largely uncontrollable, impact on the size of the budget and the deficit for any one year. For instance, an increase in unemployment by 1 percent, other things being equal, could add about $9 billion to outlays due to increased unemployment benefits paid out, as well as increased outlays for Social Security, food stamps, and public assistance. But increasing unemployment has a compounding effect on the deficit by decreasing tax revenues at the same time spending goes up. Thus the 1 percent increase in unemployment could increase the deficit by $25 billion.[19] Rising interest rates, which plagued the economy in the late 1970s and early 1980s, mean that the government must pay more to finance the debt. A rise of 1 percent in interest rates in 1981 meant an increase in 1982 outlays of $4.5 billion.[20]

When the economy is expanding it can absorb increasing outlays without too much dislocation (providing the deficit is under control); but when total production does not expand, the effect can be devastating to the federal budget. A decrease of 1 percent in economic growth can increase the deficit by $19 billion because of fewer taxes paid and greater outlays for unemployment and other programs.[21]

A president who wants to cut spending and decrease the deficit is thus at the mercy of the economy. If it performs well, deficits automatically decrease without any tough policy decisions. If the economy falters, the deficit will grow despite any but drastic changes. And any attempt to increase revenues or decrease spending may aggravate rather than help the declining economy.

With federal spending dominated by Social Security, other entitlement programs, and the defense budget, the remaining portion is quite small. Much of the remainder is made up of interest on the debt as well as federal salaries and other things not easily controllable. In its first term the Reagan administration made significant cuts in social programs, including education, training, housing, nutrition, and welfare. Significant new cuts are increasingly difficult to find in the shrinking "all other" portion of the budget. Defense and entitlements cannot escape any serious attempt to cut federal spending. A president who wants to make serious inroads on the deficit in the federal budget must look to the largest programs: Social Security, medical care, and defense, as well as to some increase in tax revenues.[22]

FISCAL POLICY: THE EFFECT OF THE BUDGET ON THE ECONOMY

Just as a president faces major constraints in any attempt to control the federal budget, he faces even more intractable problems in trying to control the economy. Given our capitalist values, presidents do not want to control the economy in any detail, but there have been periods of optimism about how much the government could do to smooth out the business cycles of inflation and recession. Two of those periods were the 1960s and the early 1980s.

As a result of the Great Depression in the 1930s and the recovery resulting from the deficit spending for World War II, the ideas of Keynesian economics came to have a large impact in the United States. The basic assumption of the Keynesian approach was that the government could help smooth out the business cycle by active stimulation of the economy during a recession, that is, deficit spending. The flip side of this was that when the economy recovered and full employment was approached, the budget should run a surplus in order to pull money out of the economy and dampen inflationary pressures.

Optimism (or hubris) about how these economic tools could control the economy reached a high point during the early and mid-1960s. President Kennedy's economic advisers convinced him that economic stimulation in the form of a tax cut would prod the economy to grow despite an already existing deficit. Their predictions came true, and the economy enjoyed high growth with relatively low inflation and unemployment. In the late 1960s the economy began to heat up because of spending for President Johnson's Great Society and the Vietnam War. Johnson resisted the tax increase that his advisers proposed to dampen the growing inflation. In 1967 Johnson finally did agree to a tax hike that Congress passed in 1968, but it came too late to stem the inflation. This guns-and-butter policy with a tardy tax increase initiated an inflationary spiral that was not broken until the recession of 1981–1982.

When President Nixon came to office he considered the reduction of inflation to be his primary economic goal. But with stagflation, that is, simultaneous increases in unemployment and inflation, he resorted to an incomes policy, that is, wage and price controls. When the controls were lifted, prices jumped up again, and inflation was greatly aggravated by the oil shock of 1973. President Ford tried to fight the growing inflation with fiscal restraint, but the economy fell into the worst recession (at that time) since World War II, with unemployment at 8.5 percent. When President Carter came to office, he pursued a stimulative fiscal policy that brought unemployment down to 5.8 percent in 1979 but that also helped increase inflation to 9 percent in 1978, and, after the second oil shock, to over 13 percent.

An important cause of President Reagan's victory in 1980 was the poor state of the economy. With inflation over 13 percent, Reagan made control of the economy a major thrust of his campaign, promising a cure for the country's economic ills after his election. The centerpiece of his economic program was his embrace of supply-side economics, the main component of which was an income tax cut of 23 percent over three years. The supply-siders claimed that the tax cuts would not decrease revenues but would actually increase government receipts as a result of the economic growth that would be released. Its adherents harked back to the Kennedy tax cuts and argued that tax cuts of 23 percent would stimulate the economy to new productive heights. The economy would be stimulated not by increasing demand through government spending, but by increasing the supply of capital available to business entrepreneurs.

Monetary restraint was supposed to keep the stimulative fiscal policy from increasing inflation, and the tax cut was supposed to release capital and productive forces to turn around the economy without the usual price of a recession and high unemployment. Conventional economists of the right and left were skeptical that the supply-side approach could produce such a rapid increase in real growth while decreasing inflation and unemployment at the same time. They also doubted that rapid economic growth would be able to generate enough tax revenues to reduce the large deficits that would result from increased spending and the tax cut. "Supply-side theory was the equivalent of laughing gas when compared to the monetarists' and orthodox conservatives' devotion to chemotherapy. It is not difficult to convince people that the world would be a better place if their taxes were cut."[23] David Stockman called the Reagan administration approach "an exercise in free lunch economics."[24]

It soon became clear that the supply-side miracle was not going to happen. The combination of a tight monetary policy and high interest rates (with the prime rate at 20 percent in the spring of 1981) slowed the economy so suddenly that it fell into the deepest recession since the Great Depression. Inflation was brought down to less than 5 percent, and unemployment zoomed to more than 10 percent along with the greatest number of business failures since the 1930s.

In 1983 and 1984 the economy rebounded from the recession due to a growing money supply and stimulative deficits ($110 billion in 1982 and near $200 billion in 1983 and 1984). Joy over the rebounding economy, however, was moderated when the economic recovery did not wipe out the deficit but left a huge "structural" or "full employment" deficit. The structural deficit is that portion of the deficit due *not* to a recession but to a basic imbalance between spending and revenues. In a normal recovery the increased revenues and decreased expenditures would substantially wipe out the deficit. But due to the large tax cut and increased defense spending, the deficit would remain around $200 billion unless major changes in policy were made. The strong economic recovery in 1984 and 1985 would not be able to wipe out the deficit, which would remain between $200 and $300 billion through the early 1990s.[25] Interest rates remained at historically high real (discounting inflation) levels in spite of relatively low inflation, indicating the expectation of future inflation in the money markets.

Monetary policy, the control of the money supply by the Federal Reserve Board, plays an important role in macroeconomic performance. The Fed's policy switch to targeting monetary growth rather than interest rates in 1979 played a major role in the following recession and decrease in inflation. Cooperation from the Fed is necessary in order to pursue any coherent economic policy. Presidents have complained about the Fed's independence, and there have been threats from Congress to make it more responsive. For example, in the early 1980s Fed Chairman Paul Volcker was attacked simultaneously from the right and the left. Supply-siders felt that the tight monetary policy had undermined the recovery they had promised, and liberals felt that the level of unemployment was too high a price to pay for reducing inflation.[26]

But presidents do not have to fear too much from the recalcitrance of the Fed. The Fed chairman has often consulted with the president (and members of Congress), and it is unlikely that the Fed will pursue a policy directly at odds with the prevailing economic consensus.[27] As Herbert Stein has said: "The Federal Reserve is an independent duchy but shouldn't be confused with such foreign powers as the House Ways and Means Committee or the Kremlin. The Fed keeps in touch and wants to get along."[28] In 1993 Fed Chairman Alan Greenspan played a significant role in influencing the new Clinton administration's fiscal policy.

The lesson to draw from the experience of recent administrations is that presidents cannot substantially control the U.S. economy. First of all, presidents do not control the tools of economic policy making. In order to change spending or taxes, they must have the cooperation of Congress. Neither do they control monetary policy and the Fed. But most importantly, they do not control the multitude of economic decision makers in the private market.

Nevertheless, fiscal and monetary policy can and do make important differences and can push the economy in one direction or another. They are blunt economic instruments, though they can be decisive. Presidents, however, should not promise more than they can deliver. While overpromising may get them elected, their failure to fulfill their promises may very well result in a cynical electorate. Given the overpromising of recent presidents, it might be helpful to consult President Truman's unjustly maligned two-handed economist who would be honest and say, "on the other hand . . ."

THE REAGAN BUDGET JUGGERNAUT

Despite the inability of presidents to control the economy and the political, economic, and structural constraints on budget making, presidents do have important options. Until President Reagan came to office it was considered impossible to do much to the lame-duck budget proposal that had been a year in the making. The complexity of the document itself as well as all of the political bargains that had been struck in arriving at the totals for each program make the budget seem, if not locked in concrete, at least mired in a vat of molasses.

President Kennedy came to office promising to get the country moving again, but also with conventional ideas about balancing the budget as soon as possible. It was not until after a year in office that he recommended the fiscally stimulative tax cuts that would spur the economy. In 1961 he proposed additions of $1.7 billion to the FY1961 budget (then in effect) and $3.4 billion to the FY1962 budget. In his March 24 message to Congress he said: "This Message is not intended to present a wholly new budget. Nor is it intended to propose any new programs or expenditures in the non-defense area."[29]

When President Nixon took office his main concern was the growing inflation, which, at 6.1 percent, was the highest it had been since the Korean War. Reversing his campaign promises, President Nixon on February 24 requested an extension of Lyndon Johnson's 10 percent tax surcharge. His changes to Johnson's lame-duck budget for FY1970 were piecemeal, cutting outlays by several billion dollars. Funds within the budget were shifted to reflect Nixon's priorities, with many cuts falling on domestic programs. His systematic impoundment program did not begin until later in his administration.[30]

The preparation of Jimmy Carter's transition team was more systematic than that of any of his predecessors. While Jack Watson ran the transition effort, Bowman Cutter was in charge of budget preparation. The Carter team had to move quickly once in office, because of the new budget timetable established by the 1974 Budget Act. Carter transition teams had detailed proposals prepared for each department and agency, and they reversed virtually all of the increases and decreases recommended in President Ford's lame-duck budget.

According to Dale McOmber, career OMB assistant director from 1973 to 1981, the Carter administration was prepared in a "systematic, document supported way" that was more impressive than even the Reagan takeover in 1981.[31]

Nevertheless, the changes Carter proposed were not sweeping. He added about $20 billion to total spending and about $10 billion to the deficit with the intention of stimulating the economy. But budget priorities were not shifted in any major way. As Carter said in his budget message to Congress: "The 1978 budget is essentially still President Ford's budget, with only such limited revisions as my administration has had time to make."[32]

How, then, was President Reagan able to make such drastic changes in President Carter's lame-duck budget? By March 10, only forty-nine days after taking office, he submitted to Congress a complete revision of the FY1982 budget and succeeded in passing the largest tax cut in history, initiating the largest peacetime defense buildup, and making the most drastic budget cuts. His success resulted from advanced planning, singleness of purpose, and speed of execution. The personal wills and political skills of Ronald Reagan and David Stockman were crucial to the Reagan administration's unprecedented budget victories in 1981.

The Groundwork

Much of the groundwork for the specific budget cuts was done by David Stockman during his two terms in the House. One of the initial documents, known as the "Stockman Manifesto," was an article coauthored with Congressman Jack Kemp entitled "Avoiding a GOP Economic Dunkirk."[33] They argued that swift action was necessary to avoid an economic disaster. After Stockman was designated OMB director by the president-elect, he and his staff compiled in detail cuts that were to be made, program by program. They were collected in what was known as Stockman's "Black Book." In a risky gambit, within two weeks of the inauguration, Stockman gave copies to Republican members of Congress. As expected, the "Stockman Hit List" was soon photocopied and distributed all over Washington. This wide distribution of the hit list served Stockman's purpose of absorbing some of the political fallout before the release of the official budget and showing that the administration was serious about deep cuts in social programs. It might have backfired by giving the opposition time to pull itself together, but the Democrats were in too much disarray to mount an effective counterattack on the Reagan budget proposals.

The public budget campaign featured a series of televised presidential speeches and official documents. On February 5, in a televised address, the president warned of an "economic calamity of tremendous proportions" if his program were not passed. On February 18, in a speech to a joint session of Congress, he presented his "Program for Economic Recovery" along with an inch-thick document explaining his approach to fiscal and monetary policy. This was followed on March 10 by another address to Congress and the release of *Fiscal Year 1982 Budget Revisions,* the Reagan budget proposal prepared by OMB. The president's personal political appeals to the public helped to orchestrate political pressure on the Congress to pass his budget proposals.

The Cabinet

One source of potential opposition to the proposed cuts in domestic programs was the executive branch bureaucracies that were being cut. The administration used several approaches to neutralize this potential opposition: It delayed executive appointments and carefully orchestrated cabinet-level acceptance of budget cuts. Despite the administration's intention to hit the ground running, which it was doing in the budget arena, its executive personnel appointments immediately below the cabinet level were made more slowly than in previous administrations. While this was frustrating for those concerned with managing the executive branch, it served the budget cutters well.[34]

Those appointed to run programs want to do a good job and may see budget cuts as limiting the resources they might use to accomplish their program goals, not to mention turf considerations. If budget cuts are made before positions are filled, there will be no one with any credibility in the new administration to marshal arguments against drastically cutting back programs. While some argue that the career service, the permanent bureaucrats, are a potent force in opposition to budget cuts, they are a negligible factor in this set of circumstances. They might have been able to argue convincingly against program cuts, but no one in the administration would listen to them, whereas they would have had to at least listen to a Reagan appointee.

Since the cabinet secretaries had already been appointed, a different tack was necessary with them. During the first few weeks of the administration, before the newly appointed secretaries were fully able or willing to defend their organizations, small meetings were held with Stockman, the president, and several White House aides present, along with the cabinet secretary. The new appointee was confronted with Stockman's proposed cuts and given a chance to argue against them. But that was difficult, because they wanted to be seen as team players. "They usually conceded after only a perfunctory debate."[35]

Although the new cabinet strongly supported the Reagan economic program in general and probably some cuts to their programs in particular, they may have felt railroaded to go along with decisions made by others before they were ready to take an active role in the process. But the cabinet was a small problem of bringing along the home team compared with the political challenge that faced the administration in Congress.

Persuading the Congress

"The world's so-called greatest deliberative body would have to be reduced to the status of a ministerial arm of the White House," if the Reagan economic program was to be enacted, according to David Stockman. "Rubber stamp approval, nothing less," would be necessary.[36] Even is this statement was a bit hyperbolic, it reflects the secondary role Congress played in the battle over budget priorities in 1981.

The Republican capture of the Senate in 1980 assured support for the president, and allowed the administration to focus its efforts on the House, in which the Democrats had a fifty-two-seat edge. Despite this edge, the Democrats could not mount any effective opposition, because they could not agree on a unified plan to oppose the president. Some wanted to present a complete alternative approach, while some wanted to give the administration enough rope to hang itself by approving the proposals and then blaming the president for a faltering economy and reduced domestic programs.

The natural target of the White House was the group of southern Democrats who felt politically vulnerable since they came from conservative districts that might replace them with Republicans if they were perceived to be undermining the economy by budget busting, and the president had run ahead of many of them in their own districts. This group of forty-seven Democrats became a highly visible swing block of votes that organized itself into the Conservative Democratic Forum and were known as the "Boll Weevils."[37] Since these Democrats were crucial to passage of the administration's budget program, they were both wooed by the president and subjected to White House political pressures. Similar tactics were also used on "soft" Republicans.

One source of President Reagan's success with the Congress was his affable personal style, and his active personal involvement in congressional lobbying was crucial to the administration's budget success. Other political pressures from the administration were not quite so gentle. In late April the political assistant to the President, Lyn Nofziger, coordinated a "Southern Blitz" to pressure southern Democrats to vote with the administration on its budget program. Government officials were sent to home districts of House members to focus media attention on the upcoming vote with the hope that constituents would pressure the incumbents to support the president. Trade associations, corporations, and local campaign contributors to sympathetic to the president were enlisted to put pressure on the members.[38] Letter-writing campaigns were organized, and corporations were asked to take out ads in magazines and newspapers supporting the administration's budget proposals.[39]

Electoral carrots and sticks were also used. The White House contacted Democratic campaign contributors to ask them not to contribute to the campaigns of those who voted against the president.[40] The president even promised not to campaign against southern Democrats who consistently supported his budget program.[41] There was also word that conservative Democrats who supported the administration would have easy campaigns in the 1982 elections. Paul Weyrich, director of the Committee for a Free Congress, said "there is a sense that if the (conservative Democrats) vote for Reagan in the House, they ought to get a bye in '82."[42]

All of these pressures reinforced the conservative Democrats' own sense of electoral vulnerability. They believed the voters wanted the president and the Congress to cut spending and that a vote against President Reagan's formula for cuts would be punished by the voters. They believed in President Reagan's version of his mandate.

After President Reagan sent his detailed budget revision proposals to the Congress on March 10, Congress had to take the first step in the congressional budget process by passing a first concurrent budget resolution, setting spending, revenue, and deficit targets for FY1982. The strategic decision had been made in February by the administration and its allies on the Hill to use the reconciliation process in conjunction with the first concurrent resolution. Reconciliation was set up in the 1974 Budget Act to enable the House or Senate to require committees to change reported legislation in order to conform with the second concurrent resolution.

In fiscal year 1981 the procedure was used for the first time in conjunction with the first resolution to reduce outlays by $4.6 billion and increase revenues by $3.6 billion. The Reagan plan, however, was much more ambitious. It called for budget cuts, $48.6 billion initially, to be made by changes in the laws authorizing programs and extended the cuts over fiscal years 1983 and 1984. This had the effect of putting all of the budget cuts into one package so that lawmakers had to vote for or against the whole package rather than piece by piece.

The crucial votes came in the House on May 7, when it passed the first concurrent resolution. In April the House Budget Committee reported out a Democrat-backed budget resolution calling for more spending but a smaller deficit than the administration proposal. After several weeks of the intense lobbying described above, however, sixty-three Democrats defected and, along with solid Republican backing, passed the administration-backed package known as "Gramm-Latta" by 253 to 176 on May 7. This vote was crucial because it showed that Reagan could control the Democratic House and get his unprecedented budget changes through the Congress. On May 14 the House and Senate conference committee agreed to the first concurrent resolution including reconciliation instructions requiring authorizing committees to come up with the changes in law that would provide the $36 billion in budget cuts wanted by Reagan.

Over the next few weeks legislative committees in both houses struggled to make the cuts required of them in the reconciliation instructions. As each committee made its changes, the separate bills were referred back to the budget committees to compile them in a package and bring them to the floor for a vote. In mid-June each Budget Committee reported out the budget cut packages.

As in the May vote on the first concurrent resolution, the crucial test came in the House. The House Budget Committee reported a bill compiled from the recommendations of fifteen committees that provided $37.7 billion in savings and claimed the bill included 85 percent of the cuts wanted by Reagan. Republicans and conservative Democrats, however, claimed that entitlements were not cut enough and not enough programs were put into block grants. They proposed a substitute called "Gramm-Latta II" that conformed very closely with what the administration wanted.

The administration again pulled out its heavy guns in lobbying for the Gramm-Latta substitute. The president himself telephoned or telegraphed each of the sixty-three Democrats who had voted with the administration on the first budget resolution. Compromises and concessions in the final package were made in order to win votes, some of them departures from the administration's earlier proposals.

The deciding vote came when the House defeated (210 to 217) a motion that would have allowed the Democrats to force votes on the separate pieces of the reconciliation substitute package rather than yes or no on the whole package as the Republicans wanted. The Gramm-Latta reconciliation substitute itself passed 232 to 193 on June 26. The Senate had already passed a very similar bill on June 25 by a vote of 80 to 15. The omnibus reconciliation package cut a total of $35.1 billion from the baseline established by CBO for FY1982 for a total savings of $130.6 billion for fiscal years 1982–1984.

WHAT HAVE WE LEARNED?

What have the past several presidencies taught us about presidential control of the budget? The Carter and Reagan administrations have shown that a new president can make an impact on the lame-duck budget, but that early preparation is important, and access to the OMB staff is essential. There are now precedents for early access to OMB, but these contacts have not been institutionalized because of the sensitivities and prerogatives of the outgoing president.

The executive budget cycle begins in OMB in early spring of each year and culminates in the presidential review and appeals process in late fall. In an election year this is a touchy process because of the possibility that the incumbent will not win reelection. Nevertheless, the budget of the U.S. government must be formulated, and OMB does the job as usual. When the incumbent loses in the November election, however, the end of the budget cycle does not go on as usual. Everyone realizes that it is a lame-duck budget and that the new president will change it immediately upon taking office.

All agree that, after losing an election, putting together a lame-duck budget is not a fun thing to do. As in all budgets it takes a prodigious amount of work, but everyone realizes that the work will go for naught. "There's nothing more forlorn than going through the policy disputes" when formulating the lame-duck budget, according to Charles Schultze, former BOB director (in the Johnson administration) and chairman of the Council of Economic Advisors (in the Carter administration).[43] The outgoing administration is depressed because of the election outcome, and the OMB career staff realizes that after completing its labors it will immediately have to work overtime to make all of the changes the new administration wants.

There are two main problems with the lame-duck budget. First, it is an exercise in futility, because it will be obsolete on January 20. Second, OMB staff are tied up putting it together and cannot spend time with the incoming administration whose budget will count. For these reasons the exercise of developing a full-fledged, lame-duck budget ought to be abandoned. A president who has been defeated could submit a current services budget, one that reflects the costs of maintaining policies currently in place.[44]

James T. McIntyre, director of OMB for President Carter, summarized the initial steps a president-elect ought to take to establish control over the budget: (1) Select top budget personnel quickly; (2) identify the major budget priorities for the first budget; (3) examine future implications of present budget choices, since significant changes cannot be achieved in one year; and (4) make sure that the cabinet understands and will support the president's budget priorities.[45]

We have also learned that presidents tend to overstate what they can deliver in terms of budget cutting and economic performance. Their ability to balance the budget is severely circumscribed by uncontrollable spending. Entitlements can be cut, but only if major political battles are fought. Economists and presidents have an imperfect understanding of the economy. Fiscal policy can move the economy in one direction or another, but fine-tuning is impossible. Even if the necessary knowledge did exist, presidents do not fully control the governmental institutions and political forces that determine economic outcomes.

The first year of the Reagan administration, however, taught us that presidents still can control the national agenda. By thorough preparation, speed of execution, and follow-through, the Reagan administration was able to achieve historic changes in U.S. budget priorities. A strong president is not at the mercy of a fragmented separation-of-powers system. The Reagan administration, however, did pay a price for its budget victories: Virtually all of its policy priorities except the economic program were put on the back burner. The victories were achieved only by exclusive concentration on the economic agenda. Luck was also on its side; there were no foreign or domestic crises to distract it during its early months.

After 1981, however, the Reagan administration did not come close to the budget victories it won in its first campaign. The White House would send budget proposals to Congress that demanded more domestic spending cuts and larger defense increases than even the Republican-controlled Senate would accept, much less the Democratic House.[46] The failure of the administration to compromise with Congress or reduce the deficit led to passage of the drastic Gramm-Rudman-Hollings legislation in 1985. GRH, as it was known, called for automatic cuts in the deficit until it was eliminated in 1991.

The failure of the Reagan administration to achieve its budget priorities after 1981 was due in part to the extreme nature of its proposals, which called for additional, severe domestic cuts on top of the sharp cuts of 1981. The unwillingness of the administration to compromise left much of the budget making to negotiations between the Republican Senate and the Democratic House. Congress evidently did not want to continue to act as the "rubber stamp" that David Stockman wanted it to be. The absence of presidential domination of budget priorities after 1981 highlights the exceptional nature of Reagan's first-year victories and points out the importance of moving quickly after an election to achieve major administration goals.

The deficits accumulated during the Reagan administration brought the national debt from $1 trillion in 1981 to approximately $3 trillion in 1989. The inability of the Bush or Clinton administration to substantially rein in the deficit led to the increase of the debt to $4 trillion in 1993 and $5 trillion in 1996. Because of the drastic increases in the national debt and seemingly intractable deficits, the budgetary process has changed from a bottom-up process to a top-down, deficit-driven process. The fiscal implications of continued deficit spending now dominate the public policy process.[47]

6
Moving the President's Legislative Agenda

A new president will be in an ideal position to achieve his legislative goals if he wins election by a landslide, runs ahead of most members of Congress in their states and districts, has a large partisan majority in Congress, and maintains high levels of public approval once in office. Unfortunately for most recent presidents, elections have been relatively close, their popularity has predictably decreased after a short time in office, and the effect of presidential coattails (while never great) has been decreasing.[1]

Recent changes in Congress, particularly in the House, have made it more difficult to win approval of presidential legislative programs. Congress has asserted itself more since Vietnam and Watergate, in part by passing the 1974 Budget Act and the War Powers Act. It has greatly increased its staff resources: personal, committee, and institutional (CBO, GAO, CRS). It has also fragmented itself by giving more power to subcommittees, and the unifying strength of political parties has been decreasing.[2] Other factors in American society such as the increase in single-interest groups and lack of consensus on divisive political issues have also worked to decrease the president's influence in Congress.

Recent presidents have had varying degrees of success with the Congresses they have faced. John Kennedy was not particularly successful in achieving his legislative goals, while Lyndon Johnson enjoyed legendary victories with many of his and Kennedy's initiatives. After the relative lack of success of Johnson's three successors, commentators again began to compare the separation-of-powers system unfavorably with parliamentary forms of government.[3] Yet in 1981 Ronald Reagan was able to mobilize the political system behind his legislative program and win victories in his first year in office comparable to those of Franklin Roosevelt and Lyndon Johnson. Neither President Bush nor Clinton was able to approach President Reagan's impressive first-year victories in Congress.

This chapter will examine the elements of presidential success with Congress in the early months of a new administration by comparing the Carter and Reagan legislative efforts. Although Carter's success rate, as measured by *Congressional Quarterly,* was not far behind Reagan's or other recent presidents', Reagan was able to make large changes in the direction of public policy through his legislative victories and is generally thought to have had a much more effective approach to congressional relations early in his first term than President Carter. The factors of presidential success that will be analyzed are the importance of a quick start, setting up the legislative liaison operation, "courting" Congress, and choosing between the rifle and the shotgun strategies. Finally there will be a summary of the lessons learned from the Carter and Reagan first-year efforts.

Some scholars have concluded that presidential success is determined by factors not under the president's control (such as partisan majorities in each house), and that presidents can exert very little influence on Congress as a result.[4] This does not, however, mean that presidents cannot affect their legislative fortunes. The Carter administration has shown us that early mistakes can hurt a president in Congress. The Reagan administration has demonstrated that it is possible to overcome a large partisan disadvantage in one house.

The following analysis is not meant to be a full-scale balanced evaluation of the legislative records of the Carter and Reagan administrations. It underplays the important legislative successes of President Carter and the legislative stalemate (particularly over budget policy) of the post-1982 Reagan administration. The point is to highlight the importance of early legislative action and to see what lessons we can draw from these two presidencies.

THE IMPORTANCE OF A FAST START AND EARLY VICTORIES

One thing is certain: The early actions of a new administration are crucial to its legislative success. This is so both because the main legislative accomplishments of an administration are often achieved early in its first year, and also because early successes or failures can set the tone for the rest of the administration in its relations with Congress.

Those who have been involved in passing the legislative programs of presidents agree that early successes with Congress are important. George Reedy, one of President Johnson's White House aides, argues that "if a President gets along well with Congress in the beginning, he may be able to carry this over past the initial period. But if he gets off on the wrong foot, he'll never be able to shake this no matter how well he does later."[5] Even if early victories do not guarantee future success, early mistakes may hurt a president's future potential. Max Friedersdorf, Reagan's chief congressional aide, held that "enemies and mistakes made in the first week will dog a President throughout this term in office."[6]

Early blunders in Jimmy Carter's administration hurt his future legislative prospects. In Stuart Eizenstat's opinion, "I don't think Carter's image ever recovered from some of those early mistakes."[7]

Early successes will not be handed to a new president on a silver platter. The idea that a "honeymoon" with Congress naturally follows the election of a new president is greatly exaggerated. While the public is likely to be generous in its approval of new presidents, among modern presidents only Franklin Roosevelt and Lyndon Johnson enjoyed genuinely cooperative Congresses at the beginning of their administrations.[8]

Presidents must move quickly in order to take advantage of a "mandate" from the voters. The perception of a mandate is enhanced if the election victory was sizable, as it was in 1980. According to a Reagan aide: "We are going to push the mandate as far as possible. If you don't hear us say the people have spoken again and again, we won't be doing our job."[9] The theme of a Reagan mandate from the voters was effective regardless of the fact that public opinion polls did not show majority agreement of the electorate with many Reagan priorities.[10] Ideally, momentum can be built from an early string of successes that will get as much of the new president's program through the Congress as possible. The idea of momentum connotes a sense of the power of a new president and of the inevitability of his success. In the late spring and early summer of 1981, the momentum of the Reagan administration was palpable.

The most important reason for moving quickly is what Paul Light calls the policy cycle of decreasing influence. He argues that presidents begin their terms in office with a maximum of political capital that must be exploited quickly before it is dissipated. Presidents can expect that their popularity will decline in their first year in office and that they will lose party seats in the House in the midterm elections.[11] Moving quickly means introducing legislation early in the term. Light found that, from 1960 to 1982, of the items introduced in January–March of the first year, 72 percent are eventually enacted. During the next three months the rate drops to 39 percent, and from July to September it falls to 25 percent.[12] Although President Nixon intended to be an "activist" president in legislative affairs,[13] only 11 percent of his agenda had been introduced by the end of March, compared to 71 percent of Kennedy's and 38 percent of Carter's.[14] Light concludes that timing was part of the reason for Nixon's relative lack of success with the Congress.

Lyndon Johnson explained the same phenomenon without statistics: "I keep hitting hard because I know this honeymoon won't last. Every day I lose a little more political capital. That's why we have to keep at it, never letting up. One day soon, I don't know when, the critics and the snipers will move in and we will be at stalemate. We have to get all we can, now, before the roof comes down."[15] In the second year of an administration, closer to midterm elections, congressional cooperation declines: "They'll all be thinking about their reelections. I'll have made mistakes, my polls will be down, and they'll be trying to put some distance between themselves and me. They won't want to go into the fall with their opponents calling 'em Lyndon Johnson's rubber stamp."[16]

One of the prerequisites of getting legislation to Congress quickly is having a clear idea of what the administration's priorities are and having them formulated relatively specifically. This is why the preinauguration period is so important to a new administration. While the Carter administration was well prepared with much of its agenda, the energy bill was an exception, with little preinauguration planning. One of the criticisms of the bill was that it was not well thought out and that it was put together hurriedly and secretly by James Schlesinger without much consultation with Congress. Here Carter was caught in a bind: Try to move quickly or delay until there was a better product, but when the climate might not be as receptive. Carter chose the former, but did not end up with much of what he wanted in the legislation.[17]

One way to get around the problem of unformulated policy issues is to choose those that have been around a while. This is what Kennedy did in 1960. He chose issues that the Democratic party had been pushing for a number of years and made them his initial proposals to the Congress. In this way you can take existing legislation, make some changes, push to get it passed, and then take credit for the administration. As one Kennedy aide said: "We changed some bills, altered the specifics, but the basic content was there even before the campaign. Our problem was in choosing among the items. We couldn't do everything."[18]

ESTABLISHING A LEGISLATIVE LIAISON OPERATION

"The importance of liaison during the transition and the first months of the new administration cannot be overestimated," argues political scientist Stephen Wayne. "This is the time when campaign debts are due, when personnel requests threaten to overwhelm Congress, when the president appears to have all the perquisites, when the uncertainties of channels of communication and patterns of influence are greatest."[19]

The first thing a president-elect should do in establishing relations with Congress is to designate his director of legislative liaison. The sooner this is done, the sooner procedures and communications can be set up to deal with the initial flood of congressional correspondence and requests. The main functions of the legislative liaison team during the transition are ongoing liaison with Congress, scheduling meetings with the president-elect, and working on confirmation of the cabinet.[20]

Early organization is important because of the flood of communications that must be handled immediately. When Larry O'Brien was designated by John Kennedy to take over his legislative operation, he went to talk with Bryce Harlow, who handled congressional matters for President Eisenhower. When Harlow learned that O'Brien intended to handle the operation by himself and his assistant, Harlow gave him a lecture:

> You're about to ruin your president. . . . Let me explain to you why. . . . I average a hundred and twenty-five incoming telephone calls a day. Average. Bob Hampton handles the congressional appointments and presidential appointments. That office handles four hundred incoming calls a day, even now. Now then, when you first come to work in this building, and it's January 20 and it is 12:01, you won't be able to hang up this phone. For your first two years you won't be able to hang it up without it ringing, no matter how many lines you put on it. Now, if you think you can handle all that stuff by yourself and [one assistant], I'm just telling you, you're going to destroy yourself and destroy your president . . . that's absolutely mad, stark raving mad.[21]

Harlow concluded: "So he came in here and set up the same system I had."

The workload had not abated when Frank Moore came to Washington in the summer of 1976 to handle liaison for Jimmy Carter. He was immediately swamped with calls and messages from the Hill.[22] Some members of Congress were irritated when their calls did not get returned or their messages were lost. During the administration's first week in office, Moore's office received 1,100 letters from members of Congress.[23] After President Reagan was elected, the transition team received 25,000 letters, most of them requests for jobs.[24]

Confusion marked the early days of the Carter administration's legislative liaison efforts, according to Frank Moore: "We hadn't worked out our own internal staff and procedures. There was a great sense of frustration among Democrats on the Hill. People wondered, how does it work, who do you need to know? Do we go through Kirbo? Does Jordan really have the President's ear, or maybe Mondale is the guy we ought to be talking to. They wanted the game plan."[25] In addition, the early Carter White House did not seem to appreciate the importance of the congressional liaison operation. It was understaffed because of Carter's promise to cut the size of the White House, and it had trouble convincing other White House staffers of the importance and delicacy of congressional liaison.[26] Moore began with a total of thirteen people with one professional assigned to the Senate and three to the House. Although congressional liaison had forty-two people by the end of the administration, serious damage was done in early months when they were understaffed.[27]

Because of the importance of the function of legislative liaison and the overwhelming volume of initial work, it is important to have experienced people on the job. It is generally conceded that the inexperience of Frank Moore hurt the Carter administration initially. Moore had been Carter's main legislative aide in Georgia, but he had no experience with the Congress before 1976. President Reagan chose for his legislative liaison head Max Friedersdorf, who had done the same job for President Ford and who hired for his staff only those with congressional experience.

Some have argued that the location of the congressional liaison operation is important and that location in the East Wing of the White House sends an important symbolic message.[28] Congressional liaison under Moore was located in the East Wing for the first two years of the administration, but because of cramped space, it was moved to the Old Executive Office Building. This was done only after the move was fully considered by the congressional liaison staff.[29] The Old EOB, however, is virtually as close to the West Wing as is the East Wing. What may be more important is access to the president. Here the Carter congressional liaison team had an advantage over the Reagan liaison team, which reported to the president through James Baker and the troika. Moore reported directly to the president.

How the legislative liaison operation is organized is also an important issue. When Larry O'Brien headed John Kennedy's office of legislative liaison, he organized it along the political divisions in Congress with specific people assigned to the important blocks and factions. Staff members were chosen for their political rather than their substantive backgrounds.[30] This general organizational approach remained through the Johnson, Nixon, and Ford administrations but was changed by Jimmy Carter.

Carter initially chose to organize his legislative liaison team along issue lines, with staff members being chosen on the basis of their policy expertise rather than their political skills. "Instead of having specialists for the Senate and for the various blocks within the House, there would be specialists for energy issues, foreign policy issues, health issues, environmental issues, and so on."[31] This decision was made against the advice of old Washington hands,[32] and was reversed within the first six months of the administration. Political scientist Charles O. Jones concluded that "the office never fully recovered from this initial mistake."[33]

Another departure from past practice that the Carter administration made was to let cabinet secretaries choose their own legislative liaison heads. According to one White House aide in the Carter administration: "We should have filled those jobs with Jimmy Carter people, but we didn't. The President believes very strongly in cabinet government. But a result of that is that you have in the departments not Jimmy Carter people, but Joe Califano people, or Brock Adams people, or Bob Bergland people."[34] In addition, President Carter let cabinet members deal directly with Congress—in contrast with Kennedy and Johnson's tight White House control. Hubert Humphrey thought this was a mistake.[35]

The Reagan administration, which quickly gained a reputation for having a professional legislative liaison operation, consciously did three things differently from the Carter administration: It chose experienced staff for legislative liaison; it organized its staff along political rather than issue lines; and the White House played the dominant role in selecting the heads of legislative liaison in the cabinet departments. The same approach was followed by the Bush and Clinton administrations.

STRATEGIC CHOICES: COURTING CONGRESS

By strategic choices are meant decisions about the timing and orientation of the president's whole legislative program and approach to Congress rather than specific tactics used with any given piece of legislation. Important aspects of a strategic approach to congressional relations are the "courting" of Congress and the volume and focus of the president's legislative agenda. This section will contrast the approach of the Carter administration with other presidents' dealings with Congress.

When asked how the White House could best approach relations with Congress, Richard Cheney replied: "Don't sell the boat."[36] He was referring to President Carter's early decision to sell the presidential yacht, the *Sequoia*, in order to symbolize the administration's austerity. Since the 1930s other presidents had used the *Sequoia* effectively as an informal setting to do low-key congressional lobbying. Much of the "courting" of Congress has to do with creating an atmosphere of cooperation and service. Favors, primarily small ones, are done so that when support is needed on legislation in the future, members will be receptive to overtures from the White House. Small favors are used to create a friendly climate and are seen as strategic, not tactical, weapons.[37] For instance, John Ehrlichman recalls: "I made a lifelong friend of a Congressman by finding money for a sewer project in his district; and it wasn't hard to do."[38] Explicit quid pro quos are not as common as general favors in White House–Congressional relations.

According to those with experience with Congress, the little things *are* important. "A lot of times you can get a guy's vote just by having done a lot of little things. And a lot of times they'll vote against you, just out of damn spite," in Frank Moore's words.[39] According to Tom Korologos of the Reagan administration, "If you take care of the little things, the big things will take care of themselves."[40] The "little things" include appropriate deference to members of Congress. "There's really no such thing as overdoing it," said Jack Valenti of the Johnson White House. "White House staffers must treat every congressman and every senator as though they, too, were President."[41]

Little things also include knowledge of the personal preferences of members. According to Max Friedersdorf, you have to "know all of their individual idiosyncrasies and know how they think and act. You have to know when Tip O'Neill needs a cigar."[42] Ben V. Cohen, who worked the Hill for Franklin

Roosevelt, said that they were so responsive to congressional wishes that "we scarcely knew whether we were working for the President or Sam Rayburn."[43] Larry O'Brien held that it is the fragileness of congressional relations that makes the small things important. Returning phone calls quickly, off-the-record meetings with the president, and VIP tours of the White House were all used in the Kennedy and Johnson administrations to keep lines of communication to the Hill open.[44]

Early courting of Congress is begun when the president-elect goes to the Capitol to meet with congressional leaders and invites members to the transition headquarters and later to the White House. While President Carter had invited every Democratic member of Congress to the White House within the first few months of his administration,[45] he was not perceived to be successful at wooing Congress. Part of the reason for this was his personal distaste for small talk and political "back-slapping." His general approach toward congressional politics seemed to be essentially antipolitical, aggravated by a holier-than-thou attitude.[46] President Reagan, on the other hand, seemed to relish telling stories and making small talk.

Another part of courting Congress is showing respect for Congress as an institution, Like Carter, Reagan ran against the establishment in Washington; but unlike Carter, he visibly and symbolically reversed himself after he was elected. He visited the Capitol, had Majority Leader Tip O'Neill to the White House for private dinners, and generally paid his respects to Congress. While Carter went through these motions, he also gave the impression of moral superiority to Congress. He showed disdain for politics as usual and acted as if appeals to moral principle would carry the day.

Carter demonstrated this attitude by threatening to go over the heads of Congress directly to the people if Congress would not bend to his will. "I'll handle them just as I handled the Georgia legislature. Whenever I had a problem with the Georgia legislature I took the problems to the people of Georgia."[47] This was considered bad form, and members of Congress did not appreciate being compared to the Georgia legislature. It also violated one of LBJ's rules of legislative relations: Unless you are deliberately going to pick a fight with Congress, "Go to the Public Last."[48] In contrast, President Reagan was very effective in "going public" to influence Congress.[49]

STRATEGIC CHOICES: THE RIFLE OR THE SHOTGUN?

An important strategic choice that each new president must make is the range and volume of issues to be included in his legislative agenda. It may be instructive to compare the shotgun approach of President Carter with the rifle approach taken by President Reagan. President Carter entered into his diary on the eighth day of his administration: "Everybody has warned me not to take on too many projects so early in the administration, but it's almost impossible for me to delay something that I see needs to be done."[50] Looking back at the Carter administration, it seems that "everybody" had a point.

The Carter administration got off on the right foot with much advance preparation by the transition operation and won an early victory by the renewal of the president's power to reorganize the executive branch. Negotiations with the Democratic leadership in Congress began soon after the election. But after several months in office the administration had a large number of issues on the Hill, including energy proposals, income tax reforms, hospital cost control, and welfare reforms, among other initiatives.[51] "We overloaded the circuits and blew a fuse," according to Frank Moore.[52]

Many of these legislative proposals, however, had to pass through the bottleneck of the House Ways and Means Committee. According to Frank Moore, "We're talking about ten or so major things, and eight of them have to go through Ways and Means."[53] This was the sort of logjam that President Johnson, with his intimate knowledge of Congress, would have been certain to avoid. "He sent bills one at a time rather than in a clump, which would lead to automatic opposition. Also, he sent them when the agendas of the receiving committees were clear so that they could be considered right away, without time for opposition to develop and when the members most intently concerned about the bills would be most likely to support them."[54]

The congressional leadership tried to warn Carter that the plethora of legislative proposals might jeopardize the most important parts of his agenda. In early May 1977 Senator Robert Byrd asked the president not to flood them with too many proposals for new legislation because it might make the Congress look like it was dragging its feet. Tip O'Neill told him: "You have an awful lot of balls in the air at the same time."[55] Members of the administration also wanted the president to hold back on pushing legislation at Congress. In a senior staff meeting in late March Jack Watson said, "We need to do what we can to slow the President down."[56] In late April, when Carter was warned by Secretary of the Treasury Michael Blumenthal that the timing of welfare legislation would affect tax legislation, Carter responded: "I have no preferences; my preference is to move ahead with everything at once."[57]

The volume of legislation was aggravated by Carter's refusal to choose priorities among his many initiatives. On June 22 Carter was asked to name his top priorities. He answered by listing the administration's initiatives and added: "We've got about 60 or 70 other items on the domestic agenda that I'm going over with the Speaker and Majority Leader on. I won't list them all."[58] Late in 1977 the White House staff analyzed the administration's legislative program and concluded: "If Congress did nothing but act on half of the major legislative items that we'd asked them to do, they would consume all of the legislative days that were left."[59]

Soon thereafter priorities were set and the legislative menu pared down, but the consensus of scholars and commentators is that the glut during the first year of the administration hurt its legislative record. Carter felt that a more carefully modulated approach to legislation would not have helped his legislative record, but might have eased his strained relations with Congress: "With the advantages of hindsight, it now seems that it would have been advisable to have introduced our legislation in much more careful phases—not in such a rush. We would not have accomplished any more, and perhaps less, but my relations with Congress would have been smoother and the image of undue haste and confusion could have been avoided."[60]

But the question of priorities might also be a problem of perception. If an administration tries to do many things and fails on a majority of them, public perception of competence may be lower than if it tries to do only a few things and succeeds.

CARTER'S WATER PROJECTS: TACTICAL ERROR OR STRATEGIC BLUNDER?

One early incident that hurt Carter with Congress was his decision to take on sacred congressional pork barrel legislation by eliminating nineteen water projects from his budget proposal for fiscal year 1978. The decision was made in the first month of the administration based on Carter's promise to balance the budget and protect the environment. It also was to serve notice to Congress and the country that Jimmy Carter intended to keep his promises and fight tough battles even if it meant alienating some members of Congress. The buck was going to stop with him.

Bert Lance said the intention was to show the Congress who was in charge, but it turned out to be a disaster: "We alienated a large portion of the Congress: those who had projects and those who had hopes of having projects: 100 percent alienation. It was not a good decision in my judgment, but the president felt very strongly about it."[61] Members of Congress were irate, in part because they were not consulted about the decisions, but primarily because they saw the projects as crucial to their own political interests. Russell Long (who had five projects at stake) at a meeting in the White House began a denunciation of the Carter decision by announcing: "My name is Russell Long, and I am the chairman of the Senate Finance Committee."[62] The sarcastic implication as he "shouted and screamed"[63] was that the Carter White House was so out of touch that they were not aware of his political power.

The question is: Why did Carter go ahead with what turned out to be a disaster in congressional relations for his administration? It was not a case of not being adequately warned against the congressional fallout. "There was nobody of any influence who didn't recommend against it," including career OMB officials who supposedly wear green eyeshades and are impervious to political arguments. In fact OMB staff were able to trim the number of projects on the block by almost half.[64] Stuart Eizenstat recalls that "it was very much his own thing.

There was very little agency involvement. Andreus [secretary of the interior] was not brought in until almost after the fact."[65] According to Charles Schultze, chairman of the Council of Economic Advisers, "Some of the projects were atrocious," but each project had a long history of political battles, and all of the hard-won victories were threatened by Carter's move.[66]

In the end Carter lost when the Senate attached the water projects as a rider to an economic stimulus bill wanted by the administration. Carter believed that the water projects were the one disagreement that "caused the deepest breach between me and the Democratic leadership." He later felt that he should have vetoed the bill despite the rest of the provisions he needed for his economic plan. "Signing this act was . . . accurately interpreted as a sign of weakness on my part, and I regretted it as much as any budget decision I made as President."[67] Frank Moore concluded that the hit list should have been more selective and that there should have been more political preparation.[68]

The point is not to criticize President Carter for a political blunder, but to see what can be learned from the incident. It is by no means clear that a president should cave in to any political opposition when he has labeled the issue one of the public interest versus narrower concerns. By standing up to such heat the president might very well be seen as tough and heroic. The incident might have ended with fewer bad consequences had it been handled differently. First, the president should not have blindsided the members of Congress whose projects were slated for elimination. Advance consultation might not have gained their support, but it would have taken away some of the ammunition from their attacks on him. Second, he might have chosen a few of the worst projects to make the symbolic point about the public interest without taking on so many members at the same time. Finally, as he said, once he publicly challenged Congress he should have stuck with his position, rather than giving up. As it turned out, he earned the animosity of much of Congress while not gaining the moral high ground of fighting to the end for the public interest.

Something might be learned from a similar incident in Lyndon Johnson's presidency. Shortly after his landslide victory in 1964, Johnson, acting on recommendations of the Budget Bureau, decided to shut down eleven veterans hospitals. His decision was justified on the efficiency grounds of patient load, standards of care, and deterioration of buildings. When members of Congress screamed and veterans groups rose up to defend the hospitals, Johnson appointed a blue-ribbon committee that included members of Congress to study the targeted hospitals. After several months of hearings and investigation, the committee found that nine of the eleven were worth saving, and even expanding and improving. Johnson told Harry McPherson, who had been handling the case for him and who had expected a different outcome, "Tell your boys with the computers that they ought to study up on the Congress sometime." McPherson suspected that Johnson might have sent word to the committee to fold on the issue rather than let the relatively small savings to the treasury damage his relations with Congress.[69]

What can we learn from these two incidents? (1) Pick your fights carefully. (2) Before you publicly commit yourself to a fight be pretty sure that you can win it. (3) Once you publicly commit yourself, stick to your guns. These tactical suggestions beg the substantive question of what is in the public interest. But a compromise in the short run may be a worthwhile price for not damaging your long-run capacity to work with the Congress.

LEARNING FROM CARTER'S MISTAKES

In summary, the causes of the problems President Carter had in dealing with Congress can be thought of in four categories: changes in Congress, changes in the public policy agenda, President Carter's action (or inactions), and Jimmy Carter's style. Thing *had* changed since the time of Lyndon Johnson. The reforms of the 1970s had fragmented Congress and left its leadership in a less powerful position. Carter writes of the House's "almost anarchic independence," and congressional staff had tripled in the past two decades.[70] Congressional staff had grown from 5,000 to 15,000. The War Powers Act and the 1974 Budget Act had been passed to wrest back congressional power from what was perceived to be an "imperial presidency." Party discipline was in decline, and the Democratic Congress was in the habit of opposing Presidents Ford and Nixon.

But important changes in the public policy agenda would have made it difficult for any Democratic president in the late 1970s. "Carter's staff was packed at second and third levels with bright, young former congressional aides or consultants, bills in hand, who had been waiting for 1965 to come again, and thought it had," according to Richard Neustadt and Ernest May.[71] The public mood of reaction against some of the Great Society and antigovernment feeling helped put Jimmy Carter in office, but made it difficult for him to deal with Congress once he was in office.[72]

Carter's fiscal conservatism and promise to balance the budget by 1981 made it difficult to satisfy traditional liberal Democratic demands for expanded social spending. "It's impossible to exaggerate how much legislative backlog there is on the Hill," argued Stuart Eizenstat. "For eight years, for God's sake, you've had essentially negative Presidents in the sense of not having strong legislative programs that a Democratic Congress could buy. And so they developed their own legislative packages. And now that they have a Democratic President they're gung-ho to go straight forward on it."[73] In addition, there was no natural constituency for many of Carter's legislative initiatives such as energy restraints, the Panama Canal legislation, welfare reform, deregulation, or Civil Service reform.

Political analyst Nelson Polsby argues, however, that there is little more than a grain of truth to these arguments. He blames Carter's poor relations with Congress on the administration's "mistakes, ineptitude, and presidential neglect of Congress."[74] Whether or not this is hyperbole, Carter did make mistakes in dealing with Congress which can be divided into his presidential actions and his personal attitudes.

As has been discussed, Carter has been criticized for overloading the legislative agenda, failing to set clear priorities, and neglecting the finer points of lobbying Congress. He has been charged with failing to consult (and sometimes even to inform) members of Congress of matters important to them, for example, federal appointments in their states and districts and the water projects. Carter felt the congressional demand for consultation was "insatiable."[75] His reversal on the fifty-dollar tax rebate undercut some of his allies on the Hill. His energy bill was put together in secret without consultation with the members of Congress who would have to guide it through the legislative process.[76]

Finally, but not of least importance, was President Carter's attitude toward Congress. Many of the so-called blunders of the Carter administration might have been overlooked if members had perceived Carter as sympathetic toward them and understanding of their political needs. Instead, Carter took the attitude that he would always act on principle and that Congress was dominated by the seamier side of politics. Carter disapproved of compromise because he knew what was in the public interest, and he felt that members of Congress should have preferred to be right rather than be reelected.[77]

Carter's early threats to go over the heads of Congress and make his case directly to "the people" did not endear him to Congress, nor did his implied comparison of the U.S. Congress to the Georgia legislature. Carter came across to many members of Congress as a self-righteous preacher. Carter's style was essentially "antipolitical" and "holier than thou," according to political scientist Charles O. Jones, but the same Carter style that irritated Congress was also part of the appeal that got him elected.[78]

What can we learn from the Carter experience? By his own admission, Carter's relations with Congress left something to be desired, and it is likely that in the absence of many of his reported "blunders" more could have been accomplished. Many of the blunders came early in his administration, and were thus magnified in their consequences. It is also true that in line with Paul Light's cycle of increasing effectiveness, the Carter administration learned from its early mistakes and ran a much more effective legislative liaison operation after its first year.[79] Unfortunately, the reputation for bumbling gained in the early days of the administration was not reversed despite improvement in performance. This hard lesson underscores the importance of an effective transition into office.

LEARNING FROM REAGAN'S VICTORIES

President Reagan's early victories in Congress have been compared to those of Franklin Roosevelt and Lyndon Johnson. Reagan benefited from the sense of economic crisis felt by the public and from his landslide victory as well as from the lack of any crises to distract from his own agenda. (The attempted assassination did not hurt, and may have helped his legislative program.) He was able to overcome the fragmenting tendencies that frustrated his three immediate predecessors in their efforts with the Congress. But his success was qualified by the fact that he focused his legislative efforts on his economic program to the virtual exclusion of other Republican priorities. The main elements of the impressive, early legislative victories of the Reagan administration were its courting of Congress, its legislative liaison operation, and its overall legislative strategy.

Ronald Reagan began the careful courting of Congress long before he became president-elect. In 1977 he helped set up a political action committee, Citizens for the Republic, that funneled campaign money to Republican candidates. The payoff came when sixty-two of those he helped were victorious and could be expected to be grateful for his help and perceived coattails.[80] After his nomination, his aides made early contacts with members of Congress and set up a network of advisory committees for the Reagan campaign that included 160 members of Congress.[81] He made a symbolic gesture to the importance of Congress during his campaign by staging on the steps of the Capitol a show of unity on his future legislative agenda. While not specific in substance, it was intended as an important gesture. Of more substantive importance was Reagan's inclusion of Senator Paul Laxalt and Representative Thomas B. Evans, Jr., in weekly campaign strategy sessions at his headquarters in Arlington, Virginia.

After the election, Congress continued to be a major transition priority. The president-elect held a series of dinners to which he invited members of Congress. Realizing that Democratic votes would be necessary for his legislative agenda, he announced that he would retain ex-Democratic Senator Mike Mansfield as ambassador to Japan. He took particular care to court House Majority Leader Tip O'Neill, who had chafed at perceived slights from the Carter White House. He and his wife were invited to a private dinner at the White House, and he was also invited to the president's small seventieth birthday party. These were striking gestures given the ideological gap between the two men. Republican members of Congress were invited to advise the transition teams in the departments. And the president-elect sought the advice of Senators Robert Dole, John Tower, and Strom Thurmond in making his cabinet choices.

Choosing Max Friedersdorf as head of congressional liaison was important in Reagan's legislative strategy. Friedersdorf was widely respected on the Hill and selected his lobbying staff from those with strong professional experience with Congress. The intention was to show a sharp contrast with President Carter's choice of Frank Moore, who recruited a less-experienced lobbying staff. In his dealings with Congress, Reagan consciously deemphasized his campaign as an outsider to Washington. His advisers felt that President Carter's failure to make overtures to the Washington establishment had been one of the reasons for his lack of early success with the Congress.

The main elements of the Reagan legislative strategy were speed and focus. Old Washington hands and academics alike had warned that the scope of budgetary changes sought by the new administration would be virtually impossible to get through the Congress, particularly the Democratic House. The Reagan strategists realized that if it was to be done at all it had to be done quickly, both to take advantage of the "mandate" and to move before opposition could coalesce. During the first months of 1981 the Democrats were in shock from the Republican electoral victory and were unable to unite on any coherent opposition to the Reagan economic program.

The campaign for the administration's economic agenda dominated Reagan's first year in office. "We knew we had to get our bills enacted before the Labor Day recess," Max Friedersdorf said. As time passes partisan divisions become more important, members of Congress become more concerned with their constituencies and reelection, and the president's popularity declines.[82]

The second element of the strategy, focus, was intended to avoid what they felt was the Carter mistake of sending Congress too much legislation to digest. Thus the Reagan strategy systematically neglected other Republican priorities, particularly "social issues," such as busing, abortion, school prayer, and crime. According to Max Friedersdorf, "The president was determined not to clutter up the landscape with extraneous legislation."[83] This drastic limiting of presidential priorities was part of the administration's strategic approach to the presidency. It felt that the economy was the most important issue facing the country, and success on budget priorities (increasing defense spending and cutting social spending) and cutting taxes were paramount. This also allowed the president to include many complex issues within a few simple principles that Reagan argued were in the best interests of the country. President Carter had difficulty giving coherence to his many priorities and legislative initiatives.[84]

The winning of the votes of the Boll Weevils (and of other House members) covered the gamut of legislative tactics from soft sell to hardball. To garner votes for his economic package the president systematically and personally dealt with wavering members. He called them repeatedly; he invited them to the White House and Camp David and gave them small favors such as cuff links or tickets to the presidential box at the Kennedy Center. The president's personal approach was understated and soft-pedaled. He dealt with the general issues and did not get involved with the details of legislative horse-trading. His aides would follow up with specific promises and threats.[85] Personal presidential involvement was seen as crucial to the legislative success of the administration, and, according to Max Friedersdorf, Reagan spent more time on congressional affairs than at any other of his responsibilities during his first year.[86]

In bargaining with the Congress, Reagan took pains to stick to his few, simple priorities. The administration was very careful not to seem to reverse itself in order to avoid the reputation that President Carter had for flip-flopping. This does not mean that the administration was rigid or unable to make compromises.

"A typical script found the president enunciating some simple principle, followed by reports of the president resisting counterpressures with great stubbornness, then an eventual compromise sufficient for the president's proposal to win passage without the president himself appearing to engage in political bargaining, and finally a White House claim of victory."[87]

The administration also made specific compromises to win votes in Congress, such as the "rental" of Democrat John Breaux's vote in exchange for a pledge on sugar price supports or a compromise on peanut price supports.[88] When the carrots of favors and compromises did not do the job, the sticks of political hardball were brought out. One of the main tactics was going directly to the voters.[89] It is ironic that President Carter was criticized so severely on the Hill for *threatening* to go over the heads of Congress to the people if legislators would not give him what he wanted. President Reagan did not threaten; he just did it. He put pressure on Congress by a series of televised speeches to the nation as well as personal appeals to groups around the country by himself and members of his administration. In the battle for the administration's tax bill, the president in a televised speech asked people to call their representatives and demand support for his bill. With the help of donated corporate phone banks, the volume of calls at the Capitol switchboard doubled.[90]

One of the most potent tactics was the use of electoral leverage. There was the threat that big political action money would be used against those who opposed the President's program.[91] There was also the promise that conservative organizations, such as the Committee for the Survival of a Free Congress, and the Fund for the Conservative Majority, would not campaign against Democrats voting the right way.[92] There was even a presidential promise not to campaign against southern Democrats who consistently supported his budget program.[93]

How did President Reagan achieve virtually all of his legislative goals during his first eight months in office? He included members of Congress in his preelection and preinaugural activities. After his election he dropped most of his anti-Washington rhetoric and assiduously courted Congress, emphasizing his respect for the institution. Once in office he moved quickly to take advantage of his "mandate" from the voters and to create momentum with early victories. He strictly limited his legislative agenda to his budget and tax initiatives, to the neglect of other priorities. Finally, he became personally involved with the lobbying for his program and spent a significant proportion of his time on his legislative agenda.

The failure of President Reagan to sustain his early level of success with Congress over his two terms is not surprising, given the controversial nature of many of his legislative proposals. As calculated by *Congressional Quarterly,* his success rate in Congress dropped steadily from 82.4 percent in 1981 to 56.6 percent in 1986, and to an average of 45.0 percent in his last two years, despite his relatively high personal popularity with the public.[94] What is striking is the magnitude of his early victories in moving the Congress in new policy directions. We

can learn from this that presidential leadership can make an important difference, but that it is most effectively exercised early in a president's first term.

The emphasis in this chapter has been on the negative aspects of the
Carter administration's legislative operations and the positive aspects of the
Reagan administration's. The contrasts were systematically overstated. For
instance, President Carter said many complimentary things about Congress.
He also did many of the same things as President Reagan in courting Congress: called members, invited them to the White House, and so on. The purpose of this chapter has been to see what we can learn about getting the
presidents' legislative agenda enacted. The intention was not to present a balanced evaluation of the two presidents' approaches to public policy or their
contributions to the well-being of the Republic.

7

The Bush Transition: A Friendly Takeover

The challenges facing George Bush during his transition and early weeks in office were to distinguish himself from his predecessor, put his own stamp on the executive branch, and pursue his own policy agenda. President Bush was the first president elected to succeed a predecessor of his own party since 1928 and the first sitting vice president to be elected in his own right since 1836. But succeeding the president he served as vice president proved to be a mixed blessing. The easy parts of the Bush transition were several: he had President Reagan's help, Republican party loyalists held leadership positions in the executive branch, and no great changes in policy were necessary.

The difficult aspects of President Bush's transition were a mirror reflection of the easy side. Bush could not be seen to be rejecting his predecessor, yet he had to define his own presidency. He could not dismiss Reagan executives too roughly, yet he had to make room for his own appointments. He could not change policy directions too sharply, yet he had to set a distinctive direction for his own administration. To complicate these challenges, he was facing a Congress with the fewest partisan seats of any newly elected president in the twentieth century.[1] It was dominated by Democrats who had become used to opposing the Reagan administration and who thought they had as plausible a mandate to govern as had the president.

TRANSITION PLANNING AND SYMBOLIC CHANGES

Whatever the planning in 1988 that went into the preparations of the two candidates for the presidency, the experience with the large Reagan transition bureaucracy in 1980–1981 was enough to ensure that the transition organization of 1988–1989 would be considerably smaller in size. The Bush transition teams in departments and agencies were low-level contact points rather than the policy-oriented and personnel channels that the Carter and Reagan transition teams were.[2] The Bush teams were smaller, more disciplined, and less threatening to departments and agencies than in 1980–1981.[3]

At Christmas of 1987 Chase Untermeyer offered to undertake a low-visibility transition planning operation. Bush agreed, though he insisted on extreme discretion, since at that time it was by no means certain that Bush would survive the Republican primaries, much less be elected the next November. Later in the campaign it became likely that Untermeyer would become the director of Presidential Personnel in a future Bush administration. Nevertheless, Bush forbade him to take any steps to assemble the beginnings of a personnel operation. He could not set up an office, establish mail-handling operations, create computer programs, or even recruit his own staff, much less do any actual personnel planning. Bush also insisted that the small operation be entirely separate from the campaign and from the Office of the Vice President.[4]

President Reagan paved the way for the hoped-for Bush transition in unprecedented ways. In contrast with the lukewarm support Presidents Eisenhower and Johnson gave their vice presidents, Reagan campaigned long and hard for Bush, traveling many thousands of miles and visiting key states. Personnel changes in the cabinet in 1988 were molded to fit Bush priorities: Attorney General Meese resigned; and secretaries of education (Lauro Cavazos), treasury (Nicholas Brady), and justice (Richard Thornburgh) were appointed after assuring that they were acceptable to Bush and would be kept on in his administration. Immediately after the election, resignations were requested from all Reagan political appointees so that a newly inaugurated President Bush would not be the one to deliver the bad news.

Despite all of these careful preparations, President-elect Bush faced a difficult situation in the transition to his own presidency. His campaign made it clear that he saw no need for basic changes in direction from the Reagan presidency; there would be policy continuity between the two presidencies. As he said in his campaign kickoff speech: "We don't need radical new directions. We need strong and steady leadership. We don't need to remake society, we just need to remember who we are."[5] This made it more difficult for Bush to establish his own administration and not seem merely to preside over a third Reagan term.

Thus in his first months in office President Bush engaged in what might be called "the semiotics of dissimilarity," that is, symbolic changes to distinguish himself from his popular predecessor.[6] In his acceptance speech at the Republican National Convention in the summer of 1988, Bush spoke of his goal of a "kinder, gentler America." (Nancy Reagan is said to have remarked, "Kinder and gentler than *whom*?") Bush clearly saw the Reagan administration agenda on social policy to be more punitive than was his preference. During the transition and inauguration the extended Bush family was highly visible, a subtle contrast to the Reagan family disputes, with three books by Reagan children casting unfavorable light on the Reagans as parents. The president met very publicly with African-American leaders on Martin Luther King Day ceremonies, a sharp contrast with President Reagan, who had criticized the motives of civil rights leaders in a television appearance in the last week of his presidency.[7]

The president's early public statements placed heavy emphasis on the importance that high ethical standards would play in his administration, a not-so-subtle contrast with what had become known as the "sleaze factor" in the Reagan administration. But this issue turned around to bite him several weeks later when conflict of interest concerns were raised about C. Boyden Gray, James Baker, and John Tower.[8] Early press stories emphasized the way in which George Bush would be a "hands-on" president, dealing with the details of policy issues. He also kept working hours from about 7:00 A.M. to 6:00 P.M., in contrast with Reagan's usual nine-to-five schedule. Reporters were told of the many phone calls he made every day to "keep in touch" and not allow himself to be isolated by the White House staff.

President Reagan had been criticized for refusing to hold press conferences and for not being available for reporters' questions. President Bush held more news conferences in his first eighty days in office than President Reagan did during his last two years in office. Reagan held fifty news conferences in his eight years; they were usually highly structured and lasted precisely thirty minutes.[9] During his four years President Bush held 280 press conferences, most of which were much less managed than Reagan's and often went beyond the time allotted.[10] Bush even invited reporters to social occasions at the White House and at his home in Kennebunkport, Maine. One of the ironies of these consciously planned contrasts between the two presidents was the White House claim that President Bush had a disdain for the symbolic and rhetorical aspects of the presidency, implying that Reagan emphasized symbol over substance. After a campaign in which his "handlers" played such an important role, President Bush went out of his way to present himself as spontaneous and nonscripted. "This presidency doesn't have an image maker," asserted Stephen Studdert, a White House aide.[11] According to Marlin Fitzwater, press secretary to both Presidents Reagan and Bush, "There was the basic old–New England, Yankee honesty of spirit about George Bush that made him distrustful of anything that was staged. He used to say to me, 'Don't tell me what to do, Marlin, I'm not a piece of meat. . . .' So he just resisted any efforts to stage manage him or do the basic public relations things that we wanted him to do."[12]

The symbolic distinctions also were symptoms of a deeper resentment that festered with the vice presidential staffers during the Reagan administration and who were now in charge and willing to repay former slights. For example, after the traditional changing of photographs in the White House during the inauguration, all photographs of Reagan were removed from the West Wing, even though Presidents Ford and Carter appeared in some.[13] In a film about the history of the White House produced during the Bush administration, with commentary by the

President and First Lady, film footage of all presidents since Herbert Hoover was included, with the conspicuous exception of Ronald Reagan,[14] who rated only a one-second shot of an image of his face with no mention of his name.

The cumulation of these conscious contrasts and the willingness of White House staffers to call press attention to them prompted a letter from Richard Nixon to John Sununu. Nixon admonished Sununu and told him that Bush appeared ungrateful for Reagan's support in the campaign and that he might need Reagan's support in the future. Sununu rebuked the White House staff, and Bush called Mr. Reagan to apologize.[15] Bush enjoyed an early honeymoon with the press in which he was favorably contrasted with President Reagan. He began his presidency with the same public approval ratings as had Reagan, but Bush went on to achieve record popularity while Reagan's ratings dropped off, never reaching the level of Bush's.[16]

ORGANIZING THE ADMINISTRATION

President Bush took sixty-five days to designate his cabinet, which was composed of competent, experienced people with cumulatively more than a century of experience with previous administrations.[17] In the first meeting of his cabinet, President-elect Bush said that he would tell them to "think big" and "challenge the system." "I want them to be frank; I want them to fight hard for their position. And then when I make the call, I'd like to have the feeling that they'd be able to support the president." In dealing with the Hill, he said: "We're going to have some fights with Congress, but we're not going to approach it as though we're dealing with the enemy."[18]

Bush intended to continue the cabinet council system of the second Reagan term, with three councils: Economic Policy, chaired by Treasury Secretary Brady; Domestic Policy, chaired by Attorney General Thornburgh; and National Security, chaired by the president's adviser for national security, Brent Scowcroft. The domestic and economic councils met for one hour every other week during the first six months of the administration.[19] The design of the policy development process was heavily influenced by Roger Porter, assistant to the president for economic and domestic policy. Porter had pioneered the cabinet council idea in the Ford administration and helped to implement it for President Reagan.

Porter's analysis of "multiple advocacy" as a model for advising the president also influenced the Bush White House.[20] Bush's preference was for oral briefings (in contrast to Nixon's and Carter's preferences for written option papers), and for direct confrontation of those on opposing sides of policy issues. To help the president deliberate on policy issues White House aides set up "scheduled train wrecks" in which administration officials would engage in policy disagreements and answer questions from the president. The president said that his approach to staff advice was "to get good, strong, experienced people, encourage them to express their views openly, encourage them not to hold back."[21]

While coordination with White House staff was enforced, cabinet secretaries close to the president were given significant leeway in policy development. At times in the early months of the Bush administration, cabinet secretaries took initiatives without checking with the White House first.[22] This marked a change from the Reagan administration, in which White House staffers dominated the cabinet. "The President has a lot of confidence in the Cabinet members, and he gives them a lot of latitude to act," according to Secretary to the Cabinet David Bates.[23]

The White House staff role was to act as brokers rather than to ride herd on cabinet secretaries, an appropriate role for White House staffers as long as the president's policies are being implemented. The Bush staff early in his administration was in marked contrast to the dominant White House staff of Ronald Reagan.[24] Bush was much more likely to talk directly with his cabinet secretaries and to assert personal control in policy making than was Ronald Reagan.[25] Most members of his cabinet were personal friends whom he had known for more than a decade and who played active roles in advising the president.[26]

Direct communication between the president and cabinet members is the most effective way to keep the White House staff on tap rather than on top.[27] One senior White House official characterized the Bush White House staff: "This staff is precisely what Bush wants: nice people who will not handle him or try to, people who are technically competent and without much ideology, people who will not usurp power that belongs to the President and cabinet."[28] The first year of the administration was not marred by the tensions and rivalries among its major foreign policy officials that had hurt the Nixon, Carter, and Reagan presidencies. Brent Scowcroft, Richard Cheney, and James Baker had worked together in previous administrations, and President Bush insisted on collegiality. This close relationship among the Bush national security aides was to pay off in the effective conduct of the Gulf War in 1990–1991.[29]

President Bush may have formed the most influential cabinet since President Eisenhower in terms of the willingness of the president to give cabinet secretaries the latitude within which to operate in their jurisdictions. It is ironic that President Bush, one of the few recent presidents who did not talk about "cabinet government," may have come closest to achieving it. The influence of cabinet secretaries individually, however, did not extend to them as a collectivity. The cabinet met about once a month and was "used more for a briefing session" than for policy deliberation, according to Secretary to the Cabinet David Bates.[30] The use of the full cabinet as a deliberative body had greatly diminished since its effective use by President Eisenhower. This was due to the cabinet's increased size (with fourteen cabinet departments in 1989), but more importantly to the crosscutting nature of most presidential policy issues and the president's need for advice from a broader perspective than that of individual department heads.[31]

George Bush recruited a competent White House staff marked by experience, professionalism, and a low-visibility approach to White House service. The best in White House staff service was exemplified by Brent Scowcroft, assistant to the president for National Security Affairs, who had filled the same role in the Ford administration. Scowcroft was tireless in his service to Bush, and often provided a personal sounding board to the president's thoughts about foreign affairs. Another model White House staffer was Roger Porter, who had served in the Ford and Reagan administrations and was given responsibility for domestic and economic policy staff coordination in the Bush White House. He provided experience, expertise, and sound policy analysis without engaging in public disputes over policy or status, trying to strong-arm members of the cabinet, or using his position to pursue his own policy agenda.

Bush's White House staff did not tend to interpose themselves between the president and cabinet secretaries or to have major fights with the cabinet departments because Bush knew his cabinet appointees well and, unlike Reagan, made it a habit to keep in touch with them. Thus Bush's White House Staff exhibited few major ego problems or conflicts with the cabinet, with one major exception: his chief of staff, John Sununu.[32]

Chief of Staff

Hints of future problems arose during the transition in the maneuvering over how the Bush White House would be organized. After reportedly turning down two cabinet positions and insisting on the chief of staff slot, Sununu began to define his future role in press interviews. In an interview with the *Boston Globe* Sununu gave the impression that he would play the role of a strong chief by staff by being a "strong doorkeeper," a "tough critic" of OMB's budget before the president saw it, and the setter of the daily White House agenda. Sununu was also fighting publicly over the possible role of Robert M. Teeter, who was offered the position of deputy chief of staff but whose relationship with Bush would have guaranteed him a strong voice in the White House. The problem for Teeter, and probably the reason he decided to decline a job in the administration, was that Sununu insisted that Teeter not be allowed into the Oval Office to see the president alone.[33]

This jockeying for position in public and fighting over access to the president before he even took office or made his own decisions about White House organization was unseemly and provided early warnings about how Sununu would conduct the office of chief of staff. Of course, maneuvering for position always occurs during a presidential transition, but the Meese-Baker negotiations during the Reagan transition were less acrimonious and were not fought out in public.

President Bush, who had a chief of staff when he was vice president (Craig Fuller), clearly wanted one to organize the White House and coordinate policy development. And Sununu performed well many of the traditional chief of staff roles. He made the trains run on time. He was the enforcer with respect to White House staffers, the cabinet, and Congress. He fired people. He took the heat for unpopular decisions.

Sununu presided over the senior staff meeting every day at 7:30 A.M. in the Roosevelt Room in the White House. Typically he spent from 8:00 to 9:30 A.M. in the Oval Office with the president for the national security briefing and setting priorities for the day and ended the day with the president from 4:30 to 5:00 P.M. During the day he would see the president about ten times and would spend a total of 35 to 45 percent of the day with the president.[34]

One common mistake of chiefs of staff that Sununu did not make was to reinforce a presidential weakness, as had Regan and Haldeman before him. He provided a sharp contrast in personal style to the president. He was the president's "pit bull" who would act mean and allow the president to take the "kinder and gentler" stance. Sununu, unlike most other chiefs of staff, had firm ideological convictions and advocated his own policy preferences. But what would ordinarily be a major drawback in a chief of staff worked to the president's advantage in this case. Sununu was more conservative politically than the president and was able to play a highly visible role as keeper of the conservative flame and representative of the conservative wing of the Republican party in the White House. This was useful for Bush when Sununu would stake out a very conservative position, for instance, on environmental policy. The president could then take a more moderate stance, thus reassuring conservatives that their interests were being represented in the White House while letting the president still claim to be "the environmental president."

The danger of a chief of staff who is also a policy advocate is that advice to the president might be skewed to favor the chief of staff's favored outcome. The other common danger of a strong chief of staff is that access to the president will be constricted to a trickle. But neither of these potential pitfalls was a danger to George Bush. He knew enough about the policy issues himself to be able to discount the bias of his staff. And his personal style assured that he would not become isolated, even though Sununu did control access to the Oval Office. The danger of becoming isolated was averted because the president knew his cabinet members well and kept in touch with them. They had the personal relationship with Bush that would assure they could talk with him if they needed to. The president was constantly on the phone, touching base with anyone who was involved with current policy issues.

But the president's penchant for keeping in touch, while avoiding the danger of isolation, did not entirely eliminate Sununu's attempts to control communication with the president. At times Sununu's personal policy agenda made it difficult for those in the cabinet or staff who wanted to speak with the president about a different approach to get through Sununu's gauntlet. At one point the president felt the need to open a post office box at his summer home in Kennebunkport, Maine, as a back channel so that members of his cabinet could contact him directly without Sununu's censorship.[35]

The very fact that President Bush felt compelled to set up a private post office box physically and organizationally outside the White House was an admission of organizational failure. Later, in the fall of 1991, Michael Boskin, the chair of the Council of Economic Advisers, wanted to see the president about economic policy. After several attempts had been blocked by Sununu, Boskin had to threaten to resign before Sununu would let him through.[36] In these instances John Sununu was not acting as a "neutral broker" of ideas for the president so that others would have confidence their ideas would get to the president intact if they submitted them to the White House staff. Instead, Sununu was seen as a biased filter screening out ideas he personally did not like.

Despite his rapport with the president and his ability to perform very valuable chief of staff functions, Sununu alienated members of Congress, the press, and interest groups. Sununu was also willing to alienate cabinet secretaries as well as their subordinates. He often undercut their policy proposals to the president, which may very well have been part of his job as chief of staff, policing the policy development function. When he fought HHS Secretary Louis Sullivan on civil rights policy or EPA Administrator William Reilly on environmental issues, it was arguably part of his job and carrying out the president's wishes. But the tone of his communications often left cabinet members feeling that more than policy differences were being conveyed. The gratuitous insulting of members of the administration is not a necessary part of the policy coordination function.

In defense of his behavior Sununu echoed other chiefs of staff in claiming he was merely doing the president's bidding: "I'm no freelancer. I meet with the president dozens of times during the day. . . . The president knows I'm following his agenda. . . . I know enough about the president to do exactly what he wants done. Exactly what he wants done."[37] In this statement Sununu was both claiming presidential authority for all of his own actions and subtly shifting the blame for any of them to the president.

Sununu's defense and explanation for his lack of civility were that he was doing the president's bidding: "I don't care if people hate me, as long as they hate me for the right reasons."[38] But that was the problem. Washington professionals understand that the policy preferences of the president are the responsibility of the chief of staff, and they expect him to be tough for the president. Professionals are willing to accept being beaten in the policy arena, but Sununu's gratuitous ad hominem insults and rude behavior generated resentments much greater than mere policy defeats would have.

Sununu's decline began in the spring of 1991 when the *Washington Post* reported that the chief of staff had taken more than seventy trips around the country aboard military aircraft. Almost all of the trips were designated (by the chief of staff) as official business, even though the purpose of some of them seemed to be to provide skiing trips for Sununu and his family. None of the twenty-seven trips to his home state of New Hampshire were designated as personal.[39] In addition, Sununu allowed ski-industry organizations to pay for his meals, lodging, lift tickets, and air fare for his wife.

When the disclosures caused a public scandal in May 1991, the president (whose early priority was to have an administration above ethical reproach) ordered Sununu to clear all future flights with the White House counsel's office. But in June Sununu had a White House limousine take him to New York for a stamp auction he wanted to attend and solicited corporations to provide air travel back to Washington and other trips. The president again was forced to restrict Sununu's travel practices.[40]

There is no argument here that all of Sununu's trips on government planes constituted outrageous or illegal behavior, or that White House staffers should always fly coach. Few would begrudge a few trips on official planes with occasional combinations of business with pleasure. High-level officials in Congress and the executive branch have done this for decades, and it is standard practice in corporate America. The point is that Sununu abused his privileges and pushed them to excess. His bending of the rules was routine, pervasive, and systematic. He was unable to restrain himself from taking advantage of his position and, amazingly, was unwilling to rein himself in even after the president publicly admonished him. By pushing his privileges too far Sununu became an embarrassment to the president, who was forced to defend him in public. A chief of staff should never put the president in this position.

Even though he took pride in taking flack for the president, Sununu's final mistake was to blame the president for a gaffe. At a November 1991 campaign fund-raising speech in New York President Bush remarked that people in the financial community felt that interest rates charged on credit cards were higher than necessary and that it might spur the economy if they came down a bit. The next day Senator Alphonse D'Amato (R-NY) introduced legislation to impose a legal limit on the interest rates credit card companies could charge their customers: The economic wisdom of the proposal was challenged in the financial community, and the Dow-Jones Industrial Average fell 120 points. The administration had to back away quickly from the proposed legislation and publicly argue against it.

When asked by reporters about this embarrassing episode, Sununu said that the remarks about credit card interest rates were not in the president's prepared text but that the president had "ad-libbed" them. This attempt to blame the embarrassing remarks on the president was rebutted by Marlin Fitzwater, the president's spokesman. He told reporters that the lines were in the printed text of the speech and were not ad-libbed. Some administration officials even said that Sununu himself was the author of the offending lines.[41]

The issue in this case is not whether the lines were in the speech text or not. The issue is who publicly takes the blame for an embarrassing incident. In this case Sununu publicly tried to shift blame to the president. If Sununu were lying about the speech text, his behavior was outrageous. But even if he were telling the truth, it is not the role of the chief of staff to publicly blame the president for an administration blunder. The appropriate behavior for the chief of staff is to take the heat in order to protect the president.

The final downfall and firing of Sununu took place soon after the credit card incident, which was merely the final straw. As one Bush loyalist put it, "This guy just doesn't get it. . . . He's like the guard dog who starts attacking the house guests and has to be put to sleep."[42] When the ax finally fell and the president asked for Sununu's resignation, he still would not admit to being at fault. He blamed the press, the White House staff, and pro-Israeli groups (supposedly because he was of Lebanese origin and had been active in Arab-American groups).[43] Even in his letter of resignation Sununu implied that all of his actions were at the behest of the president: "I assure you that in pit bull mode or pussy cat mode *(your choice, as always)* I am ready to help."[44]

Shortly after Sununu resigned he was replaced by Secretary of Transportation Samuel Skinner. Skinner had a reputation as a hard taskmaster but one who was supportive of his subordinates. His task was to organize the White House for the 1992 presidential campaign and to avoid the excesses of his predecessor.[45] Skinner got high marks for civility of manner and inclusiveness in structuring advice to the president. But the broader problem of the Bush presidency after the Gulf War and heading into the 1992 election year was to establish a domestic policy agenda that would convince voters that President Bush should be reelected. The administration was divided about how best to do this, and Skinner could not solve the strategic issue while gearing up the White House for the campaign. Thus in the summer of 1992, when President Bush was faring poorly in the polls and falling behind Bill Clinton, he persuaded James Baker to leave the State Department and return to the White House as chief of staff. The return of the loyal and experienced Baker, however, could not save the election for Bush.

POLITICAL APPOINTMENTS

The fact that the transition to a Bush administration was a "friendly takeover" was a mixed blessing to personnel recruiter Chase Untermeyer. On the one hand, there was no rush, as there would be with a party-turnover transition, to ensure that the opposition political party was out of office as soon as possible. Those people remaining in policy-making positions were loyal Republicans who were no threat to Bush priorities. On the other hand, since they were loyal Republicans and had supported George Bush, many hoped and expected to stay on into a Bush administration. After all, they had high-level experience, and most were by that time qualified for the positions they held.

But the Bush people felt that substantial turnover was needed to ensure that the new administration would be Bush's and not merely an extension of the Reagan administration.[46] There was no precedent since 1929 about how to deal with political holdovers from the same party after an election, but early after the election transition officials made it clear that they intended a major turnover of political personnel. While statements during the transition indicated an expected turnover in the 90 percent range, in the summer of 1989 about 35 percent of sub-cabinet appointees had also served in the Reagan administration (not necessarily in the same position).[47] By July 1990 about 22 percent of the Reagan appointees remained in the Bush administration.[48] And by the end of the administration more than half of Bush PAS appointees had experience in the Reagan administration.[49]

The Bush transition was flooded with applications and recommendations for jobs, just as other recent transitions had been. By the time of inauguration about 16,000 resumes had been collected, including a special bequest by the Heritage Foundation of a ten-foot stack of 2,500 résumés of conservatives that Heritage thought would benefit the administration. Echoing former personnel directors, one official said that choosing from among so many résumés was like "trying to take a sip from a fire hydrant."[50] After the inauguration the volume kept up, and by the end of May more than 70,000 applications and recommendations had been received (though after eliminating duplicate resumes, the total number of files was closer to 45,000), a staggering mountain of paper.[51]

The major criterion for all new presidents in their appointments is loyalty, but loyalty comes in many guises: partisan, personal, ideological. The definition for the Bush Administration was personal loyalty to Bush over many years. The administration's emphasis on personal loyalty, however, was mitigated by a heavy dose of respect for competence. Untermeyer told the story of a past mayor of Houston who spent most of his first term in office appointing his friends to positions and, because of their incompetence, had to spend most of his second term getting rid of them.[52]

Bush's cabinet members were widely praised for their experience and competence, and his appointments called attention to the irony of Bush's campaign rhetoric that the election was about ideology rather than competence. According to transition codirector Craig Fuller, if personal recruiters erred in selections, they decided "to err on the side of expertise and qualifications for the job. We don't run around with a lot of litmus paper in our pockets. We want people who are philosophically and ideologically compatible, but we're really looking for the best people we can find."[53] The Bush personnel operation was a sharp contrast with Reagan recruitment efforts, about which White House official Lyn Nofziger said: "As far as I'm concerned, anyone who supported Reagan is competent."[54]

Another significant contrast with the Reagan administration was the willingness of President Bush to consider career public servants for presidential appointments and other high-level positions. This policy decision reflected the shift in tone of President Bush from the previous administration, which saw government as part of "the problem" and distrusted career civil servants.[55] In explaining Bush's approach, political scientist Nelson Polsby characterized Bush as an American tory: "Bush is a genuine conservative, an American tory. There are known characteristics of that breed: They care about the society and the government that is handed to them; they want to keep the boat afloat. Bush is a professional in public service, which means he has respect for other professionals. Conventional wisdom means something to him. He pays attention to people who are supposed to be experts. These are qualities he does not share with his predecessor."[56]

But the Bush transition was no exception to the general rule that any new president will be attacked by his own party for not appointing enough of the "party faithful." Richard Nixon was attacked by Robert Dole for not appointing enough loyal Republicans. Jimmy Carter was attacked by the Democratic National Committee. Ronald Reagan was attacked by the right wing of his party through its White House spokesman, Lyn Nofziger, for neglecting the true "Reaganites."

President Bush was put under pressure from his own appointees in the demand for appointments. The secretary of commerce, Robert Mosbacher, Sr., who was finance chairman for the Bush campaign, publicly complained that not enough fund-raisers were being appointed by the new administration: "There's this perception . . . that fund-raisers and fund-givers are nice, interesting people to be sort of patted on the head when you need them and ignored the rest of the time because they don't really understand the process. . . . Quite a high percentage of those who have been helpful haven't gotten anything—at least 50 percent."[57]

The *New York Times* reported that there was a "must place" list of fifty major donors who wanted jobs for themselves or for their relatives. The *Times* also reported that more than a dozen major donors had been appointed to major ambassadorial posts.[58] The ratio of political to career chiefs of mission continued to remain at relatively high levels in the early months of the administration, evoking expressions of concern that some ambassadorial appointments were undermining the professionalism of U.S. diplomacy.[59]

In general, however, the Bush personnel operation was not obsessed with narrow definitions of loyalty or White House control of all appointments, as was the Reagan administration. The Bush administration, despite several major exceptions, decided to give significant leeway to cabinet secretaries to choose, in consultation with the Office of Presidential Personnel, their own management teams at the subcabinet level.[60] The argument for this approach is that cabinet secretaries are likely to be motivated to recruit qualified people and they ought to be able to have their own management teams to run their departments.

Untermeyer considered the function of the Office of Presidential Personnel to be to ensure that the political and policy interests of the president were protected. Those cabinet secretaries who were particularly close to the president (for example, James Baker, Nicholas Brady, and Robert Mosbacher) had the greatest leeway in their choice of subordinates. Others did not have a blank check, but neither did the Office of Presidential Personnel often operate with a heavy hand. Mutual accommodation was the rule. Untermeyer asserted that, as a matter of principle, "No department or agency chief will have an appointee forced down his or her throat, that is, imposed by the White House. Conversely, every decision is a presidential decision."[61]

The Bush administration did recognize the traditional patronage imperatives of U.S. politics and instructed its appointees that the Bush political operation wanted 700 or 800 (about half of Schedule C positions) reserved for campaign workers and key supporters. As one official put it during the transition, "Our people don't have agendas. They have mortgages. They want jobs."[62] A "Special Schedule C Project" was set up in the Office of Presidential Personnel to place longtime Bush supporters in departments and agencies.[63] A "scrub group," under the direction of the president's nephew, Scott Bush, saw itself as the guardian of the personnel process to assure that Bush loyalists were not neglected in the handing out of jobs.[64] Lists of people were sent to agencies with strong recommendations from the Office of Presidential Personnel, even though Schedule C appointments are legally agency-head appointments.[65] This placement of campaign personnel caused some administrative problems when departments had to absorb lists of people before subcabinet appointments had been made and before appointees had a chance to form their own management teams.[66]

The internal clearance process for Bush appointees was simple compared with the Reagan process, which had many veto points. Once Untermeyer and the cabinet secretary agreed on a person, the nomination went forward to Chief of Staff John Sununu and then to the president, with very few proposed nominations rejected by the president.[67] Unexpectedly, the Bush personnel operation functioned at a slower pace than had those of most previous administrations. A number of factors contributed to the slowness of appointments, including more thorough FBI investigations and a slower Senate confirmation process. In addition, there was no great feeling of urgency on the part of the administration to move quickly, since loyal Republicans were still in office.

On March 18, 1989, eight departments and agencies had only one Bush appointee on board, and by April 1 only 28 policy-level appointments had been confirmed by the Senate.[68] On August 10, 156 of 394 of the top executive branch positions had been filled, according to Congressional Research Service calculations, and there were not even nominations for 160 of the positions.[69] According to administration calculations, by February 6, 1990, 51 percent (323) of new Bush PAS nominees had been confirmed by the Senate.[70]

Part of the reason for the slowness in appointments was the deliberate decision by George Bush not to let Untermeyer set up an office, pre-sort personnel resumes, or even recruit his own staff before the election. Much of the personnel organizational work of the first month of the transition might have been done before the election, but Bush decided that the risk of distracting the campaign was too great.[71]

THE BUSH POLICY AGENDA

Much of the 1988 Bush campaign was about drawing symbolic distinctions between Bush and Dukakis—or, as Bush put it, the campaign was about ideology, not competence (as Dukakis had asserted). Candidate Bush also campaigned around a number of issues, including education, the environment, the drug problem, crime control, and banking reform, promising at times to be the education president or the environmental president. But his ability to propose new programs or expand existing ones was severely limited by his promise of "no new taxes," the large deficits that the Reagan administration had produced, and the Democratic Congress.

During the 1988 campaign Bush had to walk a fine line between right-wing Republican conservatives and moderates of both parties. Shortly after his victory, when asked about the mandate provided by his election, he said: "Well, I don't know whether I want to use the word *mandate*. . . . I would simply say the people have spoken, the verdict was clear, and therefore I will take what I think the prime issues of the campaign were and work constructively with Congress to attain the will of the people."[72] In his inaugural address Bush emphasized continuity and stewardship of the Reagan legacy rather than a new beginning: "Some see leadership as high drama and the sound of trumpets calling, and sometimes it is that. But I see history as a book with many pages, and each day we fill a page with acts of hopefulness and meaning. The new breeze blows, a page turns, the story unfolds."

Policy planning during the transition emphasized themes rather than new policy directions. Robert Teeter, one of Bush's top advisers, worked out a hundred-day plan that emphasized different themes that would shape the new presidency's image. Rather than attempting major policy change, he argued that the presidency "has enormous power to lead simply by focusing attention on certain things."[73] In January 1989 Bush said: "They asked me the other day about 'the one hundred days.' I said, 'we don't have to put it in terms of one hundred days. We're not coming in to correct the ills of the past, we're coming in to build on a proud record that has already been established.'"[74]

But by March 1989 complaints began to be made publicly that the administration lacked momentum, grand design, new direction, or, as George Bush put it, "the vision thing." This perception existed in part because the administration had become bogged down in the Tower nomination battle with Congress and in part because no large-scale new policy directions were seen by the administration as major priorities of the Bush presidency.

To be sure, there were a number of important initiatives: the savings and loan bailout, dealing with the Latin American debt crisis, drug initiatives, education proposals, environmental cleanup, ethics proposals, and so on; but nothing dominated the agenda or captured the public imagination. John Sununu said, "If it looks like the president and government are juggling thirty small balls, that's because they are."[75] Another official said: "We have decided to abjure a glitzy, splashy, high-profile announcement of new programs and a grand new strategy. . . . We concluded there were no obvious things we should be doing that we weren't doing that would work."[76]

In the face of criticism about the lack of vision, President Bush felt the need to confront it publicly: "I don't have an agenda where I have to get six items done. . . . I'm not thinking in terms of 100 days."[77] Later he commented, "A lot is happening. Not all of it good, but a lot is happening."[78] The administration made the argument that not every presidency ought to have a grand vision or lead the nation off on a new crusade. The Bush administration, after all, had campaigned on a platform of continuity with the major policies of the Reagan years.

The secretary to the cabinet, David Bates, observed: "It took a while to sink in. Some people on the staff were looking for a thematic approach, or tried to build events around issues. What we got instead was an approach that was reflective of the president's character: he moves in a lot of directions at once, content to keep his head down and make progress over time."[79] But one bitter former Bush staffer argued that there was "a policy vacuum at the heart of Bush's presidency. . . . There was no focus."[80] "Ours was an Administration whose expectations were so low as to be virtually invisible."[81]

The idea that each new administration ought to accomplish major agenda changes in its first hundred days is relatively new and seldom accomplished. Only unusual circumstances allow newly elected presidents to push through major legislative changes. The reasons for the lack of an early active agenda in the Bush administration included severe budget constraints and the fact that Congress was dominated by Democrats. But it also had to do with the president's own conservatism. He did not want to return to an early era, as did Reagan, but rather to conserve the status quo, including the Reagan policy changes, and seek incremental improvements.

Despite appearances of a lack of strategic vision, President Bush must be given credit for attempting to deal with some of the festering problems left over from the Reagan administration: a bailout for the savings and loan industry, the cleanup of nuclear weapons production plants, and the scandals at the Department of Housing and Urban Development. These were tough issues. On the other hand, critics pointed out that the president seemed willing to take credit for proposing major initiatives in education, the environment, and space exploration without specifying how they would be paid for.

President Bush, whose declared strength was foreign policy, took four foreign trips in his first six months in office, more than most other newly elected presidents. He demonstrated a combination of flexibility and restraint. He was able to come to an agreement with West Germany on the modernization of U.S. short-range missiles. In May he regained the initiative in arms control by countering Gorbachev's proposal on conventional weapons reductions with a proposed 20 percent U.S. troop reduction in Europe. Bush demonstrated restraint in the U.S. reaction to the killing of a U.S. hostage in the Middle East and threats to kill another. His immediate response was to use personal diplomacy with other world leaders rather than precipitous military action. He resisted congressional pressures to respond more harshly to the Chinese government's crackdown on dissidents. In his visits to Poland and Hungary he encouraged the opening of their political systems but refrained from rhetoric that would aggravate strains between the Eastern bloc countries and the Soviet Union.

The administration's policy agenda in its first year seemed to be reactive rather than strategic. It reflected the president's style, which was to be a problem solver rather than a visionary, a doer rather than a dreamer. A former chief of staff characterized the president: "He's almost like the captain on the bridge of a ship. The captain on the bridge of a ship isn't up there creating strategy. He's already got the strategy when he's at sea.[82]

Dealing with Congress

The 1988 presidential campaign was bitter and divisive and seemed to avoid substantive issues in favor of the symbolic politics of pledging allegiance to the flag and the notorious Willie Horton television spots.[83] An important part of Bush's shift away from the campaign mode was his reaching out to Congress for conciliation and looking forward to a cordial relationship. In his inaugural address Bush extended his hand to Congress: "To my friends—and yes, I do mean friends—in the loyal opposition—and yes, I mean loyal: I put out my hand. . . . This is the age of the offered hand."[84] Having himself served in the House and presided over the Senate, Bush had many friends in both chambers and on both sides of the aisle, an asset of no small value in congressional relations. In the first half of 1989 virtually all senators and more than half of the members of the House had been invited to the White House for some function.[85] One Democratic Senator remarked, "It is a tremendous asset to have a President who does not read from note cards and is well aware of what is going on and has a good feel for politics."[86]

But the early positive attitudes and good relations were interrupted by a fight over the nomination of John Tower to be secretary of defense. The battle took on a life of its own and dominated the early months of the Bush administration. The crucial decision on the part of the administration was to let the issue escalate from the fitness of John Tower to head the Department of Defense to the ability of President Bush to stand up to Congress and prevail. Once the president's power became the issue, Republicans had to fall into rank. The stakes were raised considerably, and the fight became much more partisan. If the president lost, it would be more than merely not having a particular man as secretary of defense; it would be a serious blow to the president's credibility.[87] The choice to nail the president's colors to the mast about the Tower nomination thus constituted the crucial decision of when to pick President Bush's first fight with the Democratic Congress.

After the defeat of the Tower nomination, the first time the Senate had ever rejected an initial cabinet nominee, Bush was able to recover and put the bitter fight behind him by the quick nomination of Richard Cheney, who had the respect of most members of Congress on both sides of the aisle. There was even some speculation that Cheney was Bush's first choice for secretary all along but that he chose Tower out of political obligation for the campaigning Tower had done for Bush in Texas since the 1960s.

In March 1989 Bush and Secretary of State James Baker was able to achieve a significant compromise with the Democratic Congress on an issue that had been a bitter bone of contention during the eight years of the Reagan administration. Baker was able to forge a compromise with Congress in which the United States would supply $50 million in nonmilitary aid to the Contras in Nicaragua until November 1989. The aid would continue beyond November only with the agreement of four key committee chairs and the congressional leadership, who had to be satisfied that the aid was indeed being used for nonmilitary purposes.

The president's counsel, C. Boydon Gray, publicly questioned whether this was not an unconstitutional abdication of presidential power to Congress and a violation of the separation-of-powers principle in granting, in effect, a legislative veto to Congress. Baker argued that the legislative veto issue was avoided because the agreement was contained in a letter rather than written into legislation. He also argued that this was the best deal he could get with the Democrats, particularly the liberals in the House. The alternative to the informal legislative veto, of course, was aid that extended through November, after which the administration could come back to Congress with a new request for legislation.

The tone of compromise with the Democrats in Congress on aid to the Contras also characterized Bush's approach to other legislative issues. The president decided to build both the MX and the Midgetman missiles, he accommodated legislator's concerns on the savings and loan bailout, and he indicated a willingness to be flexible on the administration's proposal to cut capital gains taxes. The bipartisan approach to legislation was enough to draw complaints from House minority whip Newt Gingrich that Bush was being too accommodating to the Democratic majority and insufficiently confrontational. Such complaints led the president to veto the proposed increase of the minimum wage, even though the difference between the administration and the Democrats in Congress was only thirty cents per hour.

The Bush administration was thus able to demonstrate its ability to deal with the Democrats in Congress despite the bruising fight over the Tower nomination. But the real test of the ability of the administration and Congress to face up to the tough issues confronting the nation was the formulation of the budget and deficit reduction.

The National Economic Commission, among others, argued that the persistence of the huge budget deficits of the 1980s constituted a serious threat to the future of the U.S. economy.[88] The administration's first budget message included a number of spending proposals in the areas of child care, the environment, education, combating drugs, and so on, but it made no major attempt to deal with the deficit. It argued that the Gramm-Rudman-Hollings deficit-reduction targets could be met for FY1990 while keeping the president's campaign promise not to increase taxes. It did this by adopting the economic assumptions of the outgoing Reagan administration, which the Congressional Budget Office pointed out were much more optimistic than those of most independent private forecasts. The Bush budget message proposed cuts in broad categories of domestic spending but did not specify which programs would be cut to reach the deficit-reduction targets without an increase in taxes.

The budget agreement reached between the White House and Congress in mid-April purported to meet the Gramm-Rudman-Hollings deficit target of $100 billion for FY1990. The agreement, however, depended on optimistic economic assumptions, projected savings in existing programs, shifting expenditures between fiscal years, taking the Postal Service off budget, and $5.3 billion in tax changes that were not specified.[89] While the accord signaled the willingness of the administration and Congress to come to agreement, it did not signify a serious effort to confront the budget crisis. Finance Committee Chairman Senator Bentsen was so skeptical of the accord that he (along with Ways and Means Chair Dan Rostenkowski) refused to attend the Rose Garden announcement ceremony.

In the summer the administration wanted the first $50 billion of the savings and loan bailout to be financed through bonds that would not be accounted through the federal budget document and thus not calculated in the deficit. In a bipartisan compromise the administration and Congress decided that 40 percent of the initial $50 billion would count in the deficit calculations and 60 percent would be raised off budget. Moreover, the 40 percent that counted would be charged against the FY1989 budget and thus would not affect the Gramm-Rudman-Hollings calculations for FY1990.

The bipartisan budget agreements in 1989 constituted a conspiracy to use gimmicks and unrealistic projections to cover up the real size of the deficit and to ignore the necessity of making difficult choices to reduce it. The argument between the administration and Congress on the budget put off the tough decisions that would have to be made on fiscal policy, but it allowed President Bush to keep his "no new taxes" pledge for the time being. The issue was finally confronted in the fall of 1990, when a significant deficit-reduction package was put together and Bush agreed to some increase in taxes.[90]

A PRESIDENCY OF CONSOLIDATION

The new Bush administration was marked by a preference for competence, not ideology. The president's style was one of reactive problem solving, not strategic vision. His approach to Congress (despite the Tower nomination) was one of compromise, not confrontation. His approach to policy disagreements was personal communication and diplomacy rather than "going public" to bring pressure to bear on Congress.

The Bush presidency in its first year might be characterized as one of consolidation, seeking a "new balance," not confrontation and change. Consolidation was necessary for three reasons: the "Reagan revolution" had worked itself out for the time being, the continuing huge deficits precluded large-scale new programs, and the continued Democratic control of Congress made compromise part of the price of governing. The Bush record with Congress reflected this reality. Only two major laws were passed in Bush's first year in office, and he achieved the lowest first-year presidential support score (as calculated by *Congressional Quarterly*) of any postwar president.[91]

The policy changes of the Reagan revolution had worked themselves out over eight years and had gone as far as political forces would allow at that time. Defense spending had increased quickly and substantially, but the increases had leveled off at the end of the administration. Opinion polls had reversed since 1980 and indicated that the public felt the country was spending enough on defense. The law that cut personal income taxes in 1981 also indexed tax brackets, and the nation was spending much more than it received in revenues. There were significant personnel cuts on the domestic side of the government, though non-means-tested entitlements continued to dominate the budget.

The huge deficits of the 1980s continued into President Bush's first year, leaving little room for new policy initiatives. Any new spending was made even more difficult by the funds that had to be spent to rescue the savings and loan system, clean up nuclear weapons production plants, and fix the fiscal mess at the Department of Housing and Urban Development. The Gramm-Rudman-Hollings straightjacket left little room for maneuver and encouraged the use of accounting gimmicks to present the appearance of deficit reduction.

The backdrop of the policy environment was the continuing reality of divided government, with the Democrats maintaining strong majorities in both houses of Congress. The 1988 elections produced few coattails, with Bush remaining behind most members. In addition, the Democrats argued that the president did not have an unambiguous mandate, since large Democratic majorities had been returned to Congress. Thus President Bush was faced with the necessity of bargaining and compromising with Congress.

In 1989 the new administration seemed to moderate some of the major trends in the modern presidency, particularly in contrast to Reagan. Press attention and high visibility for the president and his family continued, but the political tactic of "going public" for partisan leverage was restrained. The public relations and staging skills perfected by the Reagan White House were put to good use in the Bush presidency, despite the president's resistance to being managed.

The power of the White House staff and the centralization of policy control in the White House had been increasing since 1961, reaching a peak in the Reagan White House. President Bush's confidence in his cabinet secretaries and the low-key style of his White House staff moderated the trend, though the locus of power was not reversed. A more balanced relationship was established in White House–cabinet relations, and the cabinet council system of the second Reagan term was continued.

The control of political appointments by the White House personnel office reached a peak in the Reagan administration. That control was not abandoned by the Bush White House, but it was modified in favor of more cabinet input. The attacks on government and the public service that had gone on since 1968 were abandoned. The public rhetoric of President Bush about public service was much closer to that of John Kennedy than to Nixon, Carter, or Reagan.

The most important criticism of the administration's first year in office was its failure to attempt any significant attention to reductions in the continuing high budget deficits. Even OMB Director Richard Darman in the summer of 1989 condemned "our collective short-sightedness" and "reluctance adequately to address the future" that the national debt and deficits represent. According to Darman, the deficit "is the mathematical representation of our wish to buy now, pay later—or, more accurately, buy now and let others pay later."[92] Despite the fact that Congress also bears responsibility for fiscal policy, experience since the congressional Budget Act of 1974 has shown that presidential leadership is necessary for major budget changes.[93]

In sum, in his first year in office President Bush must be given high marks for his conduct of the office of the presidency, with the reservation that he did not use his transition window of opportunity to deal with the deficit problem.

8
The Clinton Transition: Hitting the Ground Walking

In his first year in office President Clinton demonstrated prodigious talents as a policy analyst, a congressional lobbyist, and a communicator, and he won several major legislative victories in his first year. His transition, nevertheless, could not be characterized as well planned, and he did not hit the ground running. After the election, most of Clinton's time was spent selecting his cabinet, and while this paid off in terms of good cabinet secretaries, the equally important task of choosing the White House staff was delayed until just before inauguration. There was very little preparation for the broader recruitment of presidential appointees in the subcabinet, and taking control of the executive branch was delayed by one of the slowest appointment records in history.

Clinton's failure to hit the ground running in terms of his policy agenda was due not to lack of preparation but rather to the failure to finalize decisions on the substance of the policies. The major Clinton policy priorities were not ready to be announced during the transition or early weeks of the administration, and so press accounts and public discussion focused upon the problems of selecting the attorney general and whether gay citizens should be allowed to serve in the military.

The purpose of the transition into the presidency ought to be to organize the administration to take control of the government, and to pursue successfully the policy agenda of the new president. The broader purposes of a new president, of course, are to provide leadership and win the confidence of the American people, but these latter goals are often dependent upon the first set of transition goals. This chapter on the Clinton transition will take up each of these issues in turn. First it will analyze the early efforts to organize the White House. Next it will examine the recruitment of presidential and other political appointees. Finally, it will take up the initial policy agenda of the Clinton administration and examine how successful it was in achieving its major goals.

Each new president is faced with opportunities and constraints. The opportunities are those things that are under the president's personal control, such as the major priorities of the administration and a certain amount of flexibility over personnel appointments. White House institutions and offices, however, are heavily influenced by what Hugh Heclo calls the "deep structure" of the presidency, that is, other peoples' expectations of what functions the White House should carry out.[1] While presidents have some leeway here, they do not have carte blanche (e.g., they cannot easily abolish most offices in the White House or run the office effectively without a chief of staff). Finally, the ultimate success of a presidency is heavily influenced by the external political environment, that is, the nature of the president's political coalition and the strength of the president's party in Congress). Thus Bill Clinton's personal preferences determined his major priorities and the people he chose to appoint, but the broad contours of his White House were shaped by existing White House structures, and his broader policy record was heavily influenced by external forces.

Bill Clinton brought to office a passion for domestic public policy that was complemented by an optimistic energy and exuberance over public policy ideas.[2] While this passion for policy had the advantage of ensuring that his domestic policy decisions would be very well informed, it also had some negative consequences. His appreciation of the complexity of issues was often so nuanced that he could argue both sides of any issue, and his desire to discuss all of the implications of policies was both his strength and his weakness. He wanted to keep his options open as long as possible and resisted coming to closure on policy issues. Even when a decision had been made, it was subject to revision upon further reflection by Clinton.[3] At the beginning of his administration, staff meetings were attended by crowds of staffers and tended to drag on and on. "He can have a 10-minute meeting in two hours," according to one of his staffers.[4] But from Clinton's perspective his open approach served him best: "I like to get people together around a table and let everybody say what they want . . . and argue and debate and fight." A "hide-bound decision-making process" will not lead to better results.[5] But Clinton's fascination with policy and politics was not matched by a concern for organization, structure, or process; this lack of concern for process led to a number of mistakes and minor flaps early in his administration.

Clinton's leadership style also affected the issues he took up and his policy and political success in his first year. Clinton's political identity was a contradictory amalgam of perspectives, often in conflict with each other.[6] Clinton had presented himself as a "New Democrat" in the campaign, with a concern for cutting the deficit and new approaches to policy problems that were pushed by the Democratic Leadership Council, which he had chaired. But his actions early in his term also appealed to traditional Democratic constituencies (appointments of women and minorities, gays in the military, family leave) and disappointed his former supporters in the DLC. Clinton wanted to be bold in proposing new solutions to old problems, but he also wanted to be accommodating and was willing to compromise in ways that made him look inconsistent. He wanted to be a populist outsider bent on basic political reform (e.g., campaign finance and lobbying reform), yet once in the capital he wanted to be accepted by insiders, and he listened to their advice.

Preelection Preparation

During the summer of 1992 a number of Democrats with experience in previous administrations undertook planning efforts meant to help Clinton organize the transition into office.[7] The Clinton campaign did not enthusiastically encourage these efforts, though it did set up a low-visibility effort of its own under John Hart.[8] More serious preparations were avoided for fear of appearing presumptuous. Clinton got spooked in the summer of 1992 when George Bush accused him of "measuring the drapes in the White House" before having won the election. According to Thomas McLarty, "The President made a conscious decision during the campaign not to set up a major transition organization. President Reagan did set up a transition team well before the election and therefore hit the ground running."[9]

Unlike the Reagan campaign, Clinton did not have a high-level person in charge of planning for a possible transition. John Hart, lawyer and convention delegate strategist for Clinton, was given the task of doing background research and liaison with the General Services Administration about office space and other provisions of the Presidential Transition Act. This effort explicitly excluded any work on personnel or policy.[10] All of the highest-level people were concerned with the campaign, and when the election was won a high-level transition structure had to be set up. Despite efforts to assure the campaign that transition planning was not intended to exclude them, suspicions remained, and a power struggle ensued. As the maneuvering went on, Mickey Kanter made a bid to be transition director but was blocked by George Stephanopoulis. When Kanter lost, many of the planning efforts that had been informally undertaken and were technically under Kanter were considered tainted, and much of the volunteer preparation, though of a high professional quality, was lost as the power struggle was settled. Thus the Clinton transition was not able to avoid the campaign-transition staff rivalry that undermined Carter's transition into office.[11]

Clinton decided to designate two transition chairs, Warren Christopher and Vernon Jordan, who would preside over the transition, with deputy directors in Washington. This compromise solution to the problem of transition direction was characteristic of Clinton, who resisted delegating anything important. Clinton also decided to run the transition out of Little Rock rather than Washington. In part this was because Clinton was still a sitting governor, but in part it was because he wanted to preserve his outsider image. The problem of running the transition far from Washington is that so much work and liaison has to be done in the capital where the government actually is. All of the powerful people wanted to stay in Little Rock with the president-elect to protect their positions. Thus it was hard to get authoritative decisions in Washington. Despite modern communications technology, many messages between the two cities were delayed, and a lot of time was lost as decisions made in Washington were ratified or rejected in Little Rock.[12] Later, Bruce Lindsey had second thoughts: "I'm absolutely convinced we shouldn't have had the campaign in D.C., but maybe the transition should have been here. It would have put us more in the frame of mind of how this city works."[13]

The trouble with refusing to delegate authority to run the transition was that all decisions, major and minor, tended to gravitate to the top until they could be decided by the president-elect. With no firm structure, paper flow process, decision-making system, or delegation of authority, the struggle for power and position becomes a maelstrom. Everyone is maneuvering to position themselves for their preferred place in the pecking order and office in the government, and those who are most aggressive fill any vacuum.[14] What gets lost in this unstructured situation is the common purpose of preparing the president-elect to take power and move with the policy agenda of the administration.

WHITE HOUSE STAFF AND ORGANIZATION

Selecting the White House Staff

The most far-reaching initial actions of a new administration are the selection of the cabinet and White House staff. From the day after the election until the end of December, the president-elect's time was dominated by the selection of the cabinet. A small group of people, primarily Al Gore, Warren Christopher, Bruce Lindsey, and Hillary Clinton, met regularly with the president-elect in the governor's mansion in Little Rock to select the cabinet. As the lists were narrowed, Clinton invited candidates to Little Rock to meet with him. In addition to experience and qualifications, personal chemistry was important, and Clinton had to feel comfortable with the people before he chose them. A large portion of the total transition time was spent choosing the cabinet.

Despite all of the time that was devoted to choosing the cabinet there was still a crunch at the end of the artificial Christmas deadline that Clinton had imposed upon himself. A significant amount of juggling occurred immediately before Clinton announced his final five choices on December 24: Michael Espy at Agriculture, Fredrico Pena at Transportation, Bruce Babbit at Interior, Zoe Baird at Justice, and Mickey Kanter as U.S. trade representative.

All of the effort that went into selecting the cabinet was successful in several ways. In assembling a cabinet that "looked like America," Clinton had achieved greater diversity in his cabinet than most of his predecessors, with four African-Americans, two Hispanics, and three women. In addition, Clinton placed women as director of EPA, ambassador to the UN, chair of the Council of Economic Advisers, deputy director (later Director) of OMB, and domestic policy adviser.[15] Despite the last-minute juggling in order to balance all of the factors, Clinton ended up with a reasonably good cabinet with respect to competence and lack of overt conflict among cabinet members or with the White House staff, although Secretary of Defense Aspin was replaced after a year in office.[16]

In spite of the time and effort that went into the selection of the cabinet, Clinton did not reverse the trend in the contemporary presidency away from relying on the cabinet and toward centralizing power in the White House. The major policy initiatives of the Clinton administration were run out of the White House, for example, health care reform, the national service initiative, trade policy (NAFTA and GATT), and deficit reduction. Neither did Clinton revert to the Eisenhower model of using his cabinet as a deliberative body. As much as Clinton liked meetings to mull over options, he did not choose his cabinet as the forum to deliberate policy issues. In fact, the cabinet met as a body only seven times in 1993. The ironic fact is that while the White House staff was more important than the cabinet to administration policy making, much more time and deliberation were devoted to choosing the cabinet.[17] Although Washington veterans recommended that the White House staff be chosen early in the transition, the decision was put off until late in the transition period. It wasn't until the week before the inauguration that the White House staff was publicly announced.[18]

The characteristics that marked the White House staff were its youth, its inexperience, and its diversity. All presidents naturally turn to their campaigns for talent in staffing the White House. These people have served them well, are certainly loyal, and have gone through the ordeal of the campaign with them. They tend to be young, ambitious, and smart. While all presidents need people with such characteristics in the White House, presidents also need the leavening that can be provided by those with Washington experience and maturity.[19] The Clinton White House was particularly marked by its youth and diversity. Of 450 White House staffers, about one-seventh, or 63, were twenty-three years old or younger, and many others were under thirty.[20]

The selection of the Clinton White House staff was also influenced by the desire to bring new (and diverse) faces into the White House and to avoid the Washington establishment.[21] The suspicion of Washington shown by the Clintons also characterized the selection of the Carter and Reagan White House staffs. Carter's top-level White House staff was marked by its lack of Washington experience, and it hurt him. Reagan had the insight to realize that, despite his anti-Washington campaign and penchant for ideological soul mates, he needed an inside professional to run his White House. So the choice of James Baker over the loyal Ed Meese to be chief of staff was a master stroke on Reagan's part and an important factor in the impressive successes in his first year in office.

While it is true that the Democrats in 1993 had a shallow bench of experienced White House professionals after twenty years of Republican presidents, there were a number of experienced Carter White House aides who were willing and might have been tapped by Clinton. But in addition to the natural bias toward campaigners there was an unfortunate bias against those with experience in the Carter White House. Perhaps this bias originated out of fear of being tagged with an association with the one-term Carter, but it was also a consequence of the hubris that affects the staffs of all new presidents-elect. As a result, at the top of the Clinton White House there were few with White House or Washington experience. Only Stephanopoulis and Paster had extensive Washington experience, though as congressional staffers rather than in the executive branch. (Vice President Gore was another exception.) After four months in office, Clinton brought in David Gergen for ballast. Gergen had White House experience in the Nixon, Ford, and Reagan administrations, and was attacked as an ambitious turncoat by Republicans. Clinton knew him personally and trusted his judgment. Gergen added a dimension of discernment about how the administration could best present itself to the country.[22]

In retrospect, the emphasis on campaigners and the exclusion of Washington insiders were reconsidered by Clinton White House officials. The differences between campaigning and governing are profound, and people who are talented in one may not be talented in the other. According to Bruce Lindsey, "We came here, we thought, to change things. Some people whose life has been around here don't want to challenge conventional wisdom. If Washington, D.C., had decided who would be President, Bill Clinton would not have been President. . . . You do need a broader view than if you'd spent your whole life and career here." But, he admitted, *"We overdid it."*[23] George Stephanopoulis observed: "On the campaign trail, you can just change the subject. But you can't just change the subject as President. You can't wish Bosnia away. You can't wish Boris Yeltsin's troubles away. You can't wish David Koresh away. You can't just ignore them and change the subject."[24] James Carville put the difference between campaigning and governing more bluntly in a February 1993 conversation with a White House staffer: "I now see this as real. When I do a campaign and f _ _ _ up, someone just loses. But if you f _ _ _ up, you f _ _ _ up the country."[25]

Since the White House staff now plays the dominant role in any administration, more time spent on selection would pay off. In addition, selecting major White House staffers earlier in the transition would let them get to work on organizing the White House and preclude much of the maneuvering for position that took place during the transition. In retrospect, President Clinton as well as Stephanopoulis and Lindsey felt that the White House staff should have been selected much earlier in the transition.[26]

Whether or not the lack of planning or the tardy appointment of the White House staff had anything to do with it, the Clinton White House experienced considerable turnover in its first two years. After two years in the office Clinton had had two chiefs of staff, five deputy chiefs of staff, five personnel directors, three press secretaries, three counsels, two congressional liaison directors, two political affairs directors, two directors of administration, two scheduling directors, and two cabinet secretaries.

Cutting the White House Staff

One of the campaign promises that Clinton kept that just as well might have been forgotten was his promise to cut the White House staff by 25 percent. The decision was made against the advice of a number of experienced advisers, but after having dropped the middle-class tax cut and reversed himself on Haitian immigration, Clinton decided in the spring of 1993 that this was one promise he had to keep. The initial problem was 25 percent of what? The full complement of government personnel assigned to the White House numbers was well over 3,000, and more than 3,500 counting those less than full-time.[27] The next logical base would be the Executive Office of the President, which numbered about 2,200 in 1992.[28] Perhaps the most meaningful base would be the White House Office, the major unit within the EOP, which numbered 461 in 1992. Clinton staffers, however, decided that using any of these units as the base would take too big a bite out of White House capacity. They thus decided to create their own base by subtracting from the EOP category the Office of Management and Budget (586 personnel) and the U.S. Trade Representative's Office (214). This left them a base of 1,394 as of November 1992, the last month of the Bush presidency, and the need to cut 350 to bring their total down 25 percent.

The rationale for separating these two units out is that they both contain large numbers of civil service personnel who are not political appointees but rather career civil servants. But their exclusion from the count was also arbitrary because the EOP, despite the migration of subunits in and out over the years, has a fixed, legal definition, and other presidencies since 1939 have counted all of the units when calculating its size. Thus comparing sizes of White House staffs, which the exercise was supposedly about, is difficult.

At the end of September the administration declared victory and said that the requisite 350 people had been cut and that the campaign promise had been kept. One chunk of the cuts came through the elimination of 121 people of the Office of National Drug Control Policy, which had become a dumping ground for political appointees in the Bush administration. Other cuts came from eliminating 47, mostly career, workers in the Office of Administration and cutting 39 members of the advisory Space Council. The Office of Presidential Personnel was reduced from more than 100 in January to 35 in October.[29] The remainder of the cuts came from an across-the-board cut of the other units in the EOP.

While the campaign promise had been kept, at least at the end of the fiscal year, the question remains whether it made sense to cut White House staff sig-

nificantly in the beginning of an activist presidency with an ambitious legislative agenda. In John Hart's analysis the effort failed at the symbolic level
because of the skepticism of the media and Congress.[30] According to David
Gergen, "We made a mistake . . . . It's a smaller staff with a bigger agenda, and
it makes it harder."[31] White House staffers are notoriously overworked, often
spending evenings and weekends at their offices, and are prone to professional
burnout. The argument against shrinking the White House staff is that if the
policy initiatives of the administration fail, having cut the White House staff
will not save the presidency. On the other hand, if the administration succeeds
in dealing with the major issues facing the nation, the people will not care. The
American people will not begrudge the president the professional staff needed
to do the job. The real issue is which functions should be handled in the White
House and how to assure high quality advice to the president. The number of
staffers in the White House, by whatever definition, is not as important as these
two questions. Once these questions are answered, the staffing levels will flow
from them.[32]

Managing the White House: Access and Policy Structures

Access to the president. One of the early problems in the Clinton White House
was the role played by several former Clinton campaigners. They became
known as the "consultants" because they decided not to take jobs with the
administration but rather to maintain their independence on the outside and
merely work part-time for the administration as consultants. They included former campaign aides James Carville and Paul Begalla, campaign media adviser
Mandy Grunwald, and the campaign's pollster, Stanley Greenberg. Their advice
to the president was often to keep in mind the traditional Democratic constituency, and they often advised the president to consider the potential negative
political consequences of his efforts to reduce the deficit.[33]

Early in the administration there was a fight for the mind of the president
over the issue of deficit control versus the campaign promises for a middle-class
tax cut and investments in workforce training. The consultants had direct access
to Clinton in meetings and in memos that were not staffed out or vetted or even
seen by the White House staff. They met regularly with the president to give him
political advice, and they excluded White House staffers on the artificial distinction that they were concerned only with politics, not policy. Of course, what the
consultants wanted to affect was administration policy, particularly the deficit-
reduction package being prepared in the spring of 1993. They were concerned
with the negative effect that deficit reduction might have on the president's
polls. White House economic advisers weighed more heavily the long-term
implication that large deficits might have on the future of the U.S. economy.

The problem was not so much that the consultants had their eyes on short-
term political gains rather than long-term economic consequences of the budget

package. Nor was the problem that the president was listening to outsiders; presidents should be able to consult with whomever they choose. The problem was that their advice to the president was not being monitored or coordinated with input from the rest of the White House staff. They had privileged access with no check save the president's own mind. At one level, if this is what the president wants, he should get it. On the other hand, if important advice to the president about a major policy of the administration is unmonitored and unchecked by contrasting perspectives, the president is less likely to get a balanced perspective on the policies in question. According to Bowman Cutter, deputy director of the NEC: "You don't want unequal access to the President," not because it's unfair to policy advocates, but because "it's unfair to the President."[34] This balancing function is one that should be performed by the chief of staff.

The influence of the consultants was so evident that Congressman Frank Wolf (R-VA) called for them to file financial disclosure forms, as was required by members of the White House staff. Wolf's implication was that the consultants were influencing policy and might be making special pleas that could influence the financial well-being of themselves or their other clients. While the consultants protested "We do not lobby," the White House directed them to file financial disclosure forms in 1994.[35]

In terms of public accountability, the issue was one of making public any possible connections between their advice and personal financial interest they might have had in administration policy. But in terms of effective management of the White House, the issue was one of how advice to the president should be managed. The consensus of presidential scholars is that policy development must be carefully managed and that advice to the president must be carefully monitored so that the president gets the most balanced perspective possible before making policy decisions.

In addition to the consultants, Clinton's White House allowed broad access to the president. In the first years of the administration, eight to ten people had walk-in privileges to the Oval Office; they could use their own judgment in deciding whether an issue deserved the president's time.[36] Other Clinton friends had access to the White House and occasionally influenced personnel and policy. Susan Thomases, a New York lawyer and friend of Mrs. Clinton, often visited the White House and influenced the selection of White House staffers and presidential appointees.[37] Harry Thomasson, a Hollywood producer and friend of the Clintons, had an office in the East Wing and played a role in the firing of White House travel office workers in the spring of 1993.[38]

The broader issue is the question of access to the president. It is important not only because of the need to use the president's limited time wisely but also because whom the president sees can affect his perspective on public policy issues. While the president is the final arbiter, the chief of staff should play a monitoring role to ensure a balance of perspectives and to say "no" to large egos who want to use more of the president's time than is warranted. As McLarty saw it, "My role is to organize and facilitate people to see him."[39] It is the chief of staff's job to monitor and coordinate access, not to control or exclude. McLarty should have been monitoring this, but just as H. R. Haldeman kept Nixon isolated because Nixon wanted it that way, so McLarty had to allow the level of access that Clinton wanted.

Policy process structures: DPC, NEC, and NSC. The volunteer working group on White House organization prepared a document to brief Clinton on White House organization and operations. Among other issues it addressed, the report suggested a three-council policy development structure. The National Security Council would play its traditional role, and in addition there would be a Domestic Policy Council and an Economic Security Council. Clinton took the group's advice and established the National Economic Council by Executive Order 12835 on January 25, 1993, although its members totaled eighteen rather than the eleven suggested in the report.[40] The Domestic Policy Council was also established by Executive Order on August 16, 1993, numbering twenty-three rather than the thirteen recommended in the report. Each of these policy development structures will be discussed briefly.

The principals of the Domestic Policy Council seldom met as a body, though some of the deputies had regular meetings during 1993. It often played a facilitating role on interdepartmental issues, depending on which policy area was under consideration.[41] The DPC, chaired by Carol Rasco, functioned as a staff capacity and facilitator rather than as a regularized policy development body. It could be expected that the broad range of domestic policies would not present the opportunity for a coherent policy development process as do the more established models for national security policy making or even economic policy making. Domestic policy issues were most often dealt with by special working groups and task forces, the foremost example of which was the health care task force.

One of Clinton's campaign themes was the centrality of a healthy economy to national security in the post–cold war era. To symbolize this conviction and to provide an appropriate structure for economic policy making in his administration, he established the National Economic Council in the White House Office. The NEC was to play a role comparable to that of the National Security Council and be headed by a director comparable to the president's assistant for National Security Affairs.[42]

The key to the success of the NEC as an advisory and coordinating structure was Clinton's choice of its director, Robert Rubin, a former Wall Street investment banker. Rubin's calm demeanor and the trust placed in him by the president made him one of Clinton's most effective senior staffers. By all accounts Rubin was a "neutral broker" in the formulation of the administration's economic policy. He was neutral in the sense that he assured that everyone who ought to be heard on an economic issue was heard directly or their views were faithfully represented. Turf fights among White House staffers and cabinet secretaries were minimized.[43] When there was significant disagreement among presidential advisers over policy, Rubin set up debates before the president to ensure that the opposing arguments were presented most forcefully. Members of the cabinet were allowed to append dissents to major policy memoranda that Rubin sent to the president if they felt strongly about an issue. Because of his conscientiousness in representing all perspectives fairly, Rubin seldom suffered end runs to the president around his process.

Although Rubin considered himself to be a neutral broker, he also felt free to be an advocate for whatever policy he considered to be most wise. In his judgment both roles are possible, "as long as you are excruciatingly careful to make sure your own views do not taint the fairness of the process."[44] In commenting on the administration's economic policy-making process Labor Secretary Robert Reich said, "The end runs are very few and far between. . . . I have known the President for 25 years. . . . I could easily call him up on the telephone and chew his ear . . . but also there's no reason to do that as long as my views are fairly conveyed to him."[45]

Despite the large membership of the NEC (eighteen), the key meetings included primarily those officials most involved with economic policy making: treasury secretary, OMB director, CEA chair, labor secretary, and Rubin's two deputies, Bowman Cutter and Gene Sperling. Rubin and the process he established were most effective in brokering the initial deficit-cutting package in the spring of 1993, one of the policy triumphs of the Clinton administration.

The Clinton administration's effective structure for economic policy making provided a contrast with the Bush administration's infighting. During the Bush administration OMB Director Darman and John Sununu were determined to dominate the economic policy agenda and worked to exclude Treasury Secretary Brady and CEA Director Michael Boskin. Sununu's efforts to block Boskin went so far that in October 1991 Boskin threatened to resign unless he got to see the president.[46]

But just the opposite organizational situation existed in the national security area, where the NSC policy development process was not as coherent as it was in the Bush administration. The Bush administration's national security team worked together smoothly, based on the trust developed over years of common experience and acquaintance. The relationship between the NSC adviser and Secretary of State James Baker was not competitive as it was during the Nixon and Carter administrations, and it possessed the continuity that certainly was missing during the Reagan years.

The Clinton administration did not resurrect the rivalry between the NSC and the secretary of state, in part because of the personality and style of Anthony Lake, who, unlike Kissinger or Brzezinski, did not want to run everything from the White House. The Clinton White House NSC staff did not take a domineering approach to the policy-making process, but it went too far in the other direction. That is, it did not provide enough direction to the policy process at lower, working levels. Thus disputes and disagreements between the Departments of State and Defense on relatively minor issues would not be settled at lower levels, and the same issues would rise up the chain until they had to be confronted at top levels. Ideally in the policy process minor issues would be authoritatively settled by the NSC staff so that issues could be honed to the point that important decisions would be all that was on the table for the principals to decide. The lack of coordination at the lower levels was frustrating to participants at the Departments of State and Defense who had to wait until the president or Anthony Lake could get around to making decisions.

This problem was reflective of the relative lack of interest of the president in national security policy making in his first year in office. In concentrating the efforts of his presidency on domestic and economic policy making, Clinton neglected the national security policy process. While Clinton could be excused for not having a coherent worldview and strategic plan to guide the United States into the post–cold war twenty-first century (Bush didn't have one either), he still could have spent the time to work out a process with his national security team. But this was characteristic of Clinton. He did not value process or organization; he focused on national security issues when they came up and could not be avoided. Clinton's NEC worked because economic policy was central to his own priorities, but in national security he did not pay enough attention, and the policy process suffered as a result.

Chief of Staff

Bill Clinton has been the only Democrat to enter the presidency admitting that a chief of staff was necessary.[47] Both Ford and Carter tried to run the White House without one, and each came to admit that it would not work and that a chief of staff was necessary. But if the chief of staff plays too domineering a role, it will likely lead to disaster. Each of the four domineering chiefs of staff—Sherman Adams for Eisenhower, H. R. Haldeman for Nixon, Don Regan for Reagan, and John Sununu for Bush—resigned in disgrace after hurting his president.[48]

The transition report on White House organization recommended that Clinton install a chief of staff structure and recommended an "honest broker" model, which it contrasted to a "chief operating officer" model (strong chief of staff) on the one hand and a "spokes-of-the-wheel" model on the other. It recommended that the chief of staff set and enforce clear priorities, bring a political perspective to bear on all policy making, and "keep foreign and domestic policy in sync."[49]

Clinton received the report favorably and understood the White House history intellectually, but his personal approach to executive leadership cut against delegating any significant amount of power or decision making. Thus there was no danger that Clinton would allow a domineering chief of staff in his White

House, but there was a danger that he would be unwilling to delegate enough authority for anyone to play a traditional chief of staff role.

McLarty. In early 1992 Clinton picked a person for chief of staff who fit his own approach quite well. Thomas "Mack" McLarty had been friends with Clinton since kindergarten and had a long association with Clinton throughout his political career. McLarty had been an executive in a natural gas company (Arkla, Inc.) and had run a car dealership, but he was no stranger to politics, having served one term in the state legislature and having been a frequent emissary to Washington for Clinton over the years. Thus Clinton trusted McLarty implicitly, and McLarty's personal style held no danger that he would become the domineering chief of staff that wounded so many presidencies. He was unfailingly gracious, low-key, even tempered, and polite. He did not indulge in temper tantrums or try to belittle his subordinates as some of the dominating chiefs of staff in the past had done. He seldom got angry or raised his voice. He was so decent and considerate that he earned the sobriquet "Mack the Nice."[50] According to McLarty's approach, "A leader can be firm and direct without being insensitive. I'm not a believer in criticizing people in public. But I am a big believer in being very direct with people, which usually means being constructively critical during a one-on-one meeting."[51] Some thought that because of his pleasant demeanor he was not tough enough to be a president's chief of staff.

While McLarty had a difficult time, as explained below, it was not because he was too nice or even tempered. James Baker, Donald Rumsfeld, Richard Cheney, and Jack Watson all were even tempered and polite, yet were able to perform effectively in the traditional role of chief of staff. McLarty was not able to perform such a role because of three factors. First, he did not try, preferring instead to perform other important roles for the president. Second, the power structure of the Clinton White House did not lend itself easily to discipline or submission to the authority of a chief of staff. And, most importantly, Bill Clinton would not allow anyone to play the role of a traditional chief of staff.

From the very beginning of the administration, McLarty did not claim the traditional chief of staff's role. He did not have a major say in the staffing of the White House, a prerogative that James Baker insisted upon in 1981 and that Leon Panetta received when he took over as Clinton's chief of staff in July 1994.[52] McLarty played other important roles for the president. He was a particularly effective emissary to the Hill, especially among conservative Democrats, and he was often a delegate to the business community for Clinton. When an especially sensitive issue came up, McLarty was often the one chosen to handle it. For example, he was the one who negotiated the recruitment of David Gergen to the White House staff and the one who sought out a replacement for Les Aspin as secretary of defense. Because of his role as a special troubleshooter, McLarty spent only about one-third of his time actually managing the White House and did not necessarily attend all daily top staff meetings at the White House.[53]

The second factor in McLarty's challenge was that the Clinton White House was unique in that it had three power centers. Besides the president, important policy and political influence was wielded by Vice President Gore and Hillary Rodham Clinton. Gore was involved as an adviser and taken seriously by Clinton in most aspects of administration policy, with special clout in environmental, national security, and science issues. The First Lady played a powerful role across the board in politics, policy, and personnel. One of McLarty's assets was that he had good relations with Hillary, but her role was so powerful and pervasive that a traditional chief of staff role was extremely difficult to perform.

The third and most important factor thwarting McLarty's effectiveness was the president himself, who, despite his protestations, wanted to act as his own chief of staff. As described earlier, the president allowed the campaign consultants to come in to advise him without White House staffers present. In order to coordinate the White House effectively, the chief of staff must be privy to all important policy and political meetings. The consultants should not have had exclusive access to the president, but if Clinton allowed it, McLarty could not overrule him. Legislative Liaison Director Howard Paster complained, and eventually resigned, because McLarty did not control the access of the consultants and because Paster was being undercut in negotiations on the Hill.[54] But the real problem, of course, was the president. If Clinton wanted to make deals or concessions or change the administration's negotiating position, it was his call. And if he wanted to do it without warning Paster, that was not McLarty's fault. The chief of staff's role should be to coordinate all aspects of administration policy, including ensuring that all the players, including Paster, were informed about all relevant changes in policy. But if the president wanted to make changes, that was not under McLarty's control. Paster's real problem was with Clinton, not McLarty.

The bottom line was that Bill Clinton really wanted to be his own chief of staff. At the beginning of his presidency there was no other person who was with him to keep track of things. According to a White House aide, "No one sat with him on every meeting. . . . He was the only one who knew when two different people were arguing for the same money."[55] Clinton resisted any system that seemed to constrain his options or access to him. He enjoyed becoming engrossed in policy details and enjoyed being the only person who was aware of "all the cards in play at any given gime."[56] He would complain that meetings were too big and then complain that a particular staffer was missing. He would become engrossed in a policy and then complain that he had wasted his time on it. Critics argued that McLarty gave the president what he wanted but not what he needed and that he should have taken a much firmer approach to managing the White House. But McLarty became a lightning rod for White

House management problems and should not be criticized for refusing to over-rule the president or for not forcing a system on the White House against the will of the president.[57]

At times in the first years of Clinton's presidency, Hillary Clinton per-formed some of the functions that might be expected of the chief of staff. She could often focus the debate in a meeting and cut to the central point to demand closure on an issue. She was willing to hold people accountable and to insist on completed, high-quality staff work, and she was willing to enforce her decisions. But, of course, this was only possible because she had unquestioned authority and the president would back her up, a position McLarty was not in.[58]

Aside from the basic problem that the president did not want to be man-aged, McLarty was miscast as chief of staff. His real value to Clinton was to act as a confidential sounding board for presidential ideas, as a troubleshooter and high-level emissary. This was the role he returned to when he was replaced by Leon Pannetta in July 1994. It is indicative of McLarty's value to the president and his approach to his role that he was the one who recruited his own replace-ment and that he was the only chief of staff who was replaced and yet remained in the White House.[59]

Panetta. When Leon Panetta took over the job of chief of staff from McLarty in July 1994, he made a number of changes that were indications of how McLarty had not asserted the prerogatives that a traditional chief of staff might have. Pa-netta tightened up daily staff meetings by limiting the senior staff meetings to ten people and shifting it to 7:30 A.M. so that decisions could be made and then briefed to a larger staff meeting of thirty people at 8:15 (the order was reversed under McLarty). He insisted that all staff work that went to the president be cleared by him, that all decision memoranda be routed through him, and that any presentations to the president be rehearsed so that they were ready for presiden-tial involvement. That is, he insisted, as H. R. Haldeman had, that all issues be fully "staffed out" before going to the president.

Access to the Oval Office was tightened so that only one or two staffers, rather than ten, had "walk-in" privileges. All others had to reach the president through the chief of staff. (This does not mean that he controlled access tightly, merely that he monitored and coordinated access.) He also insisted that he have control over all White House hiring and payroll decisions. He set tighter agendas with more focus for meetings with fewer people and insisted on closure. He also installed himself on the "Principals Committee" for foreign policy decision mak-ing. All of these changes, according to one White House staffer, sent the mes-sage "Somebody's in charge, and everybody can't play."[60] Panetta characterized the situation before he became chief of staff as "very haphazard" and having "no clear lines of responsibility."[61] After taking over he began to meet weekly with the president about personnel and policy and with the cabinet every two weeks to ensure consistency of message.

While all of these changes were intended to move the White House closer to an organizational style associated with traditional chiefs of staff, it was not clear that the president was willing to delegate the full complement of authority that a traditional chief of staff would have. Panetta still was not informed of all meetings the president had. Panetta was assured that he would have broad leeway with personnel and had publicly indicated that he would replace Dee Dee Myers as press secretary when he took over. But Myers was able to convince the president to keep her at her job (with an increase in status, from deputy assistant to assistant to the president) for another six months before she was replaced by Michael McCurry.[62] While this particular personnel action was minor, it was symptomatic of Clinton's unwillingness to delegate.

This section has dealt with organizational issues in some detail. But the larger question remains of what the relationship is between how well a presidency is organized and its overall success. As will be argued later, the broad array of historical factors surrounding an administration and the way each president exerts leadership in his historical context may determine the broad outlines of success or failure. Nevertheless, it can be argued that in the ability of an administration to take control of the government and pursue its agenda, organizational factors can make a difference. There can be no doubt that effective organization played important roles in the Reagan administration's domestic triumphs immediately after the transition and the Bush administration's effectiveness during the Gulf War. As President Eisenhower pointed out, poor organization can hurt an administration (Chapter 1). Or as Bert Rockman has observed: "Staffing and organization will not solve all problems or perhaps even many of them. . . . But an effectively run White House can lead to an effectively run government and it can minimize what tennis buffs would call unforced errors."[63]

RECRUITING PRESIDENTIAL PERSONNEL

As in other aspects of the preparation for a possible Clinton presidency, the Clinton people planning personnel recruitment were hesitant to create too high a profile and preferred to err on the side of too little preparation. John Hart and a few aides did preliminary work for a personnel operation by laying out what would have to be done after the election in terms of infrastructure, office space, computer capabilities, communications equipment, and so on. But unlike Carter and Reagan, little work was done in compiling lists of potential candidates for subcabinet positions.[64] Such lists are politically vulnerable; they look bad if the press gets hold of them; and if campaigners become aware of them they will divert energies from winning the campaign to angling for a place on the right list. If a larger-scale operation is to be effective, as it was with the Reagan transition, it must be secret, controlled from the very top, and protected by top levels of the campaign.

Preelection Preparation

After the election there was a mad scramble to set up the personnel recruitment operation and bring it on-line. Jan Piercy, Hillary Clinton's college roommate, was designated to set up operations as deputy director. Former governor of South Carolina Richard Riley was designated to head up the personnel operation in Washington that numbered between 250 and 300 people, including volunteers.[65] The operation itself was impressive in the volume of résumés it handled with new scanning technology and the coding of applications for jobs among a number of categories. On the other hand, there were a fair number of paid workers and volunteers who were looking for jobs for themselves and who had their own agendas. Unlike the Reagan operation, Clinton's personnel team was not headed up by professional "headhunters" or experienced executive search professionals, though Piercy had some experience in nonprofit searches, because the Clinton team thought that such professionals would not be sufficiently politically sensitive.[66] Communications between the Washington personnel operations and the transition teams in the departments and agencies were not always effective, and each was vetting people whom the other side had not yet heard of. Each department and major agency had a person from the White House to help coordinate political appointments and to represent White House interests.[67] By the end of the first week after the election the transition headquarters had received 3,000 résumés; by February 1993 it was receiving 2,000 per day.[68]

One of the problems with the personnel operation was that most of the people closest to the president-elect were in Little Rock, and personnel decisions could not be made without them. Clinton was busy selecting the cabinet, and when names of candidates for the short lists were sent to Little Rock they often stagnated until they could be considered.

The other major problem with the personnel recruitment operation was that the director, Richard Riley, was soon designated as the new administration's secretary of education. Personnel recruitment is extremely important, highly charged, complex, sensitive, and time-sensitive. While Riley was working hard at the job, there was no way that some of his attention and energies would not be directed toward thinking about his new responsibilities at the Department of Education and his upcoming confirmation hearings. The rest of the personnel operation also was aware that he would not be around much longer, so an important element of continuity of leadership was lost early in the effort. After Riley, the operation was briefly headed by Phil Lader, then Bruce Lindsey from inauguration until the end of 1993, then Veronica Biggins for most of 1994, and Robert J. Nash beginning in 1995.

The issue of control of the executive branch was also confused by questions of how long appointees of the Bush administration would remain in office. In October James Baker sent a memo to departments and agency heads instructing all PAS appointees to submit letters of resignation immediately after the election that would be effective "at the pleasure of the President," an unusual move prior to an election.[69]

Bush appointees were informed on January 13 that their letters of resignation would be accepted by the president with the exception of one PAS appointee in each agency or department who would remain for legal purposes (to sign documents, etc.) until at least one Clinton appointee for the department was confirmed by the Senate. Bush White House officials were concerned that some Bush appointees hoped to stay on into the Clinton administration. These people were considered to be traitors by some Bush loyalists, who felt they had to be thrown out preemptively lest they turn colors and consort with the enemy. In the words of Kevin E. Moley, deputy secretary of HHS, "We've had people who are totally disloyal, traitorous in their actions if not their words—egregiously so in some cases—since Nov. 3."[70] In a memo dated January 13, 1993, Constance Horner, director of the Office of Presidential Personnel, stated, "This memo serves to inform you that the president accepts your resignation . . . effective noon, January 20."[71]

Most of the energy of the new administration in December was taken up in selecting the cabinet, and while the personnel operation was up and running at high speed, not a lot of progress was made in selecting subcabinet positions before the inauguration. Progress was also slowed by the failure to select the White House staff until mid-January; energy and time had to be devoted to this important task before turning to the subcabinet. Part of the logjam was caused by the designation of Bruce Lindsey to be head of the Office of Presidential Personnel. While he had the advantage of being close to Clinton and having his full trust and confidence, he had the same disadvantage. Lindsey was extremely busy doing a wide range of tasks for the president-elect and was not able to devote himself full-time to the personnel job. This problem carried on into the early part of the administration, when personnel lists were ready for his consideration but had to wait until he had the time to devote to the personnel aspects of his many duties.

The outgoing Bush administration perspective on Schedule C appointees, however, contrasted with its punitive approach to PAS appointees. For these lower-level appointees the Bush administration refused a Clinton transition request to accept resignations before the inauguration. "Why should we?" asked a Bush appointee. "They all know they will have to go in time, but let them go in Clinton Time—they could get a paycheck for another four or five months before the Democrats find them all, fire them all and replace them all."[72] In a memo dated January 20, director of the Office of Presidential Personnel Bruce Lindsey wrote to heads of departments and agencies that "all non-career SES terminations are to be effective close of business, January 22, 1993. . . . Schedule C terminations . . . January 21" except for "those individuals whom the new administration has asked to stay on."[73]

Diversity

As the administration moved into its early weeks in office, the outlines of the general criteria used in selecting personnel began to take shape. All new administrations want political appointees who are competent, have policy expertise, are good team players, and have a good fit with their particular positions. Most of all, new administrations want loyalty. But loyalty comes in many guises and is judged by different criteria (see Chapter 3). In the Reagan administration the dominating criterion was ideological loyalty to the conservative agenda that could be determined by a set of litmus tests. In the Bush administration the dominating criterion changed to personal loyalty to the president, most often determined by past association with Bush in public life.

For President Clinton the dominating theme of the personnel recruitment effort was diversity, which was summarized as the "EGG" standards—ethnicity, gender, and geography. While the political perspectives of appointees had to be compatible with Clinton's, there was no coherent set of policy preferences that characterized Clinton's appointments. Competence was a bottom-line criterion, but the demographic characteristics of Clinton nominees were clearly more important than specific policy preferences.[74] Their policy preference varied as widely as did Clinton's and reflected the electoral constituencies that supported Clinton's candidacy.[75] The idea of balance in the appointments process is as old as American politics. The criteria in the past were partisan, geographic, religious, ideological, and so on. In recent decades racial and gender factors have entered the criteria, and each contemporary administration has been affected by all of these criteria, though with different weight being given to each.

The Clinton administration's commitment to diversity began with the selection of the cabinet, and attention to diversity was intensified in the selection of the subcabinet and nonpresidential political appointees. The First Lady and her friend Susan Thomases played a very active role in personnel selection in general and in the search for diversity in particular. The White House usually made the selection of individuals for the higher-level subcabinet positions (Executive Levels II–III), but later in the spring and summer of 1993 its imprint was often made by insisting on "balance" in the slate of lower-level officials (EL IV–V and noncareer SES) nominees for any agency or department. Instead of nominating people for positions as they came up in the selection process, the White House would often wait until there was a list of appointees proposed for the department. Not infrequently lists suggested by cabinet secretaries were sent back for more balance. When agencies did well with respect to diversity, the White House would give them greater say in their own lower-level appointees.[76]

Though early in the administration Clinton was criticized by advocates for women, African-Americans, Hispanics, and other minorities, the search for

Nominations

Confirmations

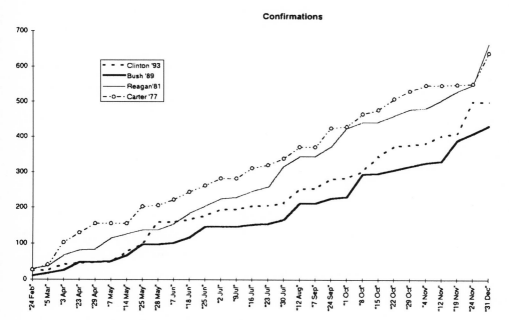

Comparisons of nominations and confirmations.
SOURCE: Executive clerk to the president, 1993.

167

diversity and balance was seen as successful by the Clinton administration and later praised by women's groups. Fifteen percent of its appointments were African-Americans (who constitute 12 percent of the population); 6 percent were Hispanics (with 9.5 percent of the population); and 46 percent were women—a record that is impressive because the pool of qualified people in these categories is relatively smaller as a result of the effects of past discrimination.[77] President Bush appointed women for 20 percent of all of his appointments, and 12.6 percent of President Reagan's appointees were women.[78] While the Clinton administration's commitment to diversity achieved some worthwhile goals in opening up positions to those formerly excluded from high-level government positions, its enthusiasm did entail some costs. Even some very high-level people who supported Clinton's diversity emphasis and helped the transition prior to inauguration thought that at times the insistence on diversity went too far. The reservations were not that appointees were unqualified but that the *best* person for the job was not always appointed and the process at times became a "numbers game."[79]

The Slowing Pace of Appointments

In addition to the diversity of the Clinton appointments, the most striking aspect of the whole appointments process was its slowness. Despite the more than 100 people working on personnel recruitment early in the administration,[80] the Clinton appointment process was decisively behind the pace of Presidents Reagan and Carter. By the end of 1993 President Clinton had 499 of his nominees confirmed by the Senate, whereas President Reagan had 662 aboard by the end of 1981 and President Carter 637 by the end of 1977. Due to a big push in mid-November Clinton was able to bring his nominations up to a comparable level to the two earlier presidents—673 as compared with 680 and 682 for Reagan and Carter, respectively.[81] Here is a comparison of total first-year appointments and nominations.

	Clinton (1993)	Bush (1989)	Reagan (1981)	Carter (1977)
All PAS	499	432	662	637
Nominations	673	501	680	682

Thus in terms of nominees confirmed, President Clinton was significantly slower than Presidents Carter and Reagan (by 136 and 161 appointments, respectively), though ahead of President Bush (by 57). The Bush delays might be explained by a lack of urgency since their PAS positions were occupied by Reagan appointees who were loyal Republicans, and no harm would be done leaving them in office for several months into the new administration.

In compiling these data the executive clerk to the president counted all PAS appointments, including part-time positions, ambassadors, U.S. attorneys and marshals, and so on. So while it is an accurate reflection of the whole appointments process, it is not focused directly on managing the executive branch. If one counts only appointments to executive branch departments and agencies, the Clinton administration was the slowest of the past six presidents, including President Bush.

If the average time from inauguration to confirmation for executive branch presidential appointees is calculated, Clinton has taken longer than any president since 1960 and probably was the slowest in history. It took President Kennedy an average of 2.4 months to get an appointee into office (down through the assistant secretary level). The average number of months from inauguration to confirmation has steadily increased, as the following data spanning 1960–1994 indicate:[82]

Kennedy	2.4 months	Reagan	5.3 months
Nixon	3.4	Bush	8.1
Carter	4.6	Clinton	8.5

For purposes of controlling the executive branch, these data are more useful than the gross number of confirmations because they include only those executives who have policy-making positions in the executive branch. These data show that Clinton was the slowest of the presidents since 1960. Was this slowness Clinton's fault or was it due to factors not under his control? The reasons for the unprecedented Clinton delays were many, though not all of them were unique to the Clinton administration. The sources of increasing delays in the appointments process reach back several decades, at least to 1960 when the White House began to develop an institutional capacity to recruit presidential nominees and thus displace political parties as the major recruitment mechanism.[83] Three factors have contributed to slowing the appointments process during this time period: "ethics" rules and regulations, the centralization of personnel recruitment in the White House, and the increasing number of political appointees.

"Ethics" regulations. Jimmy Carter emphasized "ethics" in government, and in an attempt to deal with the occasional abuse of governmental position for private gain worked for the passage of the Ethics in Government Act of 1978, which established the Office of Government Ethics. The act was intended to draw careful lines so that those in the government could not use their official positions to affect their own financial interests. Conflicts of interest were defined and remedies were established. Financial statements were required, and these could be obtained by reporters through the Freedom of Information Act. In the judgment of presidential recruiters these restrictions have had a negative effect on the willingness of some qualified people to accept presidential appointments.

President Clinton, in line with his campaign promises, tightened restrictions on postemployment career opportunities of appointed officials (PAS) serving in his administration. By executive order appointees were required to sign a pledge that for a period of five years (most restrictions in law are one or two years) they will refrain from "lobbying any department or agency with respect to which they had substantial personal responsibility," or "serving as representatives of foreign corporations or governments.[84] The additional restrictions may have prevented good candidates from working for the administration for fear that they could not return to their careers when they left government. Former Reagan White House official Michael P. Castrine said that Clinton "raised the bar so high you couldn't get some good quality people to apply for the jobs."[85]

While the prestige of high government office often overcomes most reservations, the "ethics" restrictions have increased the number of turndowns for presidential appointments. Sometimes the problem may be the divestment of stocks and assets that people prefer to keep. But often it may be the unwillingness to have one's financial situation open to a Freedom of Information Act request with the prospect of having one's assets displayed on the front page of the hometown paper.

The confirmation process may also be harrowing. Prospective appointees are sometimes unwilling to risk having political opponents of the president search their lives for embarrassing incidents. In a suicide note, President Clinton's Deputy White House Counsel Vincent Foster wrote, "I was not meant for the job or the spotlight of public life in Washington. Here ruining people is considered sport."[86] Another Clinton nominee, Henry Foster, was dismayed to find that most of the political controversy surrounding his nomination as surgeon general was about the small number of abortions he had performed rather than his career as a doctor and public leader, during which he had delivered thousands of babies.[87]

Centralization of control. As described in Chapter 3, the Reagan administration made a major change in the recruitment of political appointees by its decision to centralize control of all levels of political appointments in the White House and to deprive most cabinet secretaries of their traditional say in naming their own subcabinet teams. This had the effect of considerably slowing down Reagan's political recruiting. President Bush did not reverse the Reagan model, and it is doubtful if any future president will. President-elect Clinton made a conscious decision to emulate the Reagan approach by controlling political appointments from the White House. White House control enabled the Clintons to enforce their commitment to diversity rather than trusting the commitment of cabinet secretaries. Personnel Director Riley emphasized to cabinet secretaries-designate that White House control of subcabinet appointments would be much tighter than in the Carter administration, though the ability of the Office of Presidential Personnel to control the process lessened over 1993 as its size continued to decrease from more than 100 to 25.[88]

Clinton's decision to emulate Reagan may also have been influenced by advice from veterans of the Carter White House who felt they had trusted cabinet secretaries too much. Hamilton Jordan, Carter's top aide, urged the Clinton transition: "Don't give the Government away. We gave Cabinet officers too much latitude in selecting their key appointees, which resulted in a government staffed by people who did not share or understand our different dream.[89] Stewart Eizenstat felt that Carter's commitment to "cabinet government" hurt their administration: "One result was giving virtually carte blanche to our Cabinet appointees to make their own sub-Cabinet appointments. This in turn led to many appointees whose loyalty was mainly to the Cabinet officer and his or her own agenda, rather than to the President and our agenda."[90]

The president's personal involvement in choosing subcabinet appointees was unusual. Presidents Reagan and Bush played important roles in setting the tone for personnel selection, but most often they would go along with the consensus of their top recruiters. Clinton's personal style led him to take an active role in making individual selections, which of course was his right, but which also slowed the process since the president also had other pressing duties to attend to. The First Lady also played an important personal role across the board and with a particular concern for diversity. Running personnel selections by the First Lady for her approval provided another point that slowed the process. Reagan's personnel recruiter, Pendleton James, criticized the Clintons' hands-on, personal participation. He observed that Clinton seemed to be the starting point rather than the ending point of the personnel recruitment process: "The president should be a decision maker not a staff maker. . . . There are simply not enough hours in the day . . . for too much direct presidential involvement."[91]

Greater numbers of appointees. In addition to these problems with the appointments process, recent presidents have taken longer to establish their administrations because there are more appointments to make now than there were in the past. The total number of political appointments available to the president in 1992 exceeded 5,800, including part-time appointments and those not requiring Senate confirmation.[92] For purposes of controlling the executive branch the total is about 3,000, and the numbers have been steadily increasing over the years. Those in the highest category of political appointments in the executive branch requiring Senate confirmation, Executive Levels I–IV, have increased from 221 in 1960 to 590 in 1992; this is an important factor in explaining the increasing average number of months it takes a president to get appointees in place.[93]

But the greater number of political appointments that are not presidential have also clogged up the process, since control of many of these appointments has been drawn into the White House. The number of noncareer Senior Executive Service appointments (created in 1978) has increased from 582 in 1980 to 704 in 1992. The number of Schedule C appointments has grown from 911 in 1976 to 1,456 in 1980 to 1,699 in 1992.[94] Thus with executive branch appointments of about 3,000 plus about 500 White House appointments to make, it is not surprising that the Clinton administration took a long time to complete the task. To illustrate the increasing number of high-level positions in the executive branch, Paul Light has compiled the number of positions at different levels that increase the number of layers as well as the number of appointees in the executive branch.[95]

	1960	1992
Secretary	10	14
Deputy secretary	6	21
Under secretary	15	32
Assistant secretary	87	212
Deputy assistant secretary	78	507

The effect of these delays on the Clinton administration's policy agenda is difficult to calculate, but it certainly did not help. By April 28, 1993, the administration had more than three top officials in only two of the fourteen cabinet departments, and in seven of the departments only the secretary had been confirmed.[96] On May 1, 1994, of 325 top appointments 20.6 percent were still unfilled and 41 had no nominee pending.[97]

The lagging pace of appointments was a source of frustration to the president as well as to the rest of the administration. Bruce Lindsey said, "The delays are greater than we expected. I am not sure, really, why it takes so long, and we share the frustration" of cabinet members.[98] Clinton also expressed his frustration about the appointments process in general: "First of all, it takes too long to get anybody appointed. People who are independent and who have led interesting lives may be able to get elected to public office but may not be able to get appointed to anything. It's just ridiculous."[99]

In summary the reasons for the slowness of the Clinton appointment process include the following:

- Factors that would affect any contemporary administration—
    Financial disclosure, conflict of interest, and postemployment restrictions
    Increasing numbers of political appointees
    The centralization of personnel decisions in the White House
    Increasing sensitivity to ethical problems (e.g., "nanny" problems)
    More cautious FBI background investigations
- Factors attributable to the Clinton administration—
    The commitment to diversity
    The heavy personal involvement of the president and First Lady
    Lack of preparation and delays in getting the personnel operation into full swing
    The reduced size of the PPO in the summer and fall of 1993.

THE CLINTON POLICY AGENDA

During the campaign Bill Clinton as candidate developed a variety of issues that he promised his administration would take up if he were elected. His top priorities were clearly the economy and health care reform, but they also included a tax cut for the middle class, a program for national service, reform of the welfare system, campaign finance reform, lobbying reform, equitable treatment of gays in the military, administrative reform of the executive branch, the "Brady Bill" (handgun waiting period), and a number of other issues addressed at various times during the campaign. One of the tasks of a transition is to hone the broad range of issues from the campaign into a sharply focused set of priorities and to develop a strategy to implement the agenda at the beginning of the administration.

Initial Policy Objectives

Several ad hoc groups undertook the analysis of policy options during the campaign and put together plans for the administration to move on during its first weeks in office. A budget group worked on deficit reduction and stimulating the economy. A health care group that included several policy intellectuals who were experts in the area designed health care alternatives. Although a lot of preparatory work was done in these and other issue areas, it was not done under the sponsorship of a future official of the administration who had the authority (or clout) to ensure that the work would be seriously considered. That is, the plans had no powerful advocates, and in the power struggle that followed the election much of the preparatory work was discounted. Since White House staff appointments still had not been fully designated, policy disagreements became weapons in the battles for White House positions which seriously slowed progress on policy deliberations.[100]

Thus the failure to hit the ground running with a focused policy agenda was due not to the lack of policy preparation but to the failure to make final policy decisions and proceed with the political groundwork. There was not a clear connection between the policy planners and transition policy authority. In a sense, they had to reinvent the wheel. Looking back at the transition, Bruce Lindsey regretted that the transition was not more carefully planned: "We had working groups during the transition—welfare, economic—but we hadn't put it all together. They each came up with plans and legislation in their area, but that's as far as it went. We had no time line before we came. No one sat down and said, "If you do A, B, C, is your plate too full?" A couple of weeks into it, we realized that we had to think about it more strategically."[101]

Once the election was won, Clinton did not delegate authority to make these decisions, nor did he designate his White House staff and make it clear who would be in charge of the several areas of policy initiative. Clinton spent the bulk of the transition recruiting the cabinet while the rest of the campaign and transition personnel were jockeying over political appointments and trying to assure themselves a place in the new administration. Thus the major policy agenda issues were not settled. There was lots of action and debate, but no process, structure, or delegated authority to make authoritative decisions for the new administration short of the president-elect.

In mid-December Clinton hosted a large economic conference in Little Rock and invited a wide range of economists to debate the major issues facing the U.S. economy. Clinton was impressive as he presided over the televised discussion. He clearly knew the economic issues well and could handle them with sophistication. Some criticized him for taking valuable time out of the transition and recruitment of personnel to hold the discussions. The time and energy would have been well spent, however, if the administration had used the time to come to a consensus on what should be done in economic policy and then set about designing a strategy to implement the policies immediately upon taking office.

In a meeting on January 7, Clinton met with his economic advisers and faced the dilemma that though deficit reduction would make for a healthier economy in the long run, in the short run it might slow the economy and increase unemployment. Over the next month there was a fight for the mind of the president. The campaigners (future "consultants") argued that Clinton was not elected to reduce the deficit but rather to stimulate the economy and prepare American workers for world economic competition in the twenty-first century. In contrast, the "deficit hawks" argued that the first concern had to be deficit reduction or the bond markets would bid up interest rates because they expected increased inflation, and then the economy would spiral down.

Ordinarily the lack of agreement on the specifics of an economic policy would not be a problem, but Clinton had promised to "focus like a laser bean" on the economy, and the plan was not ready to be announced during the first weeks of the new administration. The problem was that the administration did not have a policy agenda ready for the first days and weeks of the new administration when press coverage is heaviest and expectations are high. In the first weeks of any new administration the press will predictably be looking for stories, and if the new administration does not have substantive activities planned, the press will find something to focus upon. During Clinton's first days in office the press focused on the search for the attorney general and the dispute over gays in the military, the most interesting policy conflicts available.

The economic plan was announced by Clinton on February 17, the same date that the Reagan administration announced its economic plan in 1981 (see Chapter 5). Thus, it was argued, the Clinton administration moved "extremely fast" and just as quickly as the Reagan administration had.[102] The difference, however, was that in 1981 it was clear even before Reagan was inaugurated that the direction of Reagan's economic policy would be to cut taxes, increase military spending, and cut domestic programs. The same cannot be said of the Clinton plan, which was not clearly defined because the major parts had not been agreed upon until early in February. As in the case of health care, the problem was not lack of preparation; the problem was a delay in making the major decisions.

If the policy decisions had been made in December, the transition and early weeks of the administration could have been devoted to laying the groundwork and getting OMB prepared with the details much earlier, and the public political arguments could have been made. The point here is about the tactics of transition, not the wisdom of the policies. The Reagan economic policies increased the national debt from $1 trillion in 1981 to $3 trillion by 1989. The Clinton deficit-reduction package was designed to reduce the total deficits by about $.5 trillion dollars over five years.

With the administration's budget policy still unsettled at the time of inauguration, other issues dominated publicity about the new administration. Even before the inauguration, trouble was brewing over Clinton's nominee to be attorney general, Zoe Baird. The press was running stories that she and her husband had hired illegal immigrants who did not have work permits for domestic work and they had not paid Social Security taxes for the workers until recently. The combination of a wealthy lawer (with a reported $500,000 income) not paying taxes and the prospective attorney general breaking the law provided too much of a political target, and Clinton decided to withdraw the nomination on January 21. The administration stumbled a second time in its first week when it settled on Kimba Wood as its replacement for Baird, only to withdraw her nomination when it was discovered that she also had hired an illegal alien to care for her child. Even though Wood had broken no law at the time she did it and had paid Social Security taxes, the administration decided that Wood's situation was too similar to Zoe Baird's. The administration finally settled on Janet Reno for its attorney general, and she was easily confirmed.

In his first two days in office Clinton signed several executive orders, the first to impose additional ethics guidelines that prohibited members of his administration from taking certain jobs dealing with the government for a period of time after they left government. Several other executive orders reversed those of the Bush and Reagan administrations that concerned counseling on abortion and the use of fetal tissue in scientific research as well as U.S. aid to UN population-control programs.[103]

The administration had three early legislative victories when Congress passed and Clinton signed three bills that had been vetoed by President Bush or stopped by Republicans in Congress. The Family and Medical Leave Act required employers to allow workers to take unpaid leave at the birth of a child or to care for a sick parent. The "Motor Voter" law made it easier for citizens to register to vote by making states provide for voter registration in conjunction with applying for a driver's license. The Hatch Act was liberalized to allow federal career civil servants to participate in more aspects of political campaigns while leaving in place safeguards against political coercion.

Despite these legislative victories, the headlines of the first month of the administration were dominated by the problems in the search for the attorney general and by Clinton's efforts to ensure equitable treatment for homosexuals in the armed services. Though Clinton saw the gay issue as a civil rights issue, the military establishment was dead set against any change in the status of gays, arguing that it would undermine unit cohesion and privacy. Chairman of the Joint Chiefs of Staff Colin Powell spoke out publicly against the lifting of the ban, and the rest of the Joint Chiefs spoke against it in a meeting with Clinton on January 25.[104] Just as important politically, Senator Sam Nunn (D-GA) publicly criticized Clinton's proposed change, thus legitimating other Democratic opposition, since Nunn was the Democrats' foremost national security spokesman in Congress. There were threats from the Hill that if Clinton pursued his plan by executive order Congress would pass a bill and lock the existing policy in law. Given the array of political forces against the policy and the likely defeat in Congress, Clinton accepted a compromise in which Secretary of Defense Aspin would prepare a policy on gays in the military by July 15, and in the meantime applicants to the military would not be asked about their sexual orientation.

This took the contentious issue off the front burner and newspaper headlines, but it also signaled an important defeat for the new administration. Most importantly, the issue dominated the headlines and made it seem as if the gay issue was one of the foremost priorities of the Clinton administration. If the budget policy had been ready to go earlier, the political controversy would have been over economic priorities for the country, and the gay issue would have been put into perspective as one of several items on the Clinton agenda.

The Budget Agenda

As the crises over finding the right attorney general and negotiating a compromise over gays in the military subsided, the administration was able to return the focus to its budget priorities. In a series of all-day sessions in early February, the outlines of the Clinton economic plan were hammered out. Clinton decided to drop his promise for a middle-class tax cut, increase tax rates on the affluent, and propose a broad-based energy tax. The combination of tax increases with spending cuts would reduce the deficit by $500 billion over five years, and in the short run the economy would be stimulated by an investment package. The important unveiling of the whole budget package was to come at an address to a joint session of Congress that would be televised nationally on February 17. Despite the inability of aides to get the last-minute version of the speech loaded into the TelePrompTer by the beginning of the speech (or perhaps because of it),

Clinton gave an inspired delivery, presenting much of the material from his own intimate knowledge of the details of the policies.

The day after Clinton's well-received speech the president hit the road to sell his plan to the public in town meetings, speeches, and interviews at radio and television stations. In a carefully planned blitz the whole administration was mobilized to sell the plan. Almost all of the cabinet secretaries traveled to their home states and then to carefully targeted locations. Leon Panetta met with 250 business leaders to brief them, and other groups were invited to the White House for briefings.[105] Public opinion polls indicated high approval of Clinton's plan, with 62 percent approval in a CNN/Time poll, despite the likely tax increases.[106]

The momentum from the president's speech and the carefully planned campaign to support the program lasted for a month, until the congressional votes on the concurrent resolution (which sets the outlines and totals of the budget). On March 18 the House passed the budget resolution on a party line vote of 243–183, with eleven Democrats defecting. The vote in the Senate was tougher, but after six days of lobbying and forty-five roll call votes to defeat Republican amendments, the Senate passed the budget resolution 54–45 with Senator Shelby (D-AL; since 1995, R-AL) joining the unanimous Republicans in voting no.

In order to give the economy an immediate boost that it seemed to need at the time, the administration put together a "stimulus package" that would get spending out immediately, before the next fiscal year. The Clinton package totaled $16.4 billion and included $4.3 billion in extended unemployment benefits as well as a number of special projects for training, infrastructure, and social programs that would be included in community development block grants. In addition to the money and policies involved, the issue was important because it would be Clinton's first direct confrontation with Congress.

After the package was announced it became clear to moderate Democrats that the Republicans would object to much of the plan and argue that it was irresponsible spending.[107] To stave this off, Senators David Boren (D-OK) and Representative John Breaux (D-LA) approached the White House with a scaled-down version as a proposed compromise. But the House had already passed the package right after voting on the budget resolution on March 18, and Robert Byrd (D-WV), chair of the Appropriations Committee, assured the president that he could pass the bill over Republican opposition.

The White House had miscalculated. Byrd's parliamentary maneuvering in support of the package irritated many Democrats and alienated most Republicans, who felt they did not have a fair chance to offer any amendments to the bill. But more importantly, the Republicans, who at first felt they could make some political points by decrying Democratic spending, soon realized that they might be able to defeat the bill entirely with a filibuster (an option not available to them in the expedited rules governing budget resolutions).[108] With help from Byrd's heavy-handed parliamentary tactics and the White House refusal of several offers to compromise, the Republicans were able to hold all of their moderate members and stave off any Democratic moves for cloture. Finally, on April 20, the administration gave up and withdrew the stimulus bill, with only the $4.6 billion in extended unemployment compensation passing the Senate.

The defeat of the administration on this relatively small spending bill was far greater in symbolic terms than its policy importance. First, it stopped the momentum that the administration had achieved in its total budget package. A whole month had passed, and future budget victories would be harder to wring out of Congress. Second, the administration had picked its first big fight with Congress without much awareness or planning, and it had lost. The administration and Democrats now appeared weaker, and the Republicans were more unified and emboldened to fight on other issues. Third, the Republicans were able to paint a picture of the Clinton administration as "tax and spend" Democrats, and give the impression that its budget plan was filled with "pork" rather than being the rather stringent plan the whole budget and deficit-reduction package was.

From May to August the administration fought with Congress to enact its budget priorities. The fighting was tenacious, with no Republicans voting for the deficit-reduction package and many Democrats demanding special concessions for their votes. The outcome of the budget votes, though razor thin, was successful. But the need to fight the battles through the summer of 1993 resulted in putting off health care until the fall. While exaggerating a bit, President Clinton was correct in his assessment of the budget strategy: "I think we had about a week's worth of strategy after Feb. 17 to sell this and what we needed was about three months worth of strategy . . . I believe this is my fault."[109]

The Health Care Campaign

By the end of the 1992 campaign, health care had emerged as one of the major issues to be addressed by the Clinton administration. The health care working group had draft legislation ready to go, but in January Clinton rejected its approach and decided to establish a special task force to reexamine the issues. Thus in late January 1993 Clinton announced that the administration's health care policy initiative would be headed by Hillary Clinton. He gave the task force a 100-day target to produce the administration proposal. The director of the policy development process was Ira Magaziner, who pulled together a task force of 500 experts recruited from throughout the government and private sectors. He divided the task force into thirty-four subgroups with 840 decision points or gates that had to be addressed.

Despite the felt need to move quickly with one of its most important priorities, after 100 days the administration proposal was not ready for several reasons. The task force could not come to terms with the concerns of Clinton's economic team, who thought that sweeping changes might cost too much and who favored a more incremental approach. In addition, the administration's economic plan was coming up for crucial votes, and it did not want to risk the budget votes by adding too much political and policy overload. (An earlier proposal to package health care with the budget resolution was rejected.)

The health care task force was disbanded in May 1993, and the White House team began work on formulating the administration's package, but without final presidential decisions on many key elements. It was late summer before the budget fights were over and the fall policy agenda had to be set. It was decided that when Congress reconvened in September Vice President Gore would unveil his "Reinventing Government" program before health care would be taken up and that the NAFTA issue also would be considered in the fall along with health care.[110]

Clinton finally gave his key kickoff speech on health care to Congress on September 22, 1993. The speech spelling out the principles of universal coverage and managed competition was a great success with Democrats in Congress and public opinion. A majority of the public, by almost a two-to-one margin, approved of the president's plan in October 1993.[111] Hillary Clinton received a respectful (Republican) and enthusiastic (Democratic) reception when she went to Capitol Hill to testify for the administration's health care package. But the actual text of the bill was not yet ready and did not make it to the Hill until October 27. In the meantime, some momentum was lost when the president had to deal with the crisis of twelve U.S. soldiers being killed in Somalia. At the same time, the administration was also fighting the battle over NAFTA.

The administration ended the year with the health care proposal before Congress, but the hard legislative push that would be needed to pass it in 1994 did not happen. In the end, health care reform failed in 1994 because the Democrats were divided, the Republicans were united and emboldened; interest groups spent millions to defeat the proposals; the proposal was overly ambitious and complex; and because of Clinton's 43 percent plurality, declining public approval, the Whitewater scandal, and the resistance of Americans to large governmental programs in the 1990s.

Clinton and the 103rd Congress

Despite the importance of the early actions of the administration in both symbolic and policy terms, the major policy priorities of the new Clinton administration depended upon legislative action. How did Clinton's approach to Congress compare with his predecessors' and with the prescriptions laid out in Chapter 6? Presidents were urged to begin with a quick start and early victories, and Clinton did this with the administrative actions and easy passage of the bills that President Bush had vetoed. Clinton, however, did not have much of a honeymoon with the public, and his approval ratings in the midfifties began to slide soon after he took office. The momentum he did develop with his budget speech follow-up ended with the defeat of his stimulus bill in April 1993.

At the personal level, presidents are urged in Chapter 6 to court Congress, be flexible, and be willing to use carrots and sticks in lobbying for votes on the Hill. At the agenda level, presidents are urged to move quickly in their first years to bring legislation to congressional votes, to pace their legislative demands on the Hill, and to focus their agendas by clearly setting priorities.[112] How well did Clinton perform on these latter criteria?

At the personal level Bill Clinton was an impressive lobbyer of Congress. He took pains to court members of both parties with invitations to the White House and personal phone calls. He was quite effective at the interpersonal level, combining the personal affability of Ronald Reagan with the detailed policy expertise of Jimmy Carter. In addition, he was empathetic and could communicate that he understood and sympathized with the perspective of his listener. He was willing to compromise on substance and pass out favors in seeking votes. Clinton, claiming the outsider's mantle, as had Carter and Reagan, learned from their experience by recruiting an experienced legislative insider, Howard Paster, to be his director of legislative liaison.

At the agenda level Clinton conformed less closely to prescriptions to move quickly and focus his agenda. At the very beginning of his term his primary message of budget discipline was delayed by the search for an acceptable attorney general and the issue of gays in the military. Besides these media flare-ups the administration was talking about and planning many diverse policy initiatives, including welfare reform, worker retraining, congressional campaign and lobbying reform, revamping college loan programs, national service, environmental improvement, and gun control.

As one commentator put it: "There is a tension in Clinton between the student of Presidential power and the student of policy. As a student of the presidency, he knows he should keep it simple, but as a student of policy he can't. The risk is that he knows too much. Reagan did not have that problem. For Reagan, a thematic presidency was easy because he did not know very much. All he had were broad themes on three-by-five cards. Clinton has a CD-ROM in his head."[113] It was difficult for citizens to discern one central theme or set of priorities. In May 1993 Bill Clinton admitted that he had tried to do a lot at the beginning: "One of the things that you risk when you try to get a lot of things going in a hurry—and we tried to get a lot of things going in a hurry because four years passes in a hurry—is that you wind up having people work very, very, hard but maybe getting a little out of focus. . . . And I think we can bring it—tighten the focus a little, and I think that's what we ought to do."[114] Mack McLarty agreed; "You clearly have to have a focused, concentrated plan to move your agenda forward."[115] Leon Panetta also agreed: "There were so many initiatives and so many efforts that were made that we lost the message."[116]

But Clinton's problems with Congress were more fundamental than merely tactics and timing. At a superficial level Clinton enjoyed a high legislative success rate in 1995 (as calculated by *Congressional Quarterly*), winning congressional votes on more than 86 percent of the issues upon which he took a stand. And he achieved some significant legislative victories, particularly deficit reduction and NAFTA. But at a more fundamental level he was not as successful as he had hoped or as many had expected. His major defeat was the failure to pass any kind of health care reform, but he didn't achieve many of his other legislative priorities, such as welfare reform, campaign finance reform, or lobbying reform. Much was accomplished in the first session of the 103rd Congress, but the many successes did not add up to a major Clinton agenda victory.[117]

Clinton suffered from a number of problems in his relations with Congress. Despite clear Democratic majorities, he had no natural coalition of votes for his agenda. For each major issue he had to cobble together a different combination of members to forge a winning coalition. For instance, in the two major votes on 1993 budget reconciliation and NAFTA, only 78 of 435 members of the House and 27 of 100 Senators voted with the president in both cases.[118] Democrats in Congress, despite high party unity scores, did not support him consistently or wholeheartedly. Often members of his own party did not support him in key legislative battles or demanded policy concessions or personal favors for their votes.

While the personal, tactical, and strategic decisions of presidents dealing with Congress make a difference, a consensus of scholars has developed that presidential success with Congress is largely determined by factors outside the control of presidents.[119] These scholars stress the importance of partisan balance in Congress. Bill Clinton had 57 Democrats in the Senate, the narrowest margin since Harry Truman, and 258 in the House, the narrowest margin since the large Democratic losses in 1966.[120] In addition, Clinton had no coattails, and ten House seats were lost in 1992. Few Democrats in Congress felt they owed their victory to him, and almost all of them garnered more votes than he did in their own districts (due to Ross Perot's candidacy). Combine the absence of gratitude with a lack of fear of a president with relatively low public approval ratings, and you have a formula for weak presidential influence on the Hill. There was a significant gap between Clinton's activist policy agenda and his "political opportunity level."[121]

These scholars also argue that presidential actions are not the primary determinants of members' votes. Members of Congress, rather, make up their minds on the basis of constituency pressure, ideology, and personal policy preference. Party discipline is very weak in the U.S. system, and despite the high party unity scores on roll call votes, Democrats in Congress deserted their president in important instances in the 103rd Congress. This general perspective on the relative weakness of presidential influence with Congress is summarized by George Edwards, who argues that the president is a "facilitator" rather than "director" of legislative action: "There is no systematic relationship between presidential legislative skills and congressional support for the White House."[122]

In summary, the nature of the fundamental political landscape argued against the likelihood of Clinton's success. He was elected with only a 43 percent plurality; he ran behind most members of Congress; he had fewer Democrats in Congress than other recent Democratic presidents; and his party lost seats in the election. Combine these negatives with a highly ambitious policy agenda, and you have a prescription for high conflict and low success. From this perspective we should be surprised that he did as well as he did in terms of policy success and congressional support.[123]

Conclusion:
The Strategic Presidency

If the president-elect does not want to leave his legacy to chance or be merely a caretaker in office, he must take a self-conscious strategic approach to the presidency. The policy process has become so complex, and the window of opportunity at the beginning of an administration so narrow, that only a focused effort can significantly reduce the risk of beginning an administration in disarray. This concluding chapter will examine the elements of strategic planning and the lessons learned from recent administrations about hitting the ground running with a new administration's agenda. It will then consider how initial momentum can be maintained.

Planning the strategy for a new administration cannot wait for the inauguration; it must begin immediately after election, and preferably before. Those involved in planning must take care not to seem presumptuous of victory or to seem to want to usurp the inheritance of the campaign organization. The main themes and priorities of the administration will naturally grow out of the campaign, but planning must be separate so as not to be caught up in fighting the daily fires that spring up in the heat of the campaign. The purpose of the strategic approach is to avoid dissipating administration energy from jockeying for position and fights over policy during the transition and early months of the administration. Day-to-day crises should not drive out the vision of where the presidency is going. This requires commitment from the top; it cannot be delegated to a side operation with no authoritative link to the candidate.

The first realization must be that a presidency moves through time with certain predictable cycles.[1] The four-year term is the basic cycle, the two-year cycle of congressional elections is an important break point, and the budget cycle must be confronted annually (and sometimes continually). The most important opportunity in these cycles is the predictable "honeymoon" period immediately after each inauguration in which Congress is sympathetic to a new president and during which members of his party want him to succeed. The American public also is filled with hope for the new president and public approval is often at its highest. He has not had enough time to make enemies, and the tough policy choices that will alienate some have not yet been made.

One of the ways to take advantage of this narrow window of opportunity is to make the most of the "mandate" from the people given to the president in the election. It helps if the election was a landslide, but any victory is enough to claim a mandate. Even though elections do not provide clear policy mandates, a new president can seize the opportunity to announce one. He can pull together the main themes of the campaign, choose his initial priorities, and announce that the administration has received mandate from the people. As Charles O. Jones says, "Election does not guarantee power in the American political system. Rather it legitimizes the effort of a president to lead."[2]

The Reagan administration did this quite well. Public opinion polls showed that most of the public did not agree with most administration priorities about cutting domestic programs. Nevertheless, the president announced that the people had spoken and that he was going to carry out his mandate. Announcing a mandate is a type of leadership that is expected of the president. In an unusually frank assessment, an anonymous Reagan administration aide admitted: "We were never quite as strong as we were able to give the impression of being. We pretended we had a mandate that was very much larger than it was. A tremendous number of people voted against Jimmy Carter, not for Reaganomics. Yet, we went about the country impressing them that Reagan was carrying out a mandate.[3]

Limiting the campaign priorities to be pursued is a major challenge to a new administration if initial efforts are not to be scattered and diffused. Tough choices must be made as to which campaign promises will be pursued and which will be set aside for a second term or quietly forgotten. The contrast between the Carter and Reagan presidencies is instructive here. Carter had his aides compile a list of his campaign promises (called "Promises, Promises" after a Broadway musical). Such a list can come back to haunt a president. The Carter administration used the shotgun approach to pursue many issues and refused to choose priorities during its early months in office. The Reagan administration decided early to put many of its social policy objectives on the back burners, consciously disappointing some of its constituencies, and to focus only on its economic goals. This focus was one of the key factors in enabling the Reagan administration to win such impressive victories during its early months.[4] President Bush chose to pursue a number of minor initiatives, and President Clinton's agenda was ambitious. Neither one narrowly focused his initial agenda on policies that would define his presidency.

After choosing priorities the administration must control the political agenda so that public attention and congressional debate center on the administration's priorities. Maintaining the focus on the central agenda is much easier if there is a "macrotheme" for the administration. If administration priorities can be brought together under the umbrella of one overarching theme, it will be much easier to keep public attention and support behind the president's program. This macrotheme should be something more focused than "getting the country moving again," yet broader than any specific piece of legislation or policy initiative.

With the shift of focus in American politics to the "personal presidency,"[5] the main asset of the White House is the president and the optimum use of his time must be made to support the central agenda.[6] The president must articulate the policy direction of the administration and build public and congressional support for his policies. According to the strategic approach to the presidency, the president's time is wasted if he tries to control directly departments and agencies or programs. Those are managerial details (though important ones) and should be left to his staff and appointees. The president's role is to provide leadership and central direction for the administration.

To have the maximum impact on public perception and congressional attention, the president's limited time should be used to stage events that announce policies, preferably events that make the nightly news. Mere written pronouncements of administration policies are not sufficient to have the maximum impact. Events can be presidential addresses to the public or Congress, domestic or foreign trips, support for or the vetoing of a bill, and so on. In staging an event three things must be kept in mind: the audience (primarily Congress or the general public); the medium to be used (primarily television, but also newspapers and magazines); and the message (the substance of the policy itself). The point is that presidential priorities must be demonstrated with events and actions to catch the attention of the public and Congress. Follow-through is necessary to show that the administration is serious about a policy.

This strategic approach merely sketches out an approach to focusing the administration's energy on making maximum use of the narrow window of opportunity in the beginning months of an administration. It is not a formula to control all events, which of course is impossible. It must be flexible enough to allow for compromise and unforeseen circumstances, yet it must be firm enough to provide a strategic focus for the administration that gives guidance for the use of the president's time and energy as well as providing a theme for administration officials throughout the government.

The main point of this strategic approach is that a new administration must move quickly after the election to consolidate its forces and move with its agenda. This book has traced the experience of recent administrations in taking over the government in key areas. We will turn now to abstracting some of these lessons about what is necessary to enable a new administration to hit the ground running.

MOVING QUICKLY: LESSONS LEARNED

At the same time that the strategic approach of the new administration is being set, work must begin on the major levers of governmental power that will be necessary to take control of the government. There are no cookbook formulas, but the experience of recent presidents traced in this book can give us some insights about what is most likely to give a new administration an effective start on its agenda.

Before much else can be done, the White House staff must be organized, and the important change of orientation must be made from campaigning to governing. While new presidents-elect want to move quickly on their cabinet selections, the White House staff must not be neglected. If the chief of staff and several top aides are designated early, the inevitable jockeying for position can be more easily controlled. Waiting until mid-January to name the White House staff can slow an administration, as it did for Clinton in 1993.

There is now a consensus that a chief of staff is necessary to run the White House. No president since Lyndon Johnson has successfully run the White House without one, and no one since Jimmy Carter has tried. Regardless of the president's personal style, someone short of the president must impose order on policy development, guard access to the president, and settle administration disputes that are not of presidential importance. On the other hand, if the chief of staff takes a domineering approach to the job, it is a likely prescription for disaster. *Each* of the strong chiefs of staff (Adams for Eisenhower, Haldeman for Nixon, Regan for Reagan, and Sununu for Bush) have alienated members of Congress, alienated members of their own administrations, had reputations for the lack of common civility, and had hostile relations with the press. And *each* of them resigned under varying degrees of pressure, having done harm to his own president and the presidency.

Yet the functions of the chief of staff job must be performed firmly and with a sense of civility. The job can be done well, as demonstrated by James Baker for Reagan, Jack Watson for Carter, and Don Rumsfeld and Dick Cheney for Ford. Each of them ran the White House with a firm hand, took heat for the president, and was an honest broker in the policy process.

In light of the experience of Presidents Nixon and Carter, presidents-elect should not be too optimistic about promising "cabinet government," despite the temptation to use this attractive symbol. A strong, though not necessarily domineering, White House staff is crucial to the functioning of the contemporary presidency. The trend in the modern presidency of increasing control in the White House and a diminishing role for the cabinet has not been reversed by Presidents Bush or Clinton. Predictable centrifugal forces will operate to draw cabinet secretaries in directions other than those the White House wants. The maximum White House leverage on cabinet members is at the beginning of an administration, before they have had a chance to become well acquainted with interest groups, congressional forces, and the permanent "natives" in their organizations.

The key to making sure things do not get out of hand in the departments is to set the ground rules early. The president himself must make clear what is and what is not delegated to cabinet secretaries. Which appointments are to be made by the White House and which are at cabinet discretion? What are the budget priorities of the administration? What issues are particularly important to the president, and what are the procedures of clearing policy with the White House? But an attempt to draw too much control into the White House can be counterproductive. If the White House tries to do everything, it cannot do it all well, and the expertise in departments and agencies will be wasted. Presidents are well advised to delegate to the departments and agencies those policies that are not of major presidential priority.[7]

Finally, presidents should expect loyalty and support from cabinet secretaries. The Carter administration experience demonstrated the effects of too little deference of cabinet secretaries to the White House. On the other hand, the Nixon White House seemed to expect more tight control over cabinet secretaries than the separation-of-powers systems can sustain. Presidents should be aware that, despite their understandable expectations of loyalty, there are also other legitimate claims on cabinet secretaries in the American political system.

Preparations for staffing an administration must begin early, shortly after the nominating convention. These efforts must have very low visibility because of the high potential for embarrassment. Because of the probability of leaks, compiling specific names for positions is risky, but at least a process for recruiting the best and the brightest for the administration must get under way early. Shortly after the election a personnel director with access to the president must be designated. The personnel operation, before and after inauguration, should act as a buffer for the president. If it does not, the president will be swamped with requests for jobs. The buffering effect will only occur if the president supports, rather than undercuts, the personnel operation. Presidential restraint in suspending the established personnel procedures will enhance rather than decrease the presidential control of the personnel process.

The personnel operation should have an outreach arm that will actively recruit the best people for administration positions, and not merely screen résumés that come in "over the transom." Efforts should be made to separate merit from patronage appointments. Patronage appointments cannot be ignored, and can be an important political tool, but they should not be allowed to dominate the personnel process. Procedures must be installed early to handle the flood of requests for appointments from the Hill. A delicate balance must be maintained between loyalty and competence as the criteria for choosing appointees. Neither criterion can be ignored if the administration is to expect effectiveness as well as responsiveness from its appointees.

A new administration can best ensure that its policies will be carried out effectively if it establishes policy control over the bureaucracy as quickly as possible. One way to help this along is to tone down anti-government campaign rhetoric and to try to expedite the cycle of accommodation with the career bureaucracy. Political appointees should not treat them with the hostility of a conquering army, but rather should view career employees as potential allies in carrying out the new administration's policies. It is impossible to run the government without them, and the sooner this is realized, the sooner the president's program can get to the implementation stage.

While responsiveness can be expected from most career civil servants, some "bureaucratic" resistance to the White House is inevitable. This resistance will come from Congress, interest groups, and administration appointees; it will be aided by, though not initiated by, some career bureaucrats. Blaming all resistance to the White House on career civil servants will not help solve these very real problems.

Since the budget is so crucial to policy priorities and there is so much momentum built into this rolling series of decisions, preparation to put the new administration's stamp on the budget must begin early. Planning about budget priorities by the budget staff should be under way shortly after the election, and liaison with career OMB staff to work on details should be undertaken as soon as the outgoing administration allows it.

Promising economic miracles in the campaign should be avoided as much as possible, and the constraints presented by uncontrollable spending should be appreciated. On the other hand, major budgetary change is possible by a determined administration, as the Reagan administration demonstrated. Given the intractability of our huge structural deficits, deficit politics will tend to dominate the policy debate and must be addressed as a priority by each new administration.

Congressional cooperation and support is critical to any president's agenda. The courting of Congress should be done early and often. Coordination of supporters in Congress should be initiated during the campaign. Immediately after the election the director of congressional liaison should be designated and a process for handling congressional requests for favors and appointments must be set up, because the flood of incoming mail and phone calls will be overwhelming. If the legislative liaison team members are experienced on the Hill, they will already have their personal networks ready to go without having to develop them from scratch.

When the personnel and processes for legislative liaison have been developed, the priorities of the legislative agenda should be set. Major legislative proposals should be scheduled to be submitted to Congress early in cooperation with the leadership of the president's party. Presidents should expect to devote a considerable portion of their time to congressional strategy, but the president's personal lobbying efforts should be carefully meted out. Picking the president's first confrontation with Congress should be done with careful deliberation and with the probability of victory. Carter's water projects, Bush's Tower nomination, and Clinton's stimulus package were all defeats that hurt them with Congress. Reagan's budget victories helped him establish momentum.

The irony of all of the above "musts" is that they *must* be carried out simultaneously. That is what is so overwhelming about taking control of the U.S. government. In order to do this, planning must begin before the election despite the risks of appearing to be presumptuous.

The argument in this book has been that if a new administration wants to accomplish policy goals it must move quickly to implement its agenda, but there is much to be said for caution. Richard Neustadt argues that in new administrations "ignorance of men, roles, institutions, policies and nuances" combined with arrogance and hopefulness can lead to blunders such as the Bay of Pigs invasion in John Kennedy's early months in office.[8] Charles O. Jones and William Lammers also argue that moving too quickly can lead to policy mistakes, such as some of LBJ's programs in 1956, Carter's energy plan in 1977, or Reagan's fiscal policy in 1981.[9] So the need to move quickly is no excuse to avoid careful deliberation on the part of an administration or Congress. Proposed policies should be openly deliberated, not presented full-blown after secret deliberations, as with Carter's energy plan or Clinton's health care proposals.

Despite all of the planning and preparation advocated here, much is in the hands of fate. Unexpected events not within control of the new administration may dictate actions and early priorities. A military crisis, an oil embargo, or a terrorist act may dominate the agenda of a new administration despite the elaborate planning of its strategic agenda. There is no way to plan for an unexpected crisis, but insofar as procedures have been set up to handle the key levers of control of the government dealt with here, the more energy and attention can be given to the crisis and not spent on setting up basic processes.

SHORTEN THE TRANSITION PERIOD?

After elections in which the incumbent administration has been rejected in favor of the candidate of the other party, various commentators have suggested that the time between election and inauguration be significantly shortened. This stems from frustration with watching the lame-duck administration flounder about, while the president's power diminishes steadily after the election. The newly elected president is the focus of attention and begins to accumulate power, though the formal authority to run the government will not be transferred until January 20. The diminished power of the incumbent president makes governmental policy making grind to a halt, because everybody realizes that the incoming administration will move in its own direction as soon as it takes office.

In this situation it is attractive to wish that the transfer of authority could be made much sooner. The idea is that the ambiguity of power between the president and president-elect would be settled and the newly elected president could get on with the job of running the government. This desire for the new president to be in charge of the government is reasonable, and if control of the government could be effected immediately, shortening the transition period would be a good solution to the problem of the ambiguity of power. Unfortunately, shortening the period would not solve the problem, because even though the authority of the office can be transferred, the effective control of the government is something that must be seized, and this takes time.

As should be clear from the previous chapters, it takes a considerable amount of time for a new president to take effective control of the government. The candidate has spent the previous several years immersed in the campaign for office. Time and resources cannot easily be diverted from the campaign to prepare for the transition into office. Even those (Carter and Reagan) who have done some preelection preparation have taken considerable time after the election to make the necessary decisions to begin their administrations.

Even if the choice of White House staff and cabinet members could be compressed into several weeks, budget and subcabinet personnel decisions will take considerably longer. It took the Reagan administration, despite an elaborate transition bureaucracy and transition teams, well into the summer of 1981 to complete most of its personnel appointments. It took the Bush and Clinton administrations even longer. Things would be even more hectic than they are now for a new administration if it had to run the government at the same time that it was trying to shake down its own organization and choose its appointees. It is better to have a lame-duck president clearly in control, though with diminished power, than a new president who is preoccupied with making initial appointments and basic organizational decisions while trying to run the government at the same time.

In short, it would be nice if effective control of the government could be transferred more quickly after an election. But the eleven weeks now available is not enough time to make most of the decisions that are necessary to take over the government, and for this reason the transition of a new administration into office extends well into its first year in. Shortening the time period would not enable a new administration to accomplish all of the things it has to do between election and inauguration in a shorter period of time than is now necessary. There is simply too much to do before taking office.

PROBLEMS WITH THE APPOINTMENTS PROCESS

Like the problems of deficit reduction or health care financing, there is a broad consensus that the political appointments process is broken, but there is no consensus about how to fix it. Not all agree about what the problem is, but most would agree that at least some of the following are problems: the slowing pace of presidential appointments, the growing number of political appointees, the increasing number of hierarchical layers in the departments and agencies, over-broad restrictions on career choices after serving, and the increasing intrusiveness combined with the decreasing civility of the Senate confirmations process.

The Slow Pace of Appointments

The slowing pace of presidential appointments was clearly demonstrated in Chapter 8, and there is no reason to believe the trend will not continue. The delay in getting appointees in place is a problem because a new administration cannot proceed with the implementation of its policy and programmatic agenda without the leadership of its appointees in the departments and agencies. In self-defense presidential recruiters will argue that leadership from the cabinet secretary is sufficient, but programmatic changes need hands-on attention at the assistant secretary level. Career civil servants have the experience and expertise for this leadership, but they do not have the legitimacy of presidential appointment. To implement presidential priorities someone must be able to speak authoritatively for the new administration on the Hill and commit the agency administratively. The data upon which the graphs in Chapter 8 are based were provided by the executive clerk to the president in 1993 and are presented in Table 1.

If part-time appointments are subtracted, Clinton is closer to Bush, though still behind. If recess appointments are subtracted, Carter passes Reagan. Regardless of how the data are counted, the trend is the same, and the effect on the government is negative.

As argued in Chapter 8, some of the causes of the slowness of the appointments process are under the president's control. This book has argued that presidents should set the tone and spend time with their recruiters, but President Clinton's personal participation in the selection of lower-level executives used much of his own time and slowed the process. The use of narrow criteria of loyalty also has a significant slowing effect, as it did in the Reagan administration.

One of the most important causes of the slowness of appointments is the number of political appointees. The total number of appointees available to presidents, not including judges, exceed 5,500 (Table 2). Of course, 2,000 of these are part-time, and not all are as important as those who will be running the executive branch. The number of these, including PAS, noncareer SES, and Schedule C appointees, has been increasing over the past several decades, and now totals about 3,000.

The large number of political appointees is of concern aside from the cumulative effect on the slowness of the appointments process. The large number of appointees penetrates further down into the bureaucracy and thus dilutes the

Table 1. Pace of Appointments: First-Year Nominations and
Appointments by Administration

	Clinton 1993	Bush 1989	Reagan 1981	Carter 1977
Total First-Year Appointments				
All PAS	499	432	662	637
(Part-time)	(c.65)	(17)	(65)	(68)
(Recess)	(/)	(5)	(51)	(0)
November 24				
Nominated	673	501	680	682
Confirmed	499	411	547	549
November 19				
Nominated	582	491	662	676
Confirmed	412	391	528	547
November 12				
Nominated	544	463	645	668
Confirmed	404	333	504	545
November 4				
Nominated	523	448	629	660
Confirmed	384	328	481	545
October 29				
Nominated	513	439	585	650
Confirmed	379	318	478	529
October 22				
Nominated	475	434	581	627
Confirmed	375	307	460	507
October 15				
Nominated	464	423	558	607
Confirmed	345	297	443	477
October 8				
Nominated	451	413	539	583
Confirmed	303	295	442	465
October 1				
Nominated	433	394	526	571
Confirmed	284	230	425	430
September 24				
Nominated	426	380	511	550
Confirmed	282	226	374	426
September 7				
Nominated	398	341	447	484
Confirmed	254	212	345	372
August 12				
Nominated	354	319	416	450
Confirmed	253	212	345	372
July 30				
Nominated	229	284	397	432
Confirmed	212	166	316	339
July 23				
Nominated	287	269	374	415
Confirmed	205	155	258	320
July 16				
Nominated	276	248	358	399
Confirmed	204	152	245	311

Table 1.
(Continued)

	Clinton 1993	Bush 1989	Reagan 1981	Carter 1977
July 9				
Nominated	253	222	330	378
Confirmed	194	147	227	282
July 2				
Nominated	253	222	307	368
Confirmed	194	147	227	282
June 25				
Nominated	238	222	291	345
Confirmed	177	147	203	261
June 18				
Nominated	228	205	276	332
Confirmed	166	116	183	243
June 7				
Nominated	211	176	237	296
Confirmed	159	101	153	221
May 28				
Nominated	203	146	205	283
Confirmed	159	97	137	205
May 25				
Nominated	202	146	195	276
Confirmed	99	97	137	202
May 14				
Nominated	181	136	180	NA
Confirmed	77	67	125	
May 7				
Nominated	177	127	163	NA
Confirmed	49	51	114	
April 29				
Nominated	173	96	152	215
Confirmed	49	49	83	155
April 23				
Nominated	118	96	142	195
Confirmed	46	49	81	129
April 3				
Nominated	66	46	104	161
Confirmed	43	26	67	102
March 5				
Nominated	33	29	58	74
Confirmed	26	18	37	41
February 24				
Nominated	28	21	45	59
Confirmed	25	11	30	27

NOTE: Includes all full-time presidential appointments requiring consent of the Senate (PAS), including ambassadors, U.S. attorneys, U.S. marshals, and federal judges. Also includes part-time PAS: first full year totals: Bush (17), Reagan (65), Carter (68), Clinton (35, as of October 22). Does not include foreign service officers, military officers, or public health officers.

SOURCE: Derived from data provided by the executive clerk to the president in 1993.

Table 2. Total Political Appointments Available to Presidents

PAS[1]	
Part-time	505
Ambassadors	165
U.S. attorneys and marshals	187
Executives and commissioners	663
PA[2]	
Executive branch	24
White House	438
Part-time	1,405
Agency appointments[3]	
SES[4]	711
Schedule C[5]	1,725
Total	5,823[6]

[1]Presidential appointment with the consent of the Senate.
[2]Presidential appointment not requiring Senate confirmation.
[3]Legally made by agency head, but the president can instruct appointees whom to appoint.
[4]Senior Executive Service: 10 percent of authorized total SES positions can be political appointees, about 700 of 7,000.
[5]Created in 1953, political appointments at GS 15 and below. Must have a confidential or policy-making role in the administration.
[6]Presidents can also appoint about 1,000 federal judges, who serve for life. But any individual president will only have the opportunity to make a portion of these appointments.

SOURCE: PAS data derived from information provided by the executive clerk to the president (February 19, 1992). Agency appointments data from General Accounting Office reported in the *Washington Post*, November 20, 1992, p. A23. See James P. Pfiffner, *The Modern Presidency* (New York: St. Martin's Press, 1994), p. 123.

effective control of the president and cabinet secretaries. This penetration shuts off career opportunities for civil servants and discourages them from staying in the system with their experience and expertise. It also leads to the loss of institutional memory and a short-term approach to the management of the government.[10]

These consequences are aggravated by the rapid turnover of political appointees, with an average appointee staying in a position for about two years and the time to fill a vacant position ranging from six months at the State Department to twenty months at Health and Human Services, according to GAO.[11] This instability and turnover at the top have disruptive effects in the administration of programs. When executives come and go they often take with them their own entourages of special assistants and colleagues. In addition, the further down into the bureaucracy that political levels reach, the harder it is to recruit qualified political appointees, and often marginally qualified campaign supporters are put in charge of much more experienced career civil servants.

Because of these negative effects, a number of institutions and scholars have called for decreasing the number of political appointees. The National Commission on the Public Service (the Volcker Commission) proposed cutting the number of appointees in the executive branch from about 3,000 to about 2,000.[12] The National Academy of Public Administration, in an in-depth study of presidential appointees from 1964 to 1984, also called for reducing the number of political appointees.[13] The National Academy of Sciences conducted a study of science and technology leadership in the federal government, focusing particularly on the need for high-quality talent and the disincentives for public service for scientists and engineers. In the conclusion to its final report the National Academy of Sciences called for "reducing administrative overbrush" by cutting the number of political appointees in the executive branch of the government.[14] A number of scholars have also pointed out the negative consequences of the large number of appointees and have called for a reduction in their numbers. Patricia Ingraham et al. concluded that "the demands of the appointments process have outstripped the capabilities of the Presidential Personnel Office."[15] With reductions in the federal workforce mandated by the National Performance Review and implementing legislation, the ratio of political appointees to career civil servants would increase further.

Layers

Another characteristic of the current administrative structure that is aggravated by the growing number of appointees is the increasing number of layers of administrative hierarchy in executive branch bureaucracies. Paul Light, in his book *Thickening Government*, documents this trend and argues that the layers of hierarchy are more debilitating to good management than the absolute number of appointees. In his analysis he counts the number of occupants at the top layers of the federal hierarchy (Executive Levels I–V) and shows the increase in numbers. The growth in these positions is disproportionately larger than the increase in the number of programs, and the total civilian employment of the government has been relatively flat. The number of occupants by layer of government may be compared as follows:[16]

Level	1960	1992
Secretary	10	14
Deputy secretary	6	21
Assistant secretary	87	212
Deputy assistant secretary	78	507
Total increase, I–V	451	2,393

Only a few of many layers are listed here; the totals reflect many more layers. Light argues that the number of layers is more problematic than the number of political appointees, and that many of these positions at the lower levels are occupied by career civil servants: "The numbers do not matter nearly as much as how they are distributed throughout the hierarchy. The top of the hierarchy has grown from a seventeen-layer pyramid in 1960 to thirty-two layers today, while the number of occupants has increased almost sixfold."[17]

Ethics

Other difficulties with the system's ability to recruit the most talented and qualified people from the private sector to leave their careers and spend several years in the federal government stem from the "ethics" laws and regulations. The laudable intent of these restrictions is to ensure that public officials do not take unfair advantage of their power and inside knowledge to benefit themselves financially. Thus there are prohibitions concerning conflict of interest that force appointees to divest themselves of assets, recuse themselves from certain decisions, and refrain from taking certain jobs after their government service. These restrictions, combined with financial disclosure statements, which are available to the public, are enforced by the Office of Government Ethics. These restrictions are particularly troubling in technical and defense positions. The Bush administration reportedly went through twenty-four exploratory interviews before it could find a person to accept the position of undersecretary of defense for acquisitions.[18] President Clinton tightened the rules by increasing postemployment restrictions to five years for 1,100 of the top executive in the executive branch.

While the intent of these laws is commendable, and some restrictions to ensure the fiduciary integrity of public officials are necessary, the requirements could be modified to minimize the disincentives to public service, particularly postemployment restrictions. In reflecting about the changes in defense management since his career began in the Pentagon in the 1960s, former Secretary of Defense Les Aspin said:

> The pool of topnotch civilians has shrunk because we've made so damn many reforms against revolving doors. We used to pull people from the industry into the Pentagon for a few years and then they'd go back to industry. They were a tremendous asset because they knew the field and weapon systems. That's over. Now because of legislation against revolving doors, a defense civilian must choose a career in the private or public sector, but not both. So lots of good people in the private sector stay out. We've lost that pool of people willing to do a stint in government but not make it a career.[19]

The sacrifice in privacy caused by the public disclosure of personal financial data is a high price to pay for people who may have nothing to hide. Who wants his or her personal finances displayed before the public, friends, and relatives? The laws governing financial disclosures could be modified to make the details of personal financial statements available to relevant persons in the government for judgments about conflict of interest and not available to curious reporters.

The public has the right to be assured that the decisions of government officials will not be affected by financial self-interest. But in our zeal to prevent the abuses of the few, we may also be throwing up roadblocks for the many conscientious citizens who may want to serve but are not willing to make the sacrifices now demanded of them. Closing the revolving door is justified when people use the information they gain in public service to give unfair advantage to the firms they join after public service. But we should not draw the strictures so tightly that people are prevented from pursuing their professions when they leave public service. The exchange of talent and ideas between the public and private sectors carries important benefits for our economy and government. The uncertainty that can be caused by the vague and confused set of postemployment restrictions has led to the inability to attract some highly qualified candidates to important posts.

While we should not shrink from asking our public servants to make some sacrifices that are necessary to ensure the integrity of the system, it is shortsighted and self-defeating to make the hurdles so high that our best prospects for executive positions will not consider serving. Any changes should not undercut the intent of the various ethics-in-government laws. But there is no way to prove that the existence of these laws has prevented corruption, and the risk that some scurrilous people may slip through the screen may be necessary to reduce the impediments to serving for the many highly ethical people we are trying to attract to government service.[20]

The level of salaries for presidential appointees was a problem in the late 1980s, but it was considerably alleviated by the pay raise for federal officials that took effect in 1990. The issue of pay is a politically difficult one for the federal government, and if salaries are allowed to erode again over a number of years, it will have to be revisited.

Senate Confirmation

The appointments process also suffers from declining civility and the increased politicization of the Senate confirmation process. Senators increasingly place "holds" on nominations thus preventing a vote on the nominee until their own unrelated political goals are met.[21] The media avidly pursue the backgrounds of presidential nominees, searching for embarrassing incidents. Those conducting "opposition research" by the political parties dig through personal histories searching for peccadillos that can be magnified to gain partisan leverage. Interest groups focus narrowly on the policy preferences of candidates that affect the group's concerns and oppose those candidates who do not match their own narrow preferences.

All of these developments have combined to create a nomination and appointments process that often lacks civility. Potential nominees "are not enamored at the thought of having the media and a variety of interest groups crawl all over their lives in an attempt to dig up whatever bits of dirt, or bits of things that could be called dirt . . . that turns tiny ethical molehills into vast mountains of outrage, while consigning questions of policy and ability to minor roles," according to Stephen L. Carter in his book *The Confirmation Mess.*[22] President Clinton's friend and deputy White House counsel, Vincent Foster, lamented the politicized atmosphere in Washington in his final written words: "Here ruining people is considered sport."[23] After the hearings on the nomination of Clarence Thomas, Senator John Danforth expressed his frustration with the process:

> If the president calls to say that he will nominate you for a job subject to confirmation by the Senate, just say no. . . . Why risk the reputation you have worked so hard to earn by subjecting yourself to what can become of presidential nominees. . . . The real issue is whether there are any limits to how far we can go in using a presidential nomination for the purpose of making a political point, or furthering a philosophical position, or establishing our own moral superiority or embarrassing the president of the United States, whatever party may at the time occupy the White House. Today there are no such limits, and no limits will or should be supplied by rule or law.[24]

The Supreme Court nominations of Robert Bork and Clarence Thomas illustrate these negative trends in the confirmation process. The Clinton administration suffered similar problems in a number of nominations, including those of Zoe Baird and Lani Guinier. Clinton also nominated Bobby Ray Inman to replace Les Aspin as secretary of defense, but despite Inman's distinguished record of public service and clear qualifications, he withdrew his name in January 1994 because he did not want to undergo a bruising appointments process.

All of the preceding factors have combined to make the political appointments process the "mess" that Carter writes about and justify President Clinton's conclusion—"It's just ridiculous."

Reforms and Solutions?

As the foregoing litany of the difficulties associated with the appointments process makes clear, the problem is not singular but rather a complex of interrelated issues. They are so intertwined that it would be difficult to alleviate any one symptom without solving the others. One thing that can be done about the pace of appointments is to legitimate personnel planning before the election, as has been argued previously in this book. The undertaking is just too large to wait until after the election to set up computers and design a system. The problem, of course, is that as soon as the other campaign gets wind of any preparation it will accuse the planners of presumption.

While most agree that the slow pace of appointments in recent administrations is a problem, not all would agree that there are too many appointees. Some point out that the total number of appointees is a tiny fraction of the total federal work-force and emphasize the need for a president to have loyal subordinates in the departments and agencies. Some even argue that there should be more appointees so that the bureaucracy can be forced to comply with presidential wishes.

Armed with these superficially appealing arguments, the political resistance to any significant reduction in the number of political appointees will be formidable. New presidents have obligations from the campaign and tend to see positions as a means to repay campaign debts. All PAS positions are authorized in public law, and members of Congress feel that they have more leverage over executives who must go through Senate confirmation, so Congress may not be eager to eliminate these points of access. Presidents could bring in fewer political appointees at the noncareer SES and Schedule C levels by instructing their PAS appointees to fill the positions with career civil servants. But they would meet with severe resistance from those who want to bring their own entourages with them to executive branch positions. For similar reasons, Paul Light concludes that attempts to reduce the "thickening," or layers, of the executive branch will face intense resistance and would require commensurate effort on the part of a president bent on reform. The basic problem is that the payoff for reform is in the longer-run effectiveness of the government, while the short-term political incentives all favor the status quo.

The difficulty with reforming the financial disclosure and conflict of interest restrictions is that any proposed changes can easily be made to appear to undermine the financial integrity that is the intent of current restrictions. Good-government groups will oppose these reforms, but the longer-term need to recruit the best executives for presidential appointments makes it worth the effort. The reforms proposed in the National Academy of Sciences Report, cited earlier, are a good place to start.

Finally, the problem of the declining civility of the appointments process, including Senate confirmation hearings and the attendant investigative reporting, can only be alleviated by changing behavior and is not amenable to changes in rules or laws. The challenge of reform is well illustrated by Stephen Carter's set of reasonable proposals for changing our attitudes about the appointments process, and the disjunction between those attitudinal changes and the list of proposed reforms of the process that he demonstrates are unlikely to solve the problems presented.[25]

MOLDING AN ADMINISTRATION

In addition to the preparation and initial actions of an administration advocated above, a new administration must be concerned with following through on its actions, particularly with its political appointees. Each administration has had periods of frustration when the White House perceives that the president's appointees have gone off and "married the natives." It has been argued in this book that this is to be expected and is due to strong centrifugal forces that affect each administration. But just because the tendency is inevitable does not mean that the administration is helpless.

An administration can take actions to minimize the negative effects of these forces, though they will never be completely eliminated. Heavy-handed actions, such as the Nixon administration attempt to place White House "spies" into departments and agencies, are unlikely to be effective. In this case prevention is less expensive and more effective than cure. The White House can try to counter the centrifugal tendencies in at least three ways: (1) helping its nominations through the Senate confirmation process; (2) orienting its new political appointees; and (3) continuing efforts to involve subcabinet members in the life of the administration.

Follow through on Nominations

In too many cases in recent administrations the last a candidate for a presidential appointment hears from the White House personnel office is that it has decided to forward the nomination to the Senate. The personnel office then turns its attention to other candidates, leaving the nominee to fend for him- or herself. For those who have been through the process before, this may not be a problem, but for the first-time nominee it can be intimidating. Hiring the right lawyers and accountants to fill out conflict-of-interest forms and finding the right political contacts to smooth one's way through the labyrinth of Senate confirmation are daunting tasks, particularly if the nominee must also quit a job and move a household to Washington.

The White House personnel office ought to set up a section charged with the responsibility to see to the needs of candidates for presidential positions after they have been nominated. Lawyers and accountants should assist with disclosure forms. Preparations for Senate confirmation hearings should include introductions to members of the committee involved. People should also be assigned to help facilitate the move to Washington and the search for housing.[26] The intention should be to make the nominee feel that he or she is a valued member of the new administration and not alone if difficulties should occur during confirmation hearings.

Orient New Political Appointees

Sixty percent of political appointees come from outside the federal government: 24 percent from business, 16 percent from academia, 12 percent from the legal profession, and 7 percent from state and local governments.[27] While most of these people are successful professionals, those without previous federal government experience would benefit from a briefing on the federal government.

The United States is still influenced by the Jacksonian myth that government jobs are so simple that anyone can handle them. Political appointees now have impressive educational credentials (34 percent have law degrees, 17 percent doctorates, 21 percent master's degrees, and 19 percent bachelor's degrees only), and so we seem to think that they can step into a top-level management position and function effectively with little preparation. Though the people recruited for presidential appointments are well educated and successful professionals, it is unlikely that they will have both the management skills and the political sophistication that are necessary to do a good job as a presidential appointee. Thus it is important that the government ensure that new appointees have the opportunity to be oriented to the environment of political management and to be briefed on matters specific to their jobs.

Appointees with no previous experience in the federal government must become acquainted with the external environment of their agency as well as with its internal operations. The external environment includes the omnipresence (and seeming omnipotence) of Congress. Political appointees must know how to deal with the White House staff. Each department and agency must deal with the central staff agencies in the executive branch: OMB, OPM, and GSA. The overwhelming reality is that virtually all policy questions must be coordinated with many decision makers and power centers external to the agency in question. Another factor affecting government officials is the "fishbowl" environment. The Washington press corps is constantly looking for stories, and scandals make good stories. The personal and financial lives of high government officials are not considered off-limits. People without federal government experience are unlikely to be fully prepared for these important new factors affecting their professional and personal lives.

In addition to the above external factors, political appointees must quickly master the internal operations of the agency to which they are appointed. The career staff must be won over and not alienated, if the appointee wants to work effectively. The details and history of the agency's budget must be understood as one of the primary management tools of the new executive. The constraints and flexibilities of the personnel system must be understood if one is to put together a management team. The bureaucratic routines and procedures that keep the agency operating must become automatic. Finally, the substance of the programs over which the manager has jurisdiction must be mastered.

Since the largest subset of those appointees coming from outside the government come from a business background, how well are they prepared for top federal government appointments? Certainly there are many similarities between managing business and government organizations. Both business and government managers must use human and financial resources to accomplish organizational goals. Internal management processes are more likely to be similar than external relations. But even internally, budget and personnel processes are usually more constraining in government than in the private sector. Certainly the external environment is more volatile in the public sector.

While appointees who are new to the government would be helped by an introduction to the political environment in Washington, all political appointees would benefit from orientation on certain aspects of their jobs. All presidential appointees new to an administration have a need to know certain crucial pieces of information if they are to act effectively for the president. Everybody, with or without Washington experience, needs to know what the ground rules are for this particular president.

Administrations vary as to how much discretion cabinet and agency heads are to have with respect to appointing the subcabinet as well as noncareer SES and Schedule C appointments. Budget discretion and OMB budget procedures are not identical among the administrations. How will contact with the Hill be managed? Who are the key White House staff for the administration? Does the White House want to be informed or consulted on program decisions? What are the policy areas and issues in which *this* president is particularly interested? Finally, new appointees must be oriented to the specific positions they are to fill. This agency-specific information should include the personnel, programs, congressional committees, and interest groups with which they will have to deal on the job. Despite the advocacy of knowledgeable people, the government still has no systematic orientation program for political executives new to the government, though the Reagan administration took some steps in that direction.

Learning the essential elements of political life in Washington quickly should not be left to chance. Each administration should institute a systematic orientation program for new appointees. One day of orientation should be conducted at the White House and should cover administration clearance and policy procedures, relations with Congress, dealing with the media, budget and personnel issues, and ethical/legal guidelines. An agency component of the program should include policy and program issues, authority and responsibility of the new appointee, upcoming deadlines, and congressional committees affecting the agency.[28] While it seems almost impossible to carve out two or three days from the overloaded schedules of new appointees, the payoffs in increased effectiveness and team spirit are well worth it.

Continue Team-Building Efforts

Past administrations have had problems keeping the focus of the whole administration on the central agenda and combating the centrifugal forces that pull political appointees away from the president's perspective. A new president can take positive steps to mold his administration into a working team that will actively pursue his political and policy goals. Those members of the administration with frequent access to the White House are less likely to go off in their own direction than those who feel banished to the outer reaches of the bureaucracy. There is no way that thousands of political appointees can have frequent access to the White House; nevertheless attempts can be made.

One counterweight to the centrifugal forces is to involve members of the administration in White House or Executive Office functions, both professional and social. Appointees can be brought in for receptions, speeches, or other functions. Invitation lists should include all key members of the administration, cabinet and subcabinet, political and career. Obviously, not all will be on the same lists or be invited with the same frequency. The point is to keep fresh in the minds of presidential appointees that they are valued members of the administration team. These details of presidential administration cannot be of concern to the president himself, but some member of the White House staff will have to worry about them if the administration is to maximize its potential influence in the executive branch.

John Ehrlichman recalls that when he was legal counsel in the White House he invited the counsels from the agencies and departments to the White House for a meeting. Some of them had been working for the government for eighteen years and had never been to the White House. They were impressed, and enjoyed feeling on the inside. Being able to say that you were at a White House meeting adds authority and credibility in Washington. "Many of these people were pivotal, so I made sure they and their wives got on the social list. And they knew I had put them there. It was simple to do."[29]

Another useful technique for keeping the focus of the administration on the central agenda is to hold briefings on administration policy for officials across the government. The briefings should be given by high administration officials and should be held in the White House or Old Executive Office Building. Several purposes can be filled. The briefings can be used to get information about administration policy out to key officials. They can also be used to get across the administration position on issues and keep the focus on the president's interests—political and administrative. These sessions also enable officials to defend administration policy outside of their own areas of policy expertise. The purpose is to build a team spirit and maintain morale in the administration. The president will not have the time to attend most of these briefings, but a brief appearance with a few words of encouragement will have large payoffs.

Another approach to providing some glue to hold an administration together is holding meetings attended by officials from different agencies concerned with the same policy issue. During the passage of the 1978 Civil Service Reform Act in the Carter administration there was a working group of assistant secretaries for administration chaired by Jule M. Sugarman, deputy director of the Office of Personnel Management. It met regularly to provide feedback about the implications of the proposed legislation and, after it was passed, about the problems of implementing it. This provided a valuable link among subcabinet members of the Carter administration (political and career), centered around one key administration policy initiative. A group like this, however, must have a working focus; busy executives will soon start sending deputies if the work of the group is not progressing or becomes irrelevant to their jobs.[30]

None of these efforts can guarantee a highly motivated administration, but making the effort will make it more likely that the president has a loyal team out in the bureaucracy that is concerned with the president's best interests.

PUBLIC EXPECTATIONS AND THE PRESIDENCY

The American people seem to yearn for the reassurance that *someone* is in charge of the country and that their fate is not at the mercy of mere chance. This makes us susceptible to conspiracy theories that purport to explain the nation's major economic or social problems. Whether the evil plotters behind the headlines are communists, the Trilateral Commission, or the federal bureaucracy, the willingness to believe is there. The reverse side of this tendency is the belief that a leader on a white horse can ride in and solve all of our problems. The presidency is a natural repository of all of these hopes and dreams. Presidential candidates and other successful politicians sense this yearning and use its potent political appeal in running for office.

This leads to a dynamic of inflated expectations and overpromising that is not healthy and can often result in cynicism when expectations are not fulfilled. This syndrome can be overcome only by restraint on the part of presidential candidates and more patience and appreciation of the complexity of modern society on the part of citizens and voters. As Charles O. Jones puts it, "The American Presidency carries a burden of lofty expectations that are simply not warranted by the political or constitutional basis of the office."[31]

This does not mean that voters should not hold presidents accountable or have high standards regarding the conduct of the presidency. It means that presidents should be evaluated on different criteria. *Not* Did poverty go away? *but rather* Were important improvements in the lives of many Americans made? Was it worth the cost? *Not* Was the problem of crime wiped out? *but rather* Were improvements made in controlling criminal behavior? *Not* Is the economy growing at 6 percent annually? *but rather* Was a sound basis set for continued, gradual growth of the economy? *Not* Were health care financing and access problems solved completely? *but rather* Was progress made on these difficult issues? *Not* Was the deficit eliminated? *but rather* Is the budget on a glide path toward balance? There are no quick fixes for difficult policy problems, and we should not expect them.

Some may say that if we do not aim high enough we will never accomplish anything, so we should shoot for the moon. And some say that the only way to put together a political coalition sufficient to pass any legislation is to promise more than can be accomplished. But raising expectations to unrealistic levels leads to cynicism. The desire for panaceas on the part of the electorate leads to overpromising from politicians. So what we need is a new realism as to what can be accomplished and a new system for rewarding the politicians who make realistic promises.

With respect to the presidency and transitions there are some clear implications of these themes. A major theme of this book has been that presidents must hit the ground running if they are to accomplish their goals. While this speed on the part of new administrations is necessary, citizens should not expect too much too soon. There is a danger in the hope for a second "100 days" that administrations will try to move too quickly and blunder into disaster. So citizens should be patient in waiting for a new administration to achieve its goals.

I have argued that presidential candidates must do advance planning, even before the election. Citizens and the media should not be critical of this. Candidates must be cautious that these planning activities do not overshadow the campaign or seem to be presumptuous. Citizens should understand that advance planning is necessary and not interpret this planning as arrogance on the part of the candidate. Perhaps as advance planning becomes more common, it will be perceived that "everybody does it" and thus as common sense rather than arrogance.

While this book has urged presidents to bring experienced people into the White House as principal advisers, citizens should understand that new presidents inevitably will use their campaign aides in important posts in the new administration. This is so because these people have proven their loyalty and competence in the crucible of the campaign. On the other hand, citizens should worry if a new president uses as close advisers *only* those who have been with the candidate for many years. Presidential advice is too important to be limited to only those the candidate knows intimately at the time of election. Citizens should be encouraged when a new president brings into his close circle of advisers experienced people who were not closely associated with him for many years. President Carter using Walter Mondale as a trusted adviser as well as vice president, and Ronald Reagan bringing James Baker into his White House are encouraging signs, as was David Gergen's joining the Clinton administration. On the other hand, the circling of the wagons that occurred in the last months of the Johnson and Nixon presidencies is a signal that warrants concern.

Citizens and presidential candidates should recognize that a strong White House staff is a necessary part of the presidency. This should become a matter of concern only if access to the president is too narrowly circumscribed and there is a danger of isolation. It should also be recognized that control of access is often due to the desire of the president, and not the White House staff acting against the wishes of the president.

Citizens should also expect that a strong chief of staff is a necessary part of making the White House function reasonably smoothly. Operating without one person in charge is the exception rather than the rule in the recent presidency.

The main question is how the advisory process and information flow to the president are being handled. It is the assurance that advice from different perspectives is reaching the president that matters, not the structure of the particular system that presents that advice.

We should expect that there will be conflicts between the cabinet and the White House staff. It is built into the structure of the national government and the crosscutting nature of problems being addressed. Disagreements within an administration should be accepted as part of the public policy debate, as long as they do not become destructive.

Citizens should understand that while the bureaucracy has its faults, and is often slow to change, it is not the primary cause of faulty public policies. Poorly designed public policies and resistance to presidential wishes are most often due to the constellation of political forces concerned with the issue involved. These forces are embodied in the Congress and interest groups concerned with given areas of public policies; career bureaucrats may be accomplices, but are seldom initiators.

Career public servants must help the president implement the agenda and carry out policy. The country cannot be governed without them. Thus the antibureaucratic rhetoric that strikes such a resounding chord in the electorate is counterproductive to implementing the president's program. Presidential candidates ought to moderate their attacks on the bureaucracy. They should focus their criticisms on the policies of the opposition. When the opposition is the incumbent administration there should be a sharp distinction made between the policies and appointees of the administration on the one hand and the bureaucracy that carries out those policies on the other. While technical "fixes" such as PPBS, MBO, ZBB, and NPR may be useful management techniques, they should not be presented as panaceas for all management problems. Doing so only encourages cynicism on the part of federal managers as well as citizens.

While presidents tend to blame the condition of the economy on their predecessors and promise a balanced budget by the end of their first term, citizens should make electoral decisions with a more sophisticated appreciation of the nature of economic reality. Voters should understand that presidents control only some of the many decision-making points in attempting to influence the economy. Congress, the Federal Reserve Board, and the private sector are not under presidential control. In passing around the blame or credit, Congress as well as the president most often should be made to share the praise or blame. Dumping all of the blame on Congress or voting against an incumbent president merely because of the state of the economy ignores important aspects of economic policy making. With economic policy making particularly, the long-run groundwork for economic growth is more important than short-run fixes or this quarter's statistics.

It is tactically important for new presidents to show their respect to Congress as an institution, but is also important that they recognize the constitutional role that the framers intended and U.S. historical experience has built for the Congress. Presidents are likely to feel frustrated by Congress for moving too slowly on their agendas. This frustration can lead to trying to achieve their goals through administrative rather than legislative means. When these administrative means are legal and constitutional as with most executive orders, there is no problem. But we should begin to worry when an administration becomes so frustrated that it resorts to such illegal means to achieve its goals as impounding funds or asserting political influence over the merit system.[32]

While these exhortations may seem like blowing in the wind—expecting that the negative aspects of democracy recognized since the ancient Greeks will melt away—the United States has shown over two centuries that it is not necessarily condemned to repeat the mistakes of other nations. So we should not prematurely conclude that these optimistic goals are impossible.

Notes

INTRODUCTION: TAKING OVER THE GOVERNMENT

1. Hamilton Jordan, *Crisis* (New York: G. P. Putnam's Sons, 1982), p. 402.

2. Laurin Henry, "The Transition: Transfer of Presidential Responsibility," in *The Presidential Election and Transition 1960–61,* ed. Paul T. David (Washington, D.C.: Brookings Institution, 1961), p. 213.

3. For a treatment of the definition of transition and a thorough analysis of the special problems of foreign policy during transition, see Frederick C. Mosher, W. David Clinton, and Daniel G. Lang, *Presidential Transitions and Foreign Affairs* (Baton Rouge, La.: Louisiana State University Press, 1987).

4. "Transition of the President and President-Elect," prepared under the direction of Edwin Meese and Harrison Wellford (1981), p. 13. Used with permission.

5. Memo from William D. Carey to assistant directors, office heads, and divisions chiefs, restricted to the Bureau of the Budget, dated June 3, 1960.

6. Memorandum for the heads of departments and agencies from Charles J. Zwick, director of the Bureau of the Budget, December 7, 1968.

7. Federal Personnel Manual Bulletin 273–18, January 4, 1980, singed by Alan K. Campbell. See also James P. Pfiffner, "The Carter-Reagan Transition: Hitting the Ground Running," *Presidential Studies Quarterly,* Fall 1983, p. 623.

8. Memorandum for cabinet and agency heads, subject: "An Orderly Transition of the Presidency," November 10, 1980.

9. See Laurin Henry, *Presidential Transitions* (Washington, D.C.: Brookings Institution, 1960).

10. Meese and Wellford, "Transition of the President," pp. 68–70.

11. Clark Clifford, "Memorandum on Transition," November 9, 1960, p. 2. The memorandum is in the files of Clark Clifford and is used with his permission.

12. Interview with H. R. Haldeman, Los Angeles, May 25, 1983.

13. Paul Light, *The President's Agenda* (Baltimore: The Johns Hopkins Press, 1982), p. 36.

14. Richard Neustadt, *Presidential Power* (New York: John Wiley & Sons, 1980), p. 233.

15. See John Kingdon, *Candidates for Office* (New York: Random House, 1968).

16. See Richard Neustadt, memorandum: "Organizing the Transition: A Tentative Check-List for the Weeks between Election and Inaugural." The memorandum is in the transition files of Clark Clifford.

17. See Neustadt, *Presidential Power,* pp. 220–25.

18. Neustadt, *Presidential Power,* p. 231.

19. For the definitive work on presidential transitions from 1912 to 1952, see Henry, *Presidential Transitions.*

20. Henry, *Presidential Transitions,* p. 137.

21. P.L. 88–277, 78 Stat. 153.

22. Memorandum on transition funds from Charles S. Murphy to the president dated July 22, 1968. LBJ Library.

23. Harrison Wellford, "When a Democracy Changes Hands," testimony before the Constitution Subcommittee of the Senate Committee on the Judiciary, April 24, 1984.

24. The recommendation is contained in a letter to President Nixon dated March 28, 1969. The letter is in Mr. Lincoln's files and is used with his permission.

25. Meese and Wellford, *Transition of the President,* p. 11.

26. Wellford, "When a Democracy Changes Hands."

27. See Theodore Sorensen, *Kennedy* (New York: Harper & Row, 1965), p. 251. See also Arthur Schlesinger, Jr., *A Thousand Days* (Greenwich, Conn.: Fawcett Publications, 1967), pp. 115–54.

28. Schlesinger, *A Thousand Days,* p. 118.

29. Interview with Clark Clifford by Laurin Henry, February 24, 1961, p. 2 of transcript. The transcript is in the transition files of Clark Clifford and is used with his permission.

30. Neustadt memoranda. These can be found in the Kennedy Library.

31. Neustadt memorandum, "Staffing the President-Elect," October 30, 1960, p. 2.

32. Henry interview with Clifford, p. 15.

33. Sorensen, *Kennedy,* p. 237. See also Norman Thomas and Harold Wolman, "The Presidency and Policy Formulation: The Task Force Device," *Public Administration Review,* September/October 1969, p. 459.

34. Brookings Press Release, August 21, 1960.

35. Memorandum for Mr. Kendall from Bradley Patterson dated September 16, 1960. The memo is in Bradley Patterson's files and used with his permission.

36. Memorandum for General Goodpaster and General Persons from Bradley Patterson, dated November 19, 1960. The memo is in the file of Bradley Patterson.

37. Interview with H. R. Haldeman.

38. "Easing the Transition," *Wall Street Journal,* October 25, 1968.

39. Letter from Mr. Lincoln to the author, March 15, 1983.

40. "Easing the Transition," October 25, 1968.

41. Interview with Franklin Lincoln, New York City, April 18, 1983.

42. The memorandum is in Mr. Lincoln's files and is used with his permission.

43. Memorandum to the files from Bill Blackburn, August 2, 1968, the White House. Letter from Phillip Areeda to Charles Murphy, August 12, 1968, with attached minutes of August 1 meeting. Both documents are in the LBJ Library.

44. Memorandum to the president from Charles S. Murphy, October 10, 1968. LBJ Library.

45. See Franklin Lincoln, "Presidential Transition, 1968–69," *American Bar Association Journal* 55 (June 1969), p. 529.

46. Memorandum to files from Bill Blackburn, November 8, 1968. LBJ Library.

47. See Laurin Henry, "Presidential Transitions: The 1968–69 Experience in Perspective," *Public Administration Review,* September/October 1969, p. 471.

48. Interview with Jack Watson, Atlanta, June 17, 1983.

49. Interview with Stuart Eizenstat, Washington, D. C., July 14, 1983.

50. Interview with Jule M. Sugarman, Washington, D. C., July 3, 1983.

51. Wellford, "When a Democracy Changes Hands."

52. Interview with Jack Watson.

53. See the discussion of Laurin Henry, "The Transition: From Nomination to Inauguration," in *The Presidential Election and Transition 1980–81,* ed. Paul T. David and David H. Everson (Carbondale and Edwardsville: Southern Illinois University Press, 1983), p. 198.

54. See Henry, "The Transition," for a description of the transition organization.

55. See the perceptive analysis of the operation of the transition teams by Wallace Earl Walker and Michael R. Reopel, "The Extended Presidential Transition: Domestic Policymaking and Cabinet Government in the Reagan Administration" (Paper presented at the Southern Political Science Association convention, Savannah, Ga., November 1984).

56. See Henry, "The Transition," p. 207.

57. See Richard Neustadt, "The Reagan Transition," *Presidency Research* 3, 2 (April 1981).

58. *Washington Post,* December 15, 1980.

59. Henry, "The Transition," p. 211.

60. Interview with Clark Clifford, Washington, D.C., July 15, 1983. See also Henry interview with Clifford, p. 2.

1. ORGANIZING THE WHITE HOUSE

1. Theodore Sorensen, in Samuel Kernell and Samuel Popkins, eds., *Chief of Staff* (Berkeley: University of California Press, 1986), p. 189.

2. Interview with H. R. Haldeman, Los Angeles, May 25, 1983.

3. Interview with John Ehrlichman, Santa Fe, June 3, 1983.

4. President's Committee on Administrative Management. Reorganization of the Executive Departments. Washington, D.C.: U.S. Government Printing Office, 1937, 75th Cong., 1st sess., Senate, Document no. 8, p. 5.

5. See the insightful essay by Samuel Kernell, "The Creed and Reality of Modern White House Management," in *Chief of Staff.*

6. Patrick Anderson, *The President's Men* (Garden City, N.Y.: Doubleday, Anchor Books, 1969), p. 469.

7. Comment on "Presidential Management" by Richard E. Neustadt, in *Improving the Accountability and Performance of Government,* ed. Bruce L. R. Smith and James D. Carroll (Washington, D.C.: Brookings Institution, 1982), p. 109.

8. Comment on "Presidential Management," p. 109.

9. Theodore Sorensen in Kernell and Popkin, eds., *Chief of Staff,* p. 92.

10. Bradley Patterson, "The Buck Still Stops at 1600 Pennsylvania Avenue," *The Washingtonian,* December 1980, p. 205.

11. Richard Neustadt, *Presidential Power,* rev. ed. (New York: John Wiley & Sons, 1980), p. 54.

12. Patterson, "The Buck Still Stops," p. 206.

13. Colin Campbell, *Managing the Presidency: Carter, Reagan, and the Search for Executive Harmony* (Pittsburgh: University of Pittsburgh Press, 1986), p. 93.

14. Dwight D. Eisenhower, *The White House Years: Mandate for Change, 1953–1956* (Garden City, N.Y.: Doubleday, 1963), p. 114.

15. Sherman Adams, *Firsthand Report* (New York: Popular Library, 1961), p. 57.

16. Fred I. Greenstein, *The Hidden-Hand Presidency* (New York: Basic Books, 1982), p. 139. Greenstein argues that the image of strict hierarchy and limited access of the Eisenhower presidency has been exaggerated, pp. 146–47.

17. "Advising the President," a panel discussion, *The Bureaucrat,* April 1974, p. 28. General Goodpaster felt this was an exaggeration.

18. The Wilson Center, *Jimmy Carter and the Presidency* (Washington, D.C.: The Smithsonian Institution, 1984), p. 16.

19. Greenstein, *The Hidden-Hand Presidency,* p. 147.

20. Neustadt memorandum, "Staffing the President-Elect," October 30, 1960, pp. 3–4. See also Attachment A, "Roosevelt's Approach to Staffing the White House."

21. Interview with Clark Clifford, Washington, D.C., July 15, 1983.

22. Clark Clifford, "Memorandum on Transition," November 9, 1960.

23. Theodore Sorensen, *Kennedy* (New York: Harper & Row, 1965), p. 238.

24. Jack Valenti, "Life's Never the Same after the White House Power Trip," *Washington Post National Weekly Edition,* March 19, 1984, p. 21.

25. Anderson, *The President's Men,* p. 299.

26. Quoted by Francis Rourke, "The Presidency and the Bureaucracy: Strategic Alternatives," in *The Presidency and the Political System,* ed. Michael Nelson (Washington, D.C.: CQ Press, 1984), p. 347.

27. Interview with H. R. Haldeman.

28. Interview with H. R. Haldeman.

29. Quoted in Benjamin Page and Mark Petracca, *The American Presidency* (New York: McGraw-Hill, 1983), p. 169.

30. Michael Medved, "The Shadow Presidents (New York: Times Books, 1979), p. 320. See also William Safire, *Before the Fall* (New York: Ballantine Books, 1977), p. 366.

31. Kernell and Popkin, eds., *Chief of Staff,* p. 21.

32. Quoted in Stephen Wayne, *The Legislative Presidency* (New York: Harper & Row, 1978), p. 47.

33. Wayne, *The Legislative Presidency,* p. 47.

34. See the analysis of R. Gordon Hoxie, "Staffing the Ford and Carter Presidencies," in *Organizing and Staffing the Presidency,* ed. Bradley D. Nash (New York: Center for the Study of the Presidency, 1980), p. 44.

35. Gerald R. Ford, *A Time to Heal* (New York: Harper & Row and Reader's Digest Association, 1979), p. 147.

36. See Roger Porter, *Presidential Decision Making: The Economic Policy Board* (Cambridge: Cambridge University Press, 1980), p. 35.

37. Medved, *The Shadow Presidents,* p. 335.

38. Ford, *A Time to Heal,* p. 147.

39. Quoted by Wayne, *The Legislative Presidency,* p. 52.

40. Medved, *The Shadow Presidents,* p. 339.

41. Interview with Richard Cheney, Washington, D.C., August 1, 1983.

42. Interview with Richard Cheney.

43. Joseph Califano, *Governing America* (New York: Simon & Schuster, 1981), pp. 26–27.

44. Kernell and Popkin, eds., *Chief of Staff,* pp. 71–72.

45. Interview with Stuart Eizenstat, Washington, D.C., July 14, 1983.

46. See the discussion by Campbell, *Managing the Presidency,* Chapter 4.

47. For discussions of Deaver's role, see "Making Reagan Be Reagan," *Time,* August 27, 1984, p. 21. See also Thomas DeFrank, "The President's Men," *The Washingtonian,* October 1984, p. 157.

48. Lawrence Barrett, *Gambling with History* (Garden City, N.Y.: Doubleday, 1983), pp. 76–77. Edwin Meese called Barrett's version of this incident "reasonably accurate" in an interview with the author.

49. See Barrett, *Gambling with History,* p. 89; and Chester Newland, "Executive Office Policy Apparatus: Enforcing the Reagan Agenda," in *The Reagan Presidency and the Governing of America,* ed. Lester Salamon and Michael Lund (Washington, D.C.: The Urban Institute, 1985).

50. See Morton Kondracke, "Baker Takes the Cake," *The New Republic,* February 20, 1984, p. 10.

41. "The New White House Buzzword—Burnout," *Los Angeles Times,* December 19, 1983, pp. 1, 8.

52. "The New White House Buzzword," pp. 1, 8.

53. "The New White House Buzzword," pp. 1, 8. See also Lou Cannon, "The Ideological Struggle in the White House," *Washington Post National Weekly Edition,* December 26, 1983, p. 23.

54. "Shake-up at the White House," *Time,* January 21, 1985, p. 10.

55. Bernard Weinraub, "How Donald Regan Runs the White House," *New York Times Magazine,* January 5, 1986, p. 12.

56. Ronald Brownstein and Dick Kirschten, "Cabinet Power," *National Journal,* June 28, 1986, p. 1589.

57. "Shake-up at the White House," *Time,* January 21, 1985, p. 20.

58. "And Now, from Don Regan, the Corporate White House," *Business Week,* April 29, 1985, p. 39.

59. "Regan, Inc.," *Business Week,* September 9, 1985, p. 79.

60. Weinraub, "How Donald Regan Runs the White House," *New York Times Magazine,* January 5, 1986, p. 52.

61. "Shake-up at the White House," *Time,* January 21, 1985, p. 11.

62. Phil McCombs, "McFarlane and the Web of Rumor," *Washington Post,* April 18, 1986.

63. David Stockman, *The Triumph of Politics* (New York: Harper & Row, 1986).

64. "Shake-up at the White House," *Time,* January 21, 1985, p. 20.

65. For a more thorough analysis of the Iran-Contra affair, see James P. Pfiffner, *The Modern Presidency* (New York: St. Martin's Press, 1994), pp. 200–202, 214–19.

66. *Washington Post,* February 28, 1987, p. A16.

67. Comment on "Presidential Management" by Stuart Eizenstat, in *Improving the Accountability and Performance of Government,* pp. 100–101.

68. Quoted by Thomas Cronin, *The State of the Presidency* (Boston: Little, Brown, 1980), p. 223.

69. Kernell and Popkin, eds., *Chief of Staff,* p. 143.

70. Richard Cheney, "Twenty Five Years," in Kernell and Popkin, eds., *Chief of Staff,* p. 62.

71. Kernell and Popkin, eds., *Chief of Staff,* pp. 149–51.

72. Comments presented at the Panel on White House Staff/Cabinet Relationships (at the American Political Science Association Meeting, New York City, September 4, 1981), p. 9.

73. For an elaboration of this argument, see James P. Pfiffner, "The President's Chief of Staff: Lessons Learned," *Presidential Studies Quarterly,* vol. 23, no. 1 (Winter 1993), pp. 77–102.

2. THE HOLY GRAIL OF "TRUE" CABINET GOVERMENT

1. See Richard Fenno, *The President's Cabinet* (Cambridge, Mass.: Harvard University Press, 1963). See also R. Gordon Hoxie, "The Cabinet in the American Presidency, 1789–1984," *Presidential Studies Quarterly,* Spring 1984, p. 209.

2. For discussions of cabinet making see Nelson Polsby, *Consequences of Party Reform* (New York: Oxford University Press, 1983), Chapter 3; and Polsby, *Congress and the Presidency* (Englewood Cliffs, N.J.: Prentice Hall, 1976), Chapter 2. The standard work is by Fenno, *The President's Cabinet.*

3. Harold Seidman, *Politics, Position, and Power* (New York: Oxford University Press, 1986), p. 169.

4. Quoted by Hugh Heclo, *A Government of Strangers* (Washington, D.C.: Brookings Institution, 1979), p. 97.

5. Interview with John Ehrlichman, Sante Fe, June 3, 1983.

6. Quoted by Roger Porter, *Presidential Decision Making: The Economic Policy Board* (Cambridge: Cambridge University Press, 1980), p. 13.

7. Quoted in Louis W. Koenig, *The Chief Executive* (New York: Harcourt, Brace, Jovanovich, 1969), p. 167.

8. Quoted by Bradley Patterson, *The President's Cabinet* (Washington, D.C.: ASPA, 1976), p. 106.

9. "Washington Wire," *The New Republic,* December 15, 1952, p. 3. Quoted in Stephen Hess, *Organizing the Presidency* (Washington, D.C.: Brookings Institution, 1976), p. 61.

10. Quoted in Fred I. Greenstein, *The Hidden-Hand Presidency* (New York: Basic Books, 1982), p. 119.

11. See Hess, *Organizing the Presidency,* p. 65.

12. Sherman Adams, *Firsthand Report* (New York: Popular Library, 1961), p. 57.

13. See Greenstein, *The Hidden-Hand Presidency,* p. 151.

14. R. Gordon Hoxie, ed., *The White House: Organization and Operations* (New York: Center for the Study of the Presidency, 1971), p. 4. Quoted in Hess, *Organizing the Presidency,* p. 65.

15. Quoted in Greenstein, *The Hidden-Hand Presidency,* p. 106.

16. Greenstein, *The Hidden-Hand Presidency,* p. 115.

17. Greenstein, *The Hidden-Hand Presidency,* pp. 115–16.

18. Quoted in Hess, *Organizing the Presidency,* p. 65.

19. Patterson, *The President's Cabinet,* p. 108.

20. Interview with Clark Clifford, Washington, D.C., July 15, 1983; and Clifford, "Memorandum on Transition," November 9, 1960.

21. Clifford, "Memorandum on Transition," p. 6.

22. Richard E. Neustadt memorandum, "Organizing the Transition: A Tentative Check-List for the Weeks between Election and Inaugural," p. 11. Kennedy Library.

23. Interview with Theodore Sorensen, New York City, March 25, 1985.

24. Arthur Schlesinger, Jr., *A Thousand Days* (Greenwich, Conn.: Fawcett Publications, 1967), p. 117.

25. *Christian Science Monitor,* January 12, 1963. Quoted in Koenig, *The Chief Executive,* p. 172.

26. Interview with Theodore Sorensen.

27. Schlesinger, *A Thousand Days,* p. 632.

28. J. Edward Day, *My Appointed Round: 929 Days as Postmaster General* (New York: Holt, Rinehart & Winston, 1965), p. 98.

29. "Advising the President," a panel discussion, *The Bureaucrat,* April 1974, p. 33.

30. Richard M. Nixon, *RN: The Memoirs of Richard Nixon* (New York: Grosset & Dunlap, 1978), p. 357.

31. Rowland Evans, Jr., and Robert D. Novak, *Nixon in the White House* (New York: Random House, 1971), p. 11.

32. John Ehrlichman, *Witness to Power* (New York: Simon & Schuster, 1982), p. 88.

33. Evans and Novak, *Nixon in the White House,* p. 66.

34. Ehrlichman, *Witness to Power,* pp. 110–11.

35. Interview with John Ehrlichman.

36. Interview with John Ehrlichman.

37. Ehrlichman, *Witness to Power,* pp. 112, 88.

38. Ehrlichman, *Witness to Power,* p. 108.

39. Quoted in Thomas Cronin, *The State of the Presidency* (Boston: Little, Brown, 1980), p. 266.

40. Jeb Stuart Magruder, *An American Life: One Man's Road to Watergate* (New York: Atheneum Publishers, 1974), p. 102.

41. "The System at Work," *National Journal,* January 12, 1985, p. 70.

42. Quoted in Michael Medved, *The Shadow Presidents* (New York: Times Books, 1979), p. 322.

43. Nelson Polsby, *Consequences of Party Reform,* p. 91.

44. See Seidman, *Politics, Position, and Power,* p. 114.

45. See Richard Nathan, *The American Presidency* (New York: John Wiley & Sons, 1983).

46. For a detailed analysis of the impoundment issue, see James P. Pfiffner, *The President, the Budget, and Congress: Impoundment and the 1974 Budget Act* (Boulder, Colo.: Westview Press, 1979).

47. See Hearings before the Subcommittee on Manpower and Civil Service of the House Committee on Post Office and Civil Service, *Violations and Abuses of Merit Principles in Federal Employment,* 94th Cong., 1st sess., April 10, 1975.

48. Richard Neustadt, *Presidential Power* (New York: John Wiley & Sons: 1980), p. 198.

49. See Porter, *Presidential Decision Making,* p. 35.

50. Quoted by Stephen Wayne, *The Legislative Presidency* (New York: Harper & Row, 1978), p. 54.

51. Wayne, *The Legislative Presidency.*

52. Quoted by Wayne, *The Legislative Presidency,* p. 55.

53. "The System at Work," p. 7.

54. For an analysis of the Economic Policy Board, see Porter, *Presidential Decision Making.*

55. Joseph Califano, *Governing America* (New York: Simon & Schuster, 1981), pp. 26–27.

56. Dom Bonafede, "Carter White House Is Heavy on Functions, Light on Frills," *National Journal,* February 12, 1977, p. 234.

57. Dom Bonafede, "No One Tries to Roll over Jordan in the White House," *National Journal,* April 16, 1977, p. 584.

58. Robert Shogun, *Promises to Keep* (New York: Thomas Y. Crowell, 1977), p. 192.

59. Quoted by Califano, *Governing America,* p. 410.

60. Califano, *Governing America,* p. 404.

61. Jimmy Carter, *Keeping Faith* (New York: Bantam Books, 1982), p. 59.

62. "The System at Work," p. 72.

63. Quoted by Cronin, *The State of the Presidency,* p. 273.

64. Califano, *Governing America,* pp. 404–6, 411.

65. Califano, *Governing America,* p. 431.

66. Califano, *Governing America,* p. 410.

67. Califano, *Governing America,* p. 434.

68. See Hugh Heclo, "One Executive Branch or Many?" in *Both Ends of the Avenue,* ed. Anthony King (Washington, D.C.: AEI, 1984).

69. Stockman, quoted by William Greider, "The Education of David Stockman," *The Atlantic,* December 1981, p. 33.

70. David Stockman, *The Triumph of Politics* (New York: Harper & Row, 1986), p. 113.

71. Interview with Edwin Meese, Washington, D.C., July 2, 1985.

72. "The System at Work," p. 73.

73. Interview by Colin Campbell, quoted in prepublication manuscript: "In Search of Executive Harmony: *Carter, Reagan, and the Crisis of the Presidency,"* Chapter 3, p. 16.

74. Quoted by Colin Campbell, *Managing the Presidency: Carter, Reagan, and the Search for Executive Harmony* (Pittsburgh: University Pittsburgh Press, 1986), p. 70.

75. Alexander Haig, *Caveat* (New York: Macmillan, 1984), p. 76.

76. Haig, *Caveat,* p. 77.

77. Haig, *Caveat,* p. 82.

78. See Lawrence Barrett, *Gambling with History* (Garden City, N.Y.: Doubleday, 1983), p. 72.

79. Porter, *Presidential Decision Making.*

80. See Chester Newland, "The Reagan Presidency," *Public Administration Review,* January/February 1983, p. 6.

81. Office of Planning and Evaluation, Executive Office of the President, *Strategic Evaluation Memorandum #18, Cabinet Councils and Domestic Affairs Management: An Evaluation* (The White House, June 8, 1982), p: 9. Quoted by Chester Newland, "Executive Office Policy Apparatus: Enforcing the Reagan Agenda," in *The Reagan Presidency and the Governing of America,* ed. Lester Salamon and Michael Lund (Washington, D.C.: The Urban Institute, 1985), p. 153.

82. Dick Kirschten, "With Regan Coming in the Quarterback, White House Ready to Field New Team," *National Journal,* June 15, 1985, p. 1418.

83. See Newland, "The Reagan Presidency," p. 27–28.

84. This section is based on the analysis of Campbell, *Managing the Presidency,* Chapter 3.

85. Quoted by Campbell, *Managing the Presidency,* p. 73.

86. See Campbell, *Managing the Presidency,* p. 75.

87. Haig, *Caveat,* pp. 82–83.

88. Haig, *Caveat,* pp. 85, 94.

89. Dick Kirschten, "Once Again, Cabinet Government's Beauty Lies in Being No More than Skin Deep," *National Journal,* June 15, 1985, p. 1418.

90. Ronald Brownstein and Dick Kirschten, "Cabinet Power," *National Journal,* June 28, 1986, pp. 1582–1583.

91. Quoted by Cronin, *The State of the Presidency,* p. 264.

92. Interview with Bowman Cutter, Washington, D.C., July 26, 1983.

93. Interview with John Ehrlichman.

94. See Brownstein and Kirschten, "Cabinet Power," p. 1588.

95. See Colin Campbell, *Managing the Presidency,* p. 263.

3. PERSONNEL CONTROL: STAFFING THE ADMINISTRATION

1. Quoted in *The Wall Street Journal,* August 31, 1982, p. 25.

2. Interview with John Ehrlichman, Santa Fe, June 3, 1983.

3. Interview with Donald E. Elisburg, assistant secretary of labor for employment standards in the Carter administration, conducted by the staff of the Presidential Appointee Project, National Academy of Public Administration, 1985.

4. See James P. Pfiffner, *The Modern Presidency* (New York: St. Martin's Press, 1994), p. 123; see also Chapter 8 in this volume.

5. NAPA, *America's Unelected Government* (Cambridge: Ballinger Publishing Co., 1983), p. 48.

6. See Chapter 8.

7. The Plum Book also lists those in Schedule A positions (about 100,000) and Schedule B (about 17,000). These are part of the excepted service because it is not practical to hold examinations for the positions; they include attorneys, chaplains, and National Bank examiners. Schedules A and B do not turn over with each incoming administration.

8. Arnie Miller (the head of President Carter's personnel operation), "Recruiting Presidential Appointees," Conference of Presidential Personnel Assistants, December 13, 1984, National Academy of Public Administration, Occasional Paper, p. 10.

9. Quoted in Calvin Mackenzie, *The Politics of Presidential Appointments* (New York: Free Press, 1981), p. 83.

10. Quoted by I. M. Destler, "Reorganization: When and How?" in *Federal Reorganization,* ed. Peter Szanton (Chatham, N.J.: Chatham House, 1981), p. 116.

11. "Recruiting Presidential Appointees," pp. 10, 36.

12. Interview with Theodore Sorensen, New York City, March 25, 1985.

13. See Mackenzie, *The Politics of Presidential Appointments,* p. 27.

14. "Recruiting Presidential Appointees," p. 4.

15. See Mackenzie, *The Politics of Presidential Appointments,* pp. 24–31.

16. Richard L. Schott and Dagmar S. Hamilton, *People, Positions, and Power* (Chicago: University of Chicago Press, 1983), pp. 17–18.

17. Quoted by Schott and Hamilton, *People, Positions, and Power,* p. 5.

18. Interview with John Ehrlichman.

19. "Recruiting Presidential Appointees," pp. 6–7.

20. U.S. House of Representatives, Committee on Post Office and Civil Service, *Final Report of Violations and Abuses of Merit Principles in Federal Employment,* 94th Cong., 2nd sess., December 30, 1976, p. 245.

21. Interview with Jan K. Bohren. See also U.S. House of Representatives, Committee on Post Office and Civil Service, *A Self-Inquiry into Merit Staffing: Report of the Merit Staffing Review Team,* U.S. Civil Service Commission, Committee Print No. 94-14, 94th Cong., 2nd sess., June 8, 1976.

22. Interview with Jule M. Sugarman, Washington, D.C., July 3, 1983.

23. Interview with Jack Watson, Atlanta, June 17, 1983.

24. Interview with Jack Watson.

25. See Bruce Adams and Kathryn Kavanagh-Baran, *Promise and Performance: Carter Builds a New Administration* (Lexington, Mass.: Lexington Books, 1979), pp. 11–31.

26. Interview with Jack Watson.

27. Interview with Harrison Wellford, Washington, D.C., July 14, 1983.

28. Calvin Mackenzie, "Cabinet and Subcabinet Personnel Selection in Reagan's First Year: New Variations on Some Not-So-Old Themes" (Paper presented at the American Political Science Association meeting, New York City, September 1981).

29. Mackenzie, "Cabinet and Subcabinet Personnel Selection," p. 25.

30. See Mackenzie, "Cabinet and Subcabinet Personnel Selection," and *America's Unelected Government,* p. 62.

31. See Lou Cannon, "Reagan's Appointments 'Mess' Decried," *Washington Post,* March 1, 1981; Philip Geyelin, "One-Man Wrecking Crew," *Washington Post,* April 14, 1981; James M. Perry, "Top Jobs Still Vacant in Federal Agencies as Nominations Lag," *Wall Street Journal,* April 13, 1981; "Molasses Pace on Appointments," *Time,* May 11, 1981, p. 19.

32. Dick Kirschten, "You Say You Want a Sub-Cabinet Post? Clear It with Marty, Dick, Lyn and Fred," *National Journal,* April 4, 1981, p. 564.

33. "Molasses Pace on Appointments," p. 19.

34. See William Safire, "Of Meese and Men," *New York Times,* February 2, 1981.

35. "Recruiting Presidential Appointees," pp. 6, 15.

36. Interview with Stuart Eizenstat, Washington, D.C., July 14, 1983.

37. Quoted in David Halberstam, *The Best and the Brightest* (Greenwich, Conn.: Fawcett Publications, 1969), p. 526. See also Schott and Hamilton, *People, Positions, and Power,* p. 212.

38. See Schott and Hamilton, *People, Positions, and Power,* pp. 26–33.

39. See Mackenzie, *The Politics of Presidential Appointments,* pp. 52–53.

40. Interview with H. R. Haldeman, Los Angeles, May 25, 1983.

41. Quoted in John S. McClenahen, "The Perils of Executives in Government Jobs," *Industry Week,* November 12, 1979, p. 88.

42. Quoted by Hedrick Smith, "Conservatives Cite Gains in Top Posts," *New York Times,* March 8, 1981, p. 24.

43. See Mackenzie, *The Politics of Presidential Appointments,* p. 72.

44. Dom Bonafede, "The New Right Preaches a New Religion, and Ronald Reagan Is Its Prophet," *National Journal,* May 2, 1981, p. 779. See also Rowland Evans, Jr., and Robert D. Novak, "Reaganism without Reaganites," *Washington Post,* January 23, 1981.

45. Quoted by Howell Raines, "Nofziger Thrives on Tough Reputation," *New York Times,* June 25, 1981, p. B12.

46. Quoted by Elizabeth Drew, "A Reporter at Large," *The New Yorker,* March 16, 1981, pp. 91–92.

47. Quoted by Fred Barnes, "Who's in Charge," *The Washingtonian,* August 1983, p. 130.

48. See Mackenzie, "Cabinet and Subcabinet Personnel Selection," pp. 16, 20. See also Howell Raines, "White House Headhunter Feels the Heat," *New York Times,* May 3, 1981, p. E3, and Lou Cannon, "Appointments by White House Take Right Turn," *Washington Post,* June 18, 1981, pp. 1, 12–13.

49. Quoted in Mackenzie, *The Politics of Presidential Appointments,* p. 33.

50. Interview with Jack Watson.

51. Theodore Sorensen, "The Transition Agenda," memorandum to George McGovern on the possible transition of the presidency, November 1972, p. 8. The memorandum is in Mr. Sorensen's personal files and is used with his permission.

52. Interview with Frank Carlucci, deputy secretary of defense in the Reagan administration, conducted by the staff of the Presidential Appointee Project, National Academy of Public Administration (NAPA), 1985.

53. Interview with Graham Claytor, deputy secretary of defense in the Carter administration, conducted by the staff of the NAPA Presidential Appointee Project, 1985.

54. Interview with John Gardner, conducted by the staff of the NAPA Presidential Appointee Project, 1985. See also Schott and Hamilton, *People, Positions and Power,* pp. 206–7.

55. Dean Mann with Jamison Doig, *The Assistant Secretaries* (Washington, D.C.: Brookings Institution, 1965), p. 265.

56. Mann with Doig, *The Assistant Secretaries,* p. 99.

57. See Richard Nathan, *The Plot That Failed* (New York: John Wiley & Sons, 1975), p. 50.

58. Interview with H. R. Haldeman.

59. Interview with John Ehrlichman.

60. Interview with Stuart Eizenstat.

61. See Mackenzie, *The Politics of Presidential Appointments,* p. 68.

62. "Recruiting Presidential Personnel," p. 13.

63. Quoted by Cannon, "Appointments by White House," pp. 1, 12–13.

64. Interview with Edwin Meese, Washington, D.C., July 2, 1985.

65. For Haig's account of his choice of the subcabinet, see *Caveat* (New York: Macmillan, 1984), pp. 64–66. Haig says that he was the one who proposed to the president that William Clark be his deputy secretary.

66. Rowland Evans, Jr., and Robert D. Novak, "Cleaning Out the Kitchen," *Washington Post,* March 20, 1981.

67. "Recruiting Presidential Appointees," pp. 4, 18.

68. "Recruiting Presidential Appointees," p. 10.

69. "Recruiting Presidential Appointees," p. 20.

70. Interview with Elliot Richardson, conducted by the staff of the NAPA Presidential Appointee Project, 1985.

71. The letter is contained in the files of the LBJ Library, Collection: Gen FG11-8 (May 27, 1965), Box 70.

72. Pendleton James, *Wall Street Journal,* August 31, 1982, p. 25.

73. Quoted in Mackenzie, *The Politics of Presidential Appointments,* p. 46.

74. See Mackenzie, *The Politics of Presidential Appointments,* p. 46.

75. Jimmy Carter, *Keeping Faith* (New York: Bantam Book, 1982), p. 61.

76. Interview with Frederick Malek, Washington, D.C., July 1983.

77. Schott and Hamilton, *People, Position, and Power,* p. 15.

78. "Recruiting Presidential Appointees," p. 20.

79. "Recruiting Presidential Appointees," p. 23.

80. See Laurin Henry, *Presidential Transitions* (Washington, D.C.: Brookings Institution, 1960), pp. 655–57.

81. *Code of Federal Regulations,* vol. 5, Part 213.

82. *Federal Register,* vol. 46, no. 115 (June 16, 1981), p. 31405.

83. See Mackenzie, *The Politics of Presidential Appointments,* pp. 79–88.

84. Mackenzie, *The Politics of Presidential Appointments,* p. 86.

4. PRESIDENTIAL CONTROL OF THE BUREAUCRACY

1. Theodore Sorensen, *Kennedy* (New York: Harper & Row, 1965), p. 281.

2. Richard M. Nixon, *RN: The Memoirs of Richard Nixon* (New York: Grosset & Dunlap, 1978), p. 355.

3. *Public Papers of the Presidents 1971,* pp. 448, 465.

4. H. R. Haldeman, *The Ends of Power* (New York: Times Books, 1978), p. 149.

5. Rowland Evans, Jr., and Robert D. Novak, *Nixon in the White House* (New York: Random House, 1971), p. 12.

6. Nixon, *RN,* p. 676.

7. Nixon, *RN,* p. 677; Haldeman, *The Ends of Power,* p. 150.

8. Interview with H. R. Haldeman, Los Angeles, May 25, 1983.

9. Frederick Malek, *Washington's Hidden Tragedy* (New York: Free Press, 1978), p. 97.

10. Richard Nathan, *The Administrative Presidency* (New York: John Wiley & Sons, 1983).

11. See Ronald Moe, "Executive Branch Reorganization: An Overview," Senate Government Operations Com. reprint, March 1978.

12. Nathan, *The Administrative Presidency,* pp. 35–38.

13. See James P. Pfiffner, *The President, the Budget, and Congress: Impoundment and the 1974 Budget Act* (Boulder, Colo.: Westview Press, 1979.)

14. See Hearings before the Subcommittee on Manpower and Civil Service of the House Committee on Post Office and Civil Service, *Violations and Abuses of Merit Principles in Federal Employment,* 94th Cong., 1st sess., April 10, 1975.

15. *Congressional Quarterly,* October 16, 1976, p. 3009.

16. Interview with Howard Messner, who held top career positions in OMB and the Environmental Protection Agency, July 13, 1983.

17. James Sundquist, "Jimmy Carter as Public Administrator," *Public Administration Review,* January/February 1979, pp. 3, 8.

18. See Edie N. Goldenberg, "The Permanent Government in an Era of Retrenchment and Redirection," in *The Reagan Presidency and the Governing of America,* ed. Lester Salamon and Michael Lund (Washington, D.C.: Urban Institute, 1985), p. 390.

19. Woodrow Wilson, "The Study of Administration," *Political Science Quarterly,* June 1887, reprinted in Frederick C. Mosher, *Basic Literature of American Public Administration, 1787–1950* (New York: Holmes and Meier, 1981).

20. Max Weber, "Politics as a Vocation," in *From Max Weber,* ed. H. H. Gerth and C. W. Mills (New York: Oxford University Press, 1946), p. 95.

21. See Goldenberg, "The Permanent Government," pp. 384–85.

22. Joel D. Aberbach, Robert D. Putnam, and Bert Rockman, *Bureaucrats and Politicians in Western Democracies* (Cambridge, Mass.: Harvard University Press, 1981), p. 6.

23. For a sophisticated statement of this position, see Terry M. Moe, "The Politicized Presidency," in *The New Direction in American Politics,* ed. John E. Chubb and Paul E. Peterson (Washington, D.C.: Brookings Institute, 1985), p. 265.

24. Hugh Heclo, "The In and Outer System: A Critical Assessment," in *The In and Outers,* ed. G. Calvin Mackenzie (Baltimore: The Johns Hopkins Press, 1987).

25. For a discussion of several different interpretations of the role of civil servants see Goldenberg, "The Permanent Government." See also Paul Light, "When Worlds Collide: The Political/Career Nexus," in *The In and Outers,* ed. Mackenzie.

26. See Richard Rose, "Steering the Ship of State: One Tiller but Two Pairs of Hands (Centre for the Study of Public Policy, University of Strathclyde, Scotland, 1986), p. 8.

27. Hugh Heclo, *A Government of Strangers* (Washington, D.C.: Brookings Institution, 1977), Chapter 4.

28. See Hugh Heclo, "Executive Budget Making," in *Federal Budget Policy in the 1980s,* ed. Gregory Mills and John Palmer (Washington, D.C.: Urban Institute, 1984).

29. Interview with John Ehrlichman, Santa Fe, June 3, 1983.

30. Interview with Theodore Sorensen, New York City, March 25, 1985.

31. Interview with Jack Watson, Atlanta, June 17, 1983.

32. Interview with Harrison Wellford, Washington, D.C., July 14, 1983.

33. Quoted in *PA Times,* January 1, 1985.

34. All presidential appointees who were still alive and whose addresses could be verified were polled. The response rate was 56 percent. See the final report, "Leadership in Jeopardy: the Fraying of the Presidential Appointments System," 1985.

35. Each of these quotations is taken from the transcripts of interviews of the NAPA Presidential Appointee Project. The interviews were conducted by Jeremy Plant and Michael Hansen.

36. "Exploring the Clinton Transition: Views from the Career Civil Service" (Paper presented at the 1993 American Political Science Convention, Washington, D.C., p. 61). See also "Does Familiarity Breed Acceptance?: Trends in Career-Noncareer Relations in the Reagan Administration," *Administration and Society,* vol. 23, no. 2 (August 1991), pp. 247–266; and "Reinventing All Over Again: The Clinton Transition in the Bureaucracy" (Paper presented at the 1994 APSA Convention, New York City).

37. NAPA Presidential Appointee Project, interview with Richard Lyng, assistant secretary of agriculture for President Nixon, and secretary of agriculture for President Reagan.

38. Interview with a career executive, Washington, D.C., 1983.

39. Quoted by Hugh Heclo, *A Government of Strangers,* p. 177.

40. Hugh Heclo, "OMB and the Presidency—The Problem of Neutral Competence," *The Public Interest,* Winter 1975, pp. 80–82.

41. NAPA Presidential Appointee Project, interview with Erich Evered, administrator, Energy Information Administration, 1981–1984.

42. "Leadership in Jeopardy," 1985.

43. For an extreme argument that career executives cannot be trusted, see Michael Sanera, "Implementing the Agenda," in *Mandate For Leadership II,* ed. Stuart Butler, Michael Sanera, and Bruce Weinrod (Washington, D.C.: The Heritage Foundation, 1984). For a rebuttal see James P. Pfiffner, "Political Public Administration," *Public Administration Review,* March/April 1985, p. 352.

44. Gregory H. Gaertner, Karen N. Gaertner, and Irene Devine, "Federal Agencies in the Context of Transition," *Public Administration Review,* September/October 1983, p. 424.

45. See James P. Pfiffner, "Political Appointees and Career Executives: The Democracy-Bureaucracy Nexus in the Third Century," *Public Administration Review,* January/February, 1987, p. 57.

46. Dwight Ink, "Agency Shutdown: The Ultimate Challenge," *PA Times,* December 15, 1981.

47. Joel D. Aberbach and Bert A. Rockman, "Clashing Beliefs within the Executive Branch," *APSR,* June 1979, p. 456.

48. Richard L. Cole and David A. Caputo, "Presidential Control of the Senior Civil Service," *APSR,* June 1979, p. 399.

49. Harold Seidman, *Politics, Position, and Power* (New York: Oxford University Press, 1986).

50. Quoted in Seidman, *Politics, Position, and Power,* p. 106.

51. Interview with H. R. Haldeman, Los Angeles, May 25, 1983.

52. Jimmy Carter, *Keeping Faith* (New York: Bantam Books, 1982), p. 69.

53. "Administration of Jimmy Carter," *Weekly Compilation of Presidential Documents,* June 29, 1977, pp. 945–46.

54. Carter, *Keeping Faith,* pp. 70–71.

55. Seidman, *Politics, Position, and Power,* p. 126.

56. Seidman, *Politics, Position, and Power,* p. 132.

57. Peter Szanton, *Federal Reorganization* (Chatham, N.J.: Chatham House, 1981), p. 5.

58. Quoted in Seidman, *Politics, Position, and Power,* p. 126.

59. Seidman, *Politics, Position, and Power,* pp. 12–13.

60. Richard Polenberg, *Reorganizing Roosevelt's Government, 1936–1939* (Cambridge, Mass.: Harvard University Press, 1966), p. 8.

61. Seidman, *Politics, Position, and Power,* p. 3.

62. Szanton, *Federal Reorganization,* p. 24.

63. *Weekly Compilation of Presidential Documents,* p. 946.

64. See Louis Fisher and Ronald C. Moe, "Presidential Reorganization Authority: Is It Worth the Cost?" *Political Science Quarterly,* Summer 1981, p. 316.

65. Interview with Richard Cheney, Washington, D.C., August 1, 1983.

66. Joseph Califano, *A Presidential Nation* (New York: Norton, 1975), p. 25.

67. Califano, *A Presidential Nation,* p. 27.

68. Joseph Califano, *Governing America* (New York: Simon & Schuster, 1981), p. 281.

69. James G. March and John P. Olson, "Organizing Political Life: What Administrative Reorganization Tells Us about Government," *APSR,* December 1983, p. 286.

70. See James P. Pfiffner, "The National Performance Review in Perspective," *International Journal of Public Administration,* December 1996.

71. See James P. Pfiffner, "Management and Central Controls Reconsidered," *The Bureaucrat,* Winter 1981–1982, p. 13; and Pfiffner, "Assessment of Management Problems Project: Final Report," U.S. Office of Personnel Management, 1981.

72. See National Academy of Public Administration, *Revitalizing Federal Management,* November 1983.

73. Russell Stout, *Management or Control?* (Bloomington: Indiana University Press, 1980), p. 6.

74. For an analysis of MBO, see Richard Rose, *Managing Presidential Objectives* (New York: Free Press, 1976).

75. For a discussion of budgetary reforms, see James P. Pfiffner, "Budgeting and the 'People's Reform,'" *Public Administration Review,* March/April 1980, p. 194.

76. See James P. Pfiffner, "The Challenge of Federal Management in the 1980s," *Public Administration Quarterly,* Summer 1983, p. 162.

5. TAKING OVER THE BUDGET

1. Interview with Stuart Eizenstat, Washington, D.C., July 14, 1983.

2. Interview with H. R. Haldeman, Los Angeles, May 25, 1983.

3. Interview with Bowman Cutter, Washington, D.C., July 26, 1983.

4. Interview with Dale McOmber, Washington, D.C., July 21, 1983. McOmber was assistant director for budget review from 1973 to 1981, the top career position on the budget side of OMB.

5. Interview with Dale McOmber.

6. Interview with Samuel Cohn, Washington, D.C., July 28, 1983. Cohn was assistant director for budget review from 1966 to 1973.

7. Interview with Samuel Cohn.

8. Interview with Samuel Cohn.

9. Interview with Dale McOmber. See also Joel Havemann, "The Lame-Duck Budget That Probably Won't Last a Month," *National Journal,* January 22, 1977, p. 129.

10. Interview with Dale McOmber.

11. Interview with Dale McOmber.

12. See Royce Crocker, "Federal Government Spending and Public Opinion," *Public Budgeting and Finance,* vol. 1, no. 3 (Autumn 1981), p. 25.

13. For a compelling statement of this see David Stockman, *The Triumph of Politics* (New York: Harper & Row, 1986).

14. William Greider, "The Education of David Stockman," *The Atlantic,* December 1981, p. 43.

15. Quoted in Peter W. Bernstein, "David Stockman: No More Big Budget Cuts," *Fortune,* February 6, 1984, p. 56.

16. See Kent Weaver, "Controlling Entitlements," in *The New Direction in American Politics,* ed. John Chubb and Paul Peterson (Washington, D.C.: Brookings Institution, 1985).

17. *Historical Tables: Budget of the U.S. Government: Fiscal Year 1986,* Table 11.1.

18. Council of Economic Advisers, "Report on Indexing Federal Programs" (Washington, D.C.: GPO, 1981), p. 3. See also Kent Weaver and Alice Keck Whitfield, "Automatic Government: The Politics of Indexation" (Paper presented at the annual meeting of the Association for Public Policy Analysis and Management, October 1985).

19. President Reagan press conference reported in *Congressional Quarterly Weekly Reports,* December 26, 1981, p. 2605.

20. *Budget of the U.S. Government: Fiscal Year 1982,* p. 60.

21. *Budget: Fiscal Year 1982,* p. 59.

22. For a closer analysis of budget and economic options in the late 1980s, see James P. Pfiffner, ed., *The President and Economic Policy* (Philadelphia: ISHI Publications, 1986).

23. Hugh Heclo and Rudolph Penner, "Fiscal and Political Strategy in the Reagan Administration," in *The Reagan Presidency,* ed. Fred I. Greenstein (Baltimore: The Johns Hopkins Press, 1983), p. 27.

24. Stockman, *The Triumph of Politics,* p. 8.

25. Congressional Budget Office, *The Economic and Budget Outlook: Fiscal Years 1986–1990,* February 1985, p. xiv.

26. See Alberta Sbragia, "Monetary Policy and Monetary Theory: The Poverty of Choice," in *The President and Economic Policy,* ed. Pfiffner.

27. See John Woolley, "Federal Reserve and the Politics of Monetary Policy," in *The President and Economic Policy,* ed. Pfiffner.

28. *Fortune,* September 6, 1983, p. 39.

29. "Message on Budget and Fiscal Policy," submitted to Congress March 24, 1961, reprinted in *Congressional Quarterly 1961, Almanac,* p. 899.

30. For a detailed analysis of the impoundment issue see James P. Pfiffner, *The President, the Budget, and Congress: Impoundment and the 1974 Budget Act* (Boulder, Colo.: Westview Press, 1979).

31. Interview with Dale McOmber.

32. Quoted in *Congressional Quarterly Weekly Report,* February 26, 1977, p. 351.

33. David Stockman and Jack Kemp, "Avoiding a GOP Economic Dunkirk," *Washington Post,* December 14, 1980, sec. C, p. 1.

34. See William Safire, "Of Meese and Men," *New York Times,* February 2, 1981.

35. Stockman, *The Triumph of Politics,* p. 112.

36. Stockman, *The Triumph of Politics,* p. 159.

37. See *CQ Weekly Report,* June 13, 1980, p. 1023; and *Washington Post,* April 26, 1981, p. 1.

38. See Elizabeth Drew, "A Reporter in Washington," *The New Yorker,* June 8, 1981, p. 138.

39. *CQ Weekly Report,* June 13, 1981, p. 1023.

40. *CQ Weekly Report,* June 13, 1981, p. 1023.

41. *CQ Weekly Report,* June 13, 1981, p. 1023.

42. *Washington Post,* April 26, 1981, p. A10.

43. Interview with Charles Schultze, Washington, D.C., July 12, 1983. Schultze was BOB director for Lyndon Johnson and chairman of the Council of Economic Advisers for Jimmy Carter.

44. See the recommendation in "Transition of the President and the President-Elect," prepared under the direction of Edwin Meese and Harrison Wellford (1981), p. 68.

45. Interview with James T. McIntyre, Washington, D.C., May 9, 1986.

46. See Robert Reichauer, "The Congressional Budget Process," in *Federal Budget Policy in the 1980s,* ed. Gregory B. Mills and John L. Palmer (Washington, D.C.: Urban Institute Press, 1984).

47. For an analysis of how the budgetary process has been transformed by these fiscal constraints, see James P. Pfiffner, "The President and the Postreform Congress," in *The Postreform Congress,* ed. Roger H. Davidson (New York: St. Martin's Press, 1992), pp. 211–32.

6. MOVING THE PRESIDENT'S LEGISLATIVE AGENDA

1. See George C. Edwards, III, *Presidential Influence in Congress* (San Francisco: W. H. Freeman, 1980).

2. See William Crotty, *American Parties in Decline* (Boston: Little, Brown, 1984). See also Austin Ranney, "The President and His Party," in *Both Ends of the Avenue,* ed. Anthony King (Washington, D.C.: American Enterprise Institute, 1983).

3. See Lloyd N. Cutler, "To Form a Government," *Foreign Affairs,* Fall 1980, p. 126.

4. See Edwards, *Presidential Influence in Congress,* pp. 205–6. See also Steven A. Shull, "Legislative Adoption of Presidents' Domestic Policy Initiatives," *Presidential Studies Quarterly,* Fall, 1983, p. 551.

5. Quoted in Joel Swerdlow, "Words of Wisdom for Jimmy Carter from Presidential Adviser-Survivors of Honeymoons Gone By," Potomac Magazine, *Washington Post,* January 9, 1977.

6. Quoted in Swerdlow, "Words of Wisdom."

7. Interview with Stuart Eizenstat, Washington, D.C., July 14, 1983.

8. See Richard Neustadt and Ernest May, *Thinking in Time* (New York: The Free Press, 1986), p. 72.

9. Quoted by Paul Light, *The President's Agenda* (Baltimore: The Johns Hopkins Press, 1982), p. 30.

10. See Austin Ranney, *The American Elections of 1980* (Washington, D.C.: AEI, 1981); and Gerald Pomper et al., *The Election of 1980: Reports and Interpretations* (Chatham, N.J.: Chatham House, 1981).

11. Light, *The President's Agenda,* p. 36.

12. Light, *The President's Agenda,* p. 45.

13. Richard M. Nixon, *RN: The Memoirs of Richard Nixon* (New York: Grosset & Dunlap, 1978), p. 414.

14. Light, *The President's Agenda,* p. 44.

15. Jack Valenti, *A Very Human President* (New York: Norton, 1975), p. 144.

16. Harry McPherson, *A Political Education* (Boston: Little, Brown, 1972), p. 268.

17. See Michael Malbin, "Rhetoric and Leadership: A Look Backward at the Carter National Energy Plan," in *Both Ends of the Avenue,* ed. King.

18. Light, *The President's Agenda,* p. 50. See also Larry O'Brien's comments in Swerdlow, "Words of Wisdom."

19. Stephen Wayne, "Congressional Liaison in the Reagan White House," in *President and Congress: Assessing Reagan's First Year,* ed. Norman Ornstein (Washington, D.C.: American Enterprise Institute, 1982), p. 62.

20. Wayne, "Congressional Liaison," p. 50.

21. LBJ Library Oral History Interview of Bryce Harlow by Michael L. Gillette, pp. 51–52 of the transcript.

22. Interview with Stuart Eizenstat.

23. See Wayne, "Congressional Liaison," p. 47.

24. Wayne, "Congressional Liaison," p. 50.

25. Quoted by Robert Shogun, *Promises to Keep* (New York: Thomas Y. Crowell, 1977), pp. 207–8.

26. Interview with a Carter White House aide.

27. Telephone interview with Frank Moore, September 4, 1986.

28. See comments by Tom Korologos in Stephen J. Wayne, "Congressional Liaison in the Reagan White House: A Preliminary Assessment of the First Year," in *President and Congress: Assessing Reagan's First Year,* ed. Norman Ornstein (Washington, D.C.: American Enterprise Institute, 1982), p. 51.

29. Telephone interview with Frank Moore, September 4, 1986.

30. Eric L. Davis, "Congressional Liaison: The People and the Institutions," in *Both Ends of the Avenue,* ed. King, p. 62. See also Davis, "Legislative Liaison in the Carter Administration," *Political Science Quarterly,* Summer 1979, p. 287.

31. Davis, "Legislative Liaison," p. 298.

32. Davis, "Congressional Liaison," pp. 64–65.

33. Charles O. Jones, "Presidential Negotiations with Congress," in *Both Ends of the Avenue,* ed. King, p. 121.

34. Davis, "Congressional Liaison," p. 72.

35. Haynes Johnson, *In the Absence of Power* (New York: Viking Press, 1980), p. 168.

36. Interview with Richard Cheney, Washington, D.C., August 1, 1983.

37. See Edwards, *Presidential Influence in Congress,* p. 134.

38. Interview with John Ehrlichman, Santa Fe, June 3, 1983.

39. Shogun, *Promises to Keep,* p. 209.

40. Wayne, "Congressional Liaison," p. 51.

41. Joel Swerdlow, "How to Handle the First 100 Days," Potomac Magazine, *Washington Post,* January 9, 1977.

42. Swerdlow, "How to Handle."

43. Swerdlow, "How to Handle."

44. Johnson, *In the Absence of Power,* p. 165.

45. Stephen Wayne, *The Legislative Presidency* (New York: Harper & Row, 1978), p. 212.

46. For an analysis of Jimmy Carter's style, see Charles O. Jones, "Keeping Faith and Losing Congress: The Carter Experience in Washington," *Presidential Studies Quarterly,* Summer 1984, p. 437.

47. Quoted by Johnson, *In the Absence of Power,* p. 22.

48. See Jones, "Presidential Negotiation with Congress," p. 111.

49. For an analysis of the trend of recent presidents going public to influence Congress, see Samuel Kernell, *Going Public* (Washington, D.C.: CQ Press, 1986).

50. Jimmy Carter, *Keeping Faith* (New York: Bantam Books, 1982), p. 65.

51. See Edwards, *Presidential Influence in Congress,* p. 175.

52. Telephone interview with Frank Moore, September 4, 1986.

53. Quoted in Shogun, *Promises to Keep,* p. 197.

54. Edwards, *Presidential Influence in Congress,* p. 119.

55. Johnson, *In the Absence of Power,* pp. 163–64.

56. Shogun, *Promises to Keep,* p. 196.

57. Quoted in Laurence E. Lynn, Jr., and David deF. Whitman, *The President as Policymaker: Jimmy Carter and Welfare Reform* (Philadelphia: Temple University Press, 1981), p. 271.

58. Jimmy Carter, *Public Papers,* 1977, vol. 1, pp. 1146–47. See Malbin, "Rhetoric and Leadership," p. 245.

59. Quoted by John H. Kessel, *Presidential Parties* (Chicago: Dorsey Press, 1984), p. 61.

60. Carter, *Keeping Faith,* p. 87.

61. Interview with Bert Lance, Calhoun, Georgia, June 21, 1983.

62. Johnson, *In the Absence of Power,* p. 159.

63. Shogun, *Promises to Keep,* p. 213.

64. Interview with Bowman Cutter, Washington, D.C., July 26, 1983.

65. Interview with Stuart Eizenstat.

66. Interview with Charles Schultze, Washington, D.C., July 12, 1983.

67. Carter, *Keeping Faith,* p. 78.

68. Telephone interview with Frank Moore, September 4, 1985.

69. McPherson, *A Political Education,* p. 282.

70. Carter, *Keeping Faith,* p. 73.

71. Neustadt and May, *Thinking in Time,* p. 73.

72. See Jones, "Keeping Faith and Losing Congress," p. 441.

73. Shogun, *Promises to Keep,* p. 205.

74. Nelson Polsby, *Consequences of Party Reform* (New York: Oxford University Press, 1983), p. 106.

75. Carter, *Keeping Faith,* p. 71.

76. See Malbin, "Rhetoric and Leadership."

77. See Jones, "Keeping Faith and Losing Congress."

78. Jones, "Keeping Faith and Losing Congress," p. 437.

79. See Wayne, "Congressional Liaison," p. 48.

80. *Congressional Quarterly,* December 27, 1980, p. 3656.

81. *Congressional Quarterly,* December 27, 1980, p. 3656.

82. Wayne, "Congressional Liaison," p. 57.

83. Quoted by Wayne, "Congressional Liaison," p. 56.

84. See James Fallows, "The Passionless Presidency," *The Atlantic,* May 1979, p. 33.

85. Hedrick Smith, "Taking Charge of Congress," *New York Times,* August 9, 1981.

86. Wayne, "Congressional Liaison," p. 59.

87. Hugh Heclo and Rudolph G. Penner, "Fiscal and Political Strategy in the Reagan Administration," in *The Reagan Presidency,* ed., Fred I. Greenstein (Baltimore: The Johns Hopkins Press, 1983), p. 36.

88. Heclo and Penner, "Fiscal and Political Strategy."

89. See Kernell, *Going Public.*

90. *Congressional Quarterly,* August 1, 1981, p. 1372.

91. Smith, "Taking Charge of Congress."

92. See *Washington Post,* April 26, 1981, p. A10; *Congressional Quarterly,* July 25, 1981, p. 1325.

93. *Congressional Quarterly,* June 13, 1981, p. 1025.

94. *Congressional Quarterly,* October 25, 1986, pp. 2687–89.

7. THE BUSH TRANSITION: A FRIENDLY TAKEOVER

1. Charles O. Jones, "From Campaigning to Governing: The Challenge of Taking Over," in *Understanding the Presidency,* ed. James P. Pfiffner and Roger H. Davidson (New York: Harper Collins, 1997).

2. If Governor Michael Dukakis had won, the transition teams in departments and agencies would have been considerably smaller than the Reagan teams: two to five people, rather than the ten to twenty people of 1981. Conscious efforts would have been made to present a contrast with the 1980–1981 transition teams; interview with Harrison Wellford, Washington, D.C., October 24, 1988.

3. Interview with Constance Newman, Director of the U.S. Office of Personnel Management, Washington, D.C., June 15, 1989.

4. Interview with Chase Untermeyer, The White House, June 6, 1989.

5. Michael Duffy and Dan Goodgame, *Marching in Place: The Status Quo Presidency of George Bush* (New York: The Free Press, 1994), p. 22.

6. The phrase is *New York Times* columnist William Safire's.

7. Reagan's statement was as follows: "Sometimes I wonder if they really want what they say they want, because some of those leaders are doing very well leading organizations based on keeping alive the feeling that they're victims of prejudice," quoted by Elizabeth Drew in "Letter from Washington," *The New Yorker,* February 27, 1989, p. 78.

8. As a result both Gray and Baker divested themselves of assets or recused themselves from business interests.

9. *U.S. News & World Report,* April 17, 1989, p. 22; *Newsweek,* April 17, 1989, p. 21.

10. Marlin Fitzwater, *Call the Briefing* (New York: Times Books, 1995), p. 12; see also Eleanor Randolph, "Quieting the White House Press with Access," *Washington Post,* March 12, 1989, p. A6.

11. Burt Solomon, "Bush's Disdain for Image Making May Come to Plague His Tenure," *National Journal,* March 11, 1989, p. 602.

12. Quoted by Mark Rozell, "The Press and the Presidency," in *Understanding the Presidency,* ed. James P. Pfiffner and Roger H. Davidson (New York: HarperCollins, 1997).

13. John Anthony Maltese, *Spin Control,* 2nd ed. (Chapel Hill: University of North Carolina Press, 1994), p. 217.

14. *Within These Walls: A Visit to the White House* (Washington, D.C.: White House Historical Association, 1991), film. The author would like to thank Peter J. Wilson for assistance in obtaining this film.

15. See Rowland Evans and Robert Novak, "A Note from Saddle River," *Washington Post,* April 10, 1989, p. A9. See also *Washington Post,* April 11, 1989, p. A17, for Marlin Fitzwater's reaction to the situation.

16. See Charles O. Jones, *The Presidency in a Separated System* (Washington, D.C.: The Brookings Institution, 1994), p. 113. See also George Edwards, "George Bush and the Public Presidency: The Politics of Inclusion," in *The Bush Presidency: First Appraisals,* ed. Colin Campbell and Bert Rockman (Chatham, N.J.: Chatham House, 1991).

17. David Gergen, "Bush's Start: A Presidency 'On the Edge of a Cliff,'" *Washington Post,* March 5, 1989, p. C1.

18. *Washington Post,* January 13, 1989, p. A16.

19. Burt Solomon, "When the Bush Cabinet Convenes . . . It's a Gathering of Presidential Pals," *National Journal,* July 1, 1989, p. 1704.

20. Roger Porter, *Presidential Decision Making* (Cambridge: Cambridge University Press, 1980).

21. Quoted by Michael Duffy, "Mr. Consensus," *Time,* August 21, 1989, p. 18.

22. See Bernard Weinraub, "White House," *New York Times,* May 19, 1989, p. A14.

23. Owen Ullman, "Do Bush's People Have it?" *The Washingtonian,* June 1989, pp. 207–8.

24. Hedrick Smith argues, "The Reagan Presidency has probably been simultaneously the most centralized and staff-dominated presidency in history," *The Power Game* (New York: Random House, 1988, p. 300.

25. Ullman, "Do Bush's People Have it?," p. 116; Weinraub, "White House," p. A14.

26. Solomon, "When the Bush Cabinet Convenes," p. 1704.

27. National Academy of Public Administration, *A Presidency for the 1980s* (Washington, D.C.: NAPA, 1988), Chapter 2.

28. Quoted by Bernard Weinraub, "Unlikely Alliance Atop Bush's Staff," *New York Times,* June 19, 1989, p. B8.

29. For an analysis of presidential decision making during the Gulf War, see James P. Pfiffner, "Presidential Policy-Making and the Gulf War," in *The Presidency and the Persian Gulf War,* ed. Marcia Whicker, James Pfiffner, and Raymond Moore (Westport, Conn.: Praeger Publishers, 1993).

30. Quoted by Solomon, "When the Bush Cabinet Convenes," p. 1704.

31. For an argument that the president's cabinet should be changed to reflect this reality, see Elliot L. Richardson and James P. Pfiffner, "Our Cabinet System Is a Charade," *New York Times,* May 31, 1989; see also Richardson and Pfiffner, "Creating a Real Cabinet," *USA Today Magazine,* vol. 119, no. 2544 (September 1990), pp. 10–12.

32. In order to understand why John Sununu was chosen by Bush to be chief of staff, it is helpful to recall the desperation of Bush's political situation after the Iowa caucuses in the Republican primaries of 1988. Bush had just come in third behind Senator Robert Dole and evangelist Pat Robertson. New Hampshire had always been a rock-ribbed conservative state and a key to the Republican nomination, and Bush's conservative credentials were somewhat suspect.

But John Sununu had a plan. When an aide began to commiserate with him about the disaster of Bush's third-place finish in Iowa, Sununu explained how the situation was in fact an opportunity: "Don't you see how much good I'm going to be able to do for the next President of the United States?" (Dan Goodgame, "Big, Bad John Sununu," *Time,* May 21, 1990, p. 24). Sununu then took the offensive in calling in every favor he had earned while he was governor of New Hampshire and designed a media blitz that helped Bush win. The strategy centered around having the vice president "take the pledge" of "no new taxes" while television spots bashed Senator Dole as "senator straddle" by charging that he might consider a tax increase as one element of an attempt to shrink the deficit (David Broder, "What Bush Owes Sununu," *Washington Post,* May 1, 1991, p. A19). The strategy worked, and Bush went on to win New Hampshire and the nomination without any serious difficulties. For a more thorough analysis of the chief of staff issue and John Sununu's conduct of the office, see James P. Pfiffner, "The President's Chief of Staff: Lessons Learned," *Presidential Studies Quarterly,* vol. 23 (Winter 1993), pp. 77–102.

33. See Ann Devroy, "Sununu Swiftly Backpedals on Size of His White House Role," *Washington Post,* December 9, 1988, p. A9; and "Transition Watch," *New York Times,* December 8, 1988, p. B20.

34. See Burt Solomon, "No-Nonsense Sununu," *National Journal,* September 16, 1989, p. 2251.

35. See *Time,* September 30, 1991, p. 19; and *Newsweek,* December 30, 1991, p. 4. The existence of this avenue of communication was publicly confirmed by HSS Secretary Louis Sullivan, who admitted on television that he used the channel to communicate advice to the president; "This Week with David Brinkley," ABC News, Transcript of program of February 2, 1992, p. 13.

36. Bob Woodward, "The President's Key Men," *Washington Post,* October 7, 1992, p. A18.

37. Juan Williams, "George Bush's Flying Circus," *Washington Post,* November 24, 1991, pp. C1, C4.

38. Quoted in Maureen Dowd, "Sununu: A Case Study in Flouting the Rules,' *New York Times,* May 5, 1991, p. 34.

39. Charles Babcock and Ann Devroy, "Sununu Deems Only 4 Plane Trips 'Personal,'" *Washington Post,* April 24, 1991, pp. 1, 6.

40. *New York Times,* December 4, 1991, p. B12.

41. *New York Times,* November 23, 1991, pp. 1, 10. Duffy and Goodgame assert that Sununu had suggested the offending lines; *Marching in Place,* p. 126.

42. Quoted in Duffy and Goodgame, *Marching in Place,* p. 127.

43. Ann Devroy, "Sununu Sees Vendetta as Source of Troubles," *Washington Post,* June 26, 1991, p. A5; Sidney Blumenthal, "So Long Sununu," *Vanity Fair,* February 1992, p. 112; Burt Solomon, "Sununu Will Leave Washington with 'Low Opinion' Unchanged," *National Journal,* January 11, 1982, pp. 90–91.

44. Letter of resignation reprinted in the *New York Times,* December 4, 1991, p. B12 (emphasis added).

45. For an insightful profile of Samuel Skinner, see Marjorie Williams, "The President's Straight Man," *Washington Post Magazine,* June 7, 1992, p. 11.

46. Interview with Constance Newman, director of the U.S. Office of Personnel Management, Washington, D.C., June 15, 1989.

47. Judith Havemann, "Reagan Regime Lives on Through Appointees' Alumni Group," *Washington Post,* August 25, 1989, p. A19.

48. Joel Aberbach, "The President and the Executive Branch," in *The Bush Presidency: First Appraisals,* ed. Colin Campbell and Bert Rockman (Chatham, N.J.: Chatham House, 1991), p. 239.

49. Judith Michaels, "A View from the Top: Reflections of the Bush Presidential Appointees," *Public Administration Review,* May/June 1995, p. 276.

50. Burt Solomon, "In Person," *National Journal,* January 21, 1989, p. 140. Judith Havemann, "Bush to Get 2,500 Conservative Resumes," *Washington Post,* November 15, 1988, p. A17.

51. Interview with Chase Untermeyer, The White House, June 6, 1989.

52. Interview with Chase Untermeyer, Transition Headquarters, December 15, 1989.

53. Burt Solomon, "Bush Promised Fresh Faces," *National Journal,* January 21, 1989, p. 142.

54. Quoted by Elizabeth Drew, "A Reporter at Large," *The New Yorker,* March 16, 1981, pp. 91–92.

55. For an analysis of the problem this has caused for the management of the government, see "Politics and Performance: Strengthening the Executive Leadership System," Task Force Report to the National Commission on the Public Service [the Volcker Commission] (Washington, D.C.: The National Commission on the Public Service, 1989).

56. Quoted in Joel Aberbach, "The President and the Executive Branch," p. 236.

57. Richard L. Berke, "Ex-Finance Chairman Complains Few Jobs Go to Bush Fund-Raisers," *New York Times,* February 20, 1989, p. 1.

58. See the *New York Times* editorial "Bought, with Sewer Money," February 24, 1989, p. A32.

59. See Ann Devroy, "Envoys without Experience," *Washington Post,* July 18, 1989, p. 1; and Ronald Spires (retired undersecretary for management, the U.S. State Department), "Trashing the Foreign Service," *Washington Post,* July 23, 1989, p. D1.

60. For an argument that the White House played too heavy a role, see Robert Fulton, "Caving In to the Right," *Washington Post,* July 23, 1989, p. D1.

61. Interview with Chase Untermeyer, The White House, June 6, 1989.

62. Ann Devroy, "High Level Government Jobs Reserved for Bush Supporters," *Washington Post,* January 14, 1989, p. 1.

63. Interview with Constance Horner, Deputy Secretary of HHS, Washington, D.C., June 20, 1989. Horner later became director of Presidential Personnel for President Bush.

64. *Washington Post,* February 15, 1989, p. A23.

65. Interview with Chase Untermeyer, The White House, June 6, 1989.

66. Interview with a high-level Bush administration appointee, Washington, D.C., June 20, 1989.

67. Interview with Chase Untermeyer, The White House, June 6, 1989.

68. Judith Havemann, "Federal Vacancies Becoming Drag on Policymaking," *Washington Post,* March 18, 1989, p. A10; John Biskupic, "FBI Background Investigation Draws Intensified Scrutiny," *Congressional Quarterly,* April 1, 1989, p. 699.

69. "Executive Shortfall," Democratic Study Group Special Report, U.S. House of Representatives, no. 101–15 (August 30, 1989). See also Judith Havemann, "Half the Administration on 'Automatic Pilot'?" *Washington Post,* August 30, 1989.

70. G. Calvin Mackenzie, "Appointing Mr. (or Ms.) Right," *Government Executive,* April 1990, pp. 20–26.

71. Interview with Chase Untermeyer, The White House, June 6, 1989.

72. Quoted in Duffy and Goodgame, *Marching in Place,* p. 16.

73. Duffy and Goodgame, *Marching in Place,* p. 57.

74. Duffy and Goodgame, *Marching in Place,* p. 70.

75. Duffy and Goodgame, *Marching in Place,* p. 60.

76. Aberbach, "The President and the Executive Branch," p. 238.

77. David Gergen, "George Bush's Balky Start," *U.S. News & World Report,* January 30, 1989, p. 34.

78. "Bush's Plea 'A Lot Is Happening,'" *Newsweek,* March 29, 1989, p. 26.

79. Duffy and Goodgame, *Marching in Place,* p. 60.

80. Charles Kolb, *White House Daze* (New York: The Free Press, 1994), p. 9.

81. Kolb, *White House Daze,* p. 25.

82. Quoted by David Hoffman, "Bush: Making Himself Up as He Goes Along," *Washington Post,* August 13, 1989, p. B4.

83. See Sidney Blumenthal, *Pledging Allegiance: The Last Campaign of the Cold War* (New York: HarperPerennial, 1991); and Kathleen Hall Jamieson, *Dirty Politics: Deception, Distraction, Democracy* (New York: Oxford University Press, 1992).

84. Quoted in Charles O. Jones, "Meeting Low Expectations: Strategy and Prospects of the Bush Presidency," in *The Bush Presidency: First Appraisals,* ed. Colin Campbell and Bert Rockman (Chatham, N.J.: Chatham House, 1991), p. 54.

85. *Washington Post,* August 13, 1980, p. B4.

86. Richard Cohen, "The Gloves Are Off," *National Journal,* October 14, 1989, p. 2509.

87. Tactical errors were made by the administration. After Tower's name had been raised and it was known that he was Bush's top candidate for the job, the administration waited a number of weeks before submitting the name to the Senate, raising doubts about the administration's own judgment of Tower's fitness. In releasing parts of the FBI investigation results to Senate Republicans, but not including Senator Nunn, chairman of the Foreign Relations Committee, the administration unnecessarily alienated Nunn. It was Nunn's decision to oppose Tower in committee that sealed the fate of his nomination. The Democratic opposition to Tower was based on allegations about his drinking habits, his relations with various women, and his earning of hundreds of thousands of dollars from defense industry companies shortly after he left his position of U.S. arms control negotiator in Geneva.

88. See *The Report of the National Economic Commission* (Washington, D.C.: National Economic Commission, 1989); and the U.S. General Accounting Office, *The Budget Deficit,* GAO/OCG-89 ITR (Washington, D.C.: GAO, November 1988).

89. See Elizabeth Drew, "Letter from Washington," *The New Yorker,* May 15, 1989, pp. 87–93.

90. See Barbara Sinclair, "Governing Unheroically (and Sometimes Unappetizingly): Bush and the 101st Congress," *The Bush Presidency: First Appraisals,* ed. Colin Campbell and Bert Rockman (Chatham, N.J.: Chatham House, 1991), pp. 155–84; and James P. Pfiffner, "The President and the Postreform Congress," in *The Postreform Congress,* ed. Roger Davidson (New York: St. Martin's Press, 1991).

91. Charles O. Jones, *The Presidency in a Separated System* (Washington, D.C.: Brookings Institution, 1994), pp. 112–15, 128, 179.

92. Address to the National Press Club, "Beyond the Deficit Problem: Now-Now-Ism and 'The New Balance,'" July 20, 1989, p. 3.

93. For an argument that presidential leadership is necessary for serious deficit reduction, see James P. Pfiffner, "The President's Legislative Agenda," *The Annals,* September 1988, pp. 22–36.

8. THE CLINTON TRANSITION: HITTING THE GROUND WALKING

1. See Hugh Heclo, "The Changing Presidential Office," in *The Managerial Presidency,* ed. James P. Pfiffner, (Pacific Grove, Calif.: Brooks/Cole, 1991).

2. For an insightful article on Clinton's leadership style, see Fred I. Greenstein, "Presidential Leadership Style of Bill Clinton: An Early Appraisal," *Political Science Quarterly,* vol. 108, no. 4 (1993-1994), pp. 589–601.

3. See Michael Duffy, "The State of Bill Clinton," *Time,* February 7, 1994, p. 26. For the story of Clinton as governor of Arkansas changing his mind after a veto had been delivered to the state legislature see Chapter 1, "Unveto Man," in John Brummett, *High Wire* (New York: Hyperion, 1994).

4. Duffy, "The State of Bill Clinton," p. 28.

5. Quoted in "Clinton Deflects Criticism of Policy-Making Process," *Washington Post,* June 8, 1994, p. A17.

6. See Bert Rockman's thoughtful essay, "Leadership Style and the Clinton Presidency," in *The Clinton Presidency: First Appraisals,* ed. Colin Campbell and Bert Rockman (Chatham, N.J.: Chatham House, 1996), pp. 325–362.

7. Interview with Anne Wexler, Washington, D.C., April 24, 1995.

8. Interview with John Hart, Washington, D.C., March 3, 1995.

9. Tom Shoop, "The Facilitator," *Government Executive,* May 1994, p. 14.

10. Interview with John Hart, Washington, D.C., March 3, 1995.

11. Interview with Harrison Wellford, Washington, D.C., March 27, 1995.

12. Interview with Anne Wexler, Washington, D.C., March 24, 1995.

13. Elizabeth Drew, *On the Edge* (New York: Simon and Schuster, 1994), p. 37.

14. Remarks of Gene Sperling at a luncheon at the Brookings Institution, March 17, 1993.

15. Balance and diversity have been time-honored criteria in cabinet selection throughout U.S. history. The traditional criteria have included ideological, religious,

partisan, and geographic balance. Ethnic and gender criteria have been more recent additions. See James P. Pfiffner, *The Modern Presidency* (New York: St. Martin's Press, 1994), Chapter 5.

16. One of the ironies of Clinton's approach was that for all of the time and effort that he invested in selecting the cabinet and his special emphasis on ethics, he began with having to jettison two publicly announced candidates for attorney general, and within two and a half years three cabinet members were being investigated by independent counsels (Secretary of Agriculture Mike Espy, Commerce Secretary Ron Brown, and HUD Secretary Henry Cisneros).

17. Ann Devroy, "White House Roller-Coaster Ride Likely to Continue," *Washington Post,* April 3, 1994, p. A20.

18. Drew, *On the Edge,* p. 34.

19. See Matthew Holden, "Why Entourage Politics Is Volatile," in *The Managerial Presidency,* ed. James P. Pfiffner (Pacific Grove, Calif.: Brooks/Cole, 1991). Holden argues that presidents need staffers of three types: young, talented "gophers"; technical experts; and experienced, older peers.

20. Fiona Houston, "Youth Actively Served by Junior Clinton Aides," *New York Times,* March 28, 1993, p. 22.

21. See Drew, *On the Edge,* p. 33.

22. Commentator and political scientist Norman Ornstein quipped that Gergen was "Assistant to the President for Common Sense."

23. Quoted in Drew, *On The Edge,* pp. 33–34 (emphasis added).

24. Thomas L. Friedman, "Amid Setbacks, Clinton Team Seeks to Shake Off the Blues," *New York Times,* April 24, 1993, pp. 1, 28.

25. Quoted in Bob Woodward, *The Agenda* (New York: Simon and Schuster, 1993), p. 120.

26. Drew, *On the Edge,* pp. 36–37; Woodward, *The Agenda,* pp. 58–59.

27. See Bradley Patterson, *Ring of Power* (New York: Basic Books, 1988), p. 339.

28. For an analysis of the EOP and the White House Office, see Pfiffner, *The Modern Presidency,* Chapter 4. The numbers cited are based on the analysis of Rogelio Garcia, "President Clinton's Proposed Reduction in White House Staff," (Washington, D.C.: Congressional Research Service, 1993). See also James P. Pfiffner, "Cutting Staff No Easy Task for Clinton," *Maine Sunday Telegram,* December, 12, 1993. My analysis is also based on the fine reporting of Ann Devroy of the *Washington Post.* See her articles, "Adding Up Clinton's Cuts," September 30, 1993, p. 1; "Pruning the White House Vineyard," August 26, 1993; and "Defining the Quarter among the Dollars," April 14, 1993, among her other articles covering the cuts. On the difficulty of obtaining accurate numbers of White House staffers see John Hart, *The Presidential Branch,* 2nd ed. (Chatham, N.J.: Chatham House, 1994).

29. Tom Weko, *The Politicizing Presidency: The White House Personnel Office, 1948–1994* (Lawrence: University Press of Kansas, 1995), p. 125.

30. For an insightful analysis of the symbolic and practical aspects of the cuts, see John Hart, "The Politics of Symbolism: President Clinton's White House Staff Reductions" (Paper presented at the 1994 American Political Science Convention, New York City).

31. Burt Solomon, "A Modish Management Style Means Slip-Sliding around the West Wing," *National Journal,* October 30, 1993, p. 2607.

32. See Hart, "The Politics of Symbolism." See also Hart, *The Presidential Branch.*

33. See Woodward, *The Agenda,* pp. 93–95, 188–90, 237–41, 247–54, and passim.

34. Interview with Bowman Cutter, Washington, D.C., April 13, 1995.

35. For perspectives on "the consultants," see Woodward, *The Agenda,* pp. 188, 240, 250–57, and passim. See also Frank R. Wolf, "The White House's Outside Insiders," *Washington Post,* May 23, 1994, p. A19; Ruth Marcus, "White House Orders Consultants to Disclose Finances," *Washington Post,* June 10, 1994, p. A9; *Washington Post* editorial, June 10, 1994, p. A28; and Paul Begala, James Carville, Stanley B. Greenberg, and Mandy Grunwald, "'We Do Not Lobby,'" *Washington Post,* June 10, 1994, p. A29.

36. Eleanor Clift and Bob Cohn, "President Cliffhanger," *Newsweek,* November 22, 1993, p. 27; Solomon, "A Modish Management Style," p. 2607.

37. Drew, *On the Edge,* pp. 97, 102–103.

38. See the GAO report, "White House Travel Office Operations" (May 1994) GAO/GGD-94-132. It stated: "GAO questioned the practice of permitting nongovernment employees to have uncontrolled access to White House offices" (p. 5).

39. Burt Solomon, "A One Man Band," *National Journal,* April 24, 1993, p. 970.

40. Harrison Wellford, Donald Hawthorne, William Kelly, and Richard Neustadt, *Transition Working Plan for Reviewing the Staffing and Organization of the White House Office and Executive Office of the President,* November 2, 1992, copy in the author's files.

41. Remarks of William Galston at a lunch at the Brookings Institution, November 17, 1993; the author was present.

42. Executive Order 12835, issued on January 25, 1993. See also Paul Starobin, "The Broker," *National Journal,* April 16, 1994, pp. 887–883; John B. Judis, "Old Master," *The New Republic,* December 13, 1993, pp. 21–28; Gwen Ifil, "The Economic Czar behind the Economic Czars," *New York Times,* March 7, 1993; and Woodward, *The Agenda,* passim.

43. Interview with Bowman Cutter, Washington, D.C., April 13, 1995.

44. Starobin, "The Broker," p. 880.

45. Starobin, "The Broker," p. 879.

46. See Pfiffner, *The Modern Presidency,* pp. 80–87; Bob Woodward, "The President's Key Men," *Washington Post,* October 7, 1992, p. A18.

47. Richard Neustadt wrote a memo to John Kennedy in 1960 arguing that he should be his own chief of staff; in 1988 he wrote an article admitting that a chief of staff of some sort is a practical necessity in the contemporary presidency. Both documents are reprinted in Pfiffner, *The Managerial Presidency.*

48. For an analysis of the chief of staff dilemma—that there must be a chief of staff, but not a domineering one—see James P. Pfiffner, "The President's Chief of Staff: Lessons Learned," *Presidential Studies Quarterly,* Winter 1993, pp. 88–102.

49. Wellford et al., *Transition Workplan for Reviewing the Staffing and Organization of the White House Office and EOP,* pp. 5–6.

50. McLarty was so low-key that the *Washington Post* ran a feature story when he got mad; Lloyd Grove, "What Makes Mack Mad," (May 14, 1993), pp. B1, B8. Answer: it was a leak to the press in which a White House staffer blamed another staffer for a policy defeat.

51. Ken Adelman, "Getting a Grip," *The Washingtonian,* March 1994, p. 21.

52. See Devroy, "White House Roller-Coaster Ride," p. A20; Charles Fenyvesi, "Washington Whispers," *U.S. News & World Report,* July 18, 1994, p. 21.

53. Solomon, "A Modish Management Style," p. 2606.

54. See Woodward, *The Agenda,* pp. 230–32, 247, 319.

55. Duffy, "The State of Bill Clinton," p. 26.

56. David Lauter, "White House Awaiting Panetta's Prescription," *Los Angeles Times,* July 24, 1994, p. A24.

57. Ronald Reagan was much more "manageable" as president. As an actor he was used to following stage directions and delivering his lines effectively. As president he was effective and well known for pulling out his four-by-six cards with a script typed for him to read. His staff systems were designed to keep him on the script. The positive and negative results of this approach were demonstrated in Reagan's two terms in office, the first with James Baker as chief of staff and the second with Don Regan.

58. While Hillary Rodham Clinton could play this role at times, she would not have been an appropriate choice for chief of staff because being chief of staff is a full-time job. She also could not be the chief of staff because of the demands of her role as First Lady. In addition, she was too close to the president, and such a powerful role would have caused resentment. Finally, she was not expendable, which all chiefs of staff must be.

59. See Fred Barnes, "Big Mack," *The New Republic,* July 18 and 25, 1994, p. 10.

60. For analyses of the changes Panetta made, see Lauter, "White House Awaiting Panetta's Prescription," p. A1, A24; Elizabeth Drew, "Boss Panetta," *Washington Post,* October 2, 1994, p. C1; Rick Wartzman, "Why President Clinton Spends Exactly 62.5% More Time on Policy," *Wall Street Journal,* March 14, 1995, p. 1; Ann Devroy and Ruth Marcus, "Panetta Claims 'Authority' to Make Changes," *Washington Post,* June 29, 1994, p. A4; Burt Solomon, "Clinton's New Taskmaster Takes Charge," *National Journal,* August 6, 1994, p. 1872.

61. Wartzman. "Why President Clinton Spends 62.5% More Time on Policy," p. 1.

62. Bert Solomon, "Despite a Take-Charge Conductor, the Orchestra is Still Off Key," *National Journal,* October 1, 1994, p. 2298.

63. Bert Rockman, "Leadership Style and the Clinton Presidency," in *The Clinton Presidency: First Appraisals,* ed. Colin Campbell and Bert Rockman (Chatham, N.J.: Chatham House, 1996), p. 353.

64. Interview with John Hart, Washington, D.C., March 3, 1995.

65. For an analysis of the structure and functioning of the personnel operation, see Weko, *The Politicizing Presidency,* p. 100.

66. Interview with Roz Kleeman, Washington, D.C., September 27, 1993.

67. Interview with Thomas McFee, Washington, D.C., February 9, 1993.

68. *U.S. News & World Report,* February 1, 1993. There were 3,000 resumes at transition headquarters by November 11, 1992; Al Kamen, ". . . They Say It's What, Not Who, You Know," *Washington Post,* November 11, 1992, p. A23.

69. The Baker memo, dated October 12, 1992, was reprinted in the *Washington Post* on October 14, 1992.

70. Robert Pear, "In a Transition Tug-of-War, Bush Asks Vast Resignations," *New York Times,* January 16, 1993, pp. 1, 7.

71. Memo FROM: Constance Horner, FOR: Cabinet Secretaries and Agency Heads Presidential Appointees, SUBJECT: Letters of Resignation: dated January 13, 1993, The White House, Washington. A copy of the memo is in the author's files.

72. Ann Devroy, "Bush Team Balks," *Washington Post,* January 16, 1993, p. 1.

73. Memorandum TO: Heads of Executive Departments and Agencies, FROM: Bruce Lindsey, Director of Presidential Personnel, The White House, Washington, January 20, 1993. A copy of the memo is in the author's files.

74. See Joel D. Aberbach, "U.S. Executive Branch Politics in a Changing World," in *The U.S. after the Cold War,* ed. Herbert Dittgen and Michael Minkenberg (Pittsburgh: University of Pittsburgh Press, 1996).

75. For an analysis of how electoral constituencies were translated into pressures on the Clinton Presidential Personnel Office, see Weko, *The Politicizing Presidency,* pp. 102–103.

76. Interview with Thomas McFee, Deputy Assistant Secretary for Administration, Department of Health and Human Services, February 9, 1993.

77. Matthew Cooper, "Clinton's Focus on Diversity," *U.S. News & World Report,* March 20, 1995, pp. 35, 38; Martha Farnsworth Riche, "The Bean Count Is In!" *Washington Post,* January 23, 1994, p. C2. President Bush appointed 7 percent African-Americans. On the bench Clinton appointed 55 percent minorities, while Bush appointed 10 percent and Reagan 13 percent.

78. Rogelio Garcia, "Women Nominated and Appointed to Full-Time Civilian Positions by President George Bush, 1989–92," Congressional Research Service Report for Congress, May 26, 1993.

79. Interviews with several Clinton advisers. One cost was occasionally not putting the best-qualified person in the position. For instance, there was a general consensus that career diplomat Warren Zimmerman was the most qualified person to be assistant secretary of state for Population and Refugee Migration Affairs. His name was suggested to the White House by the State Department, but when no action was taken for almost a year, Zimmerman resigned because it was clear that the White House wanted a woman for the position; Matthew Cooper, "Clinton's Focus on Diversity," *U.S. News & World Report,* March 20, 1995, p. 35; Nelson W. Polsby, "Executive Branch Interests Differ from President's, Need His Protection," U.C. Berkeley Institute of Public Affairs, *Public Affairs Report,* March 1994, p. 4. Another cost was delays in getting Clinton people in appointive positions. For instance, the Equal Employment Opportunity Commission went without a chair for twenty months while the administration searched for the right person; Cooper, "Clinton's Focus on Diversity," p. 35. For further analysis see Joel D. Aberbach, "The Federal Executive under Clinton," in *The Clinton Presidency: First Appraisals,* ed. Colin Campbell and Bert A. Rockman (Chatham, N.J.: Chatham House, 1996), pp. 163–87. It is ironic that the agency that had responsibility for one of the administration's major priorities, equal employment opportunity, did not have a Clinton leader, in part because of the desire of the administration to find a Hispanic of Puerto Rican descent for the job; "Appointments Dithering," editorial in the *Washington Post,* June 14, 1994, p. A20.

80. For the number of people working on presidential personnel, see Weko, *The Politicizing Presidency,* pp. 100–101.

81. Data provided by the executive clerk to the president, 1993.

82. Calvin Mackenzie, quoted in Paul Light, *Thickening Government* (Washington, D.C.: Brookings Institution, 1995), p. 68. The author would like to thank Calvin Mackenzie for sharing his data on the pace of appointments. The calculation of these averages by Mackenzie was done by coding each appointment by a number corresponding to the month in which it occurred (Jan. = 1, Feb. = 2, etc.) and then dividing the total number of months by the total number of positions.

83. See Calvin Mackenzie, "Partisan Presidential Leadership: The President's Appointees," in *The Parties Respond,* ed. L. Sandy Maisel (Boulder, Colo.: Westview Press, 1990); and Weko, *The Politicizing Presidency.*

84. Text of "Clinton Policy on Post-Employment Lobbying by Political Appointees," released December 7, 1992, published by the Bureau of National Affairs, Inc., Washington, D.C.

85. Jay Matthews, "Are There ANY Skeletons in Your Closet?" *Washington Post,* May 2, 1995, p. D1.

86. The note is printed in Elizabeth Drew, *On the Edge,* p. 258.

87. On the general issue of declining civility in the appointments process, see Stephen L. Carter, *The Confirmation Mess* (New York: Basic Books, 1994).

88. Weko, *The Politicizing Presidency,* pp. 124–125.

89. Hamilton Jordan, "What Not to Do," *Washington Post,* November 9, 1992, p. A21.

90. Quoted by Thomas L. Friedman, "Clinton Taking Big Role in Picking Cabinet Aides," *New York Times,* November 18, 1992, p. A22.

91. Devroy, "Bush Team Balks," p. 1.

92. Source: Executive Clerk to the President. For details see Pfiffner, *The Modern Presidency,* p. 123.

93. Light, *Thickening Government,* p. 91. The total number of occupants of Executive Levels I–V increased from 451 in 1960 to 2,393 in 1992 (p. 192).

94. For 911 Schedule Cs in 1976 see Patricia Ingraham, "Building Bridges or Burning Them?" *Public Administration Review,* September/October 1989, p. 429. The other data come from Patricia W. Ingraham, James R. Thompson, and Elliot F. Eisenberg, "Political Management Strategies and Political/Career Relationships: Where Are We Now in the Federal Government?" *Public Administration Review,* May–June 1995, pp. 263–272.

95. Light, *Thickening Government,* pp. 191–93.

96. Jon Healey, "Administration Fills Its Slots, Congress Plays Waiting Game," *Congressional Quarterly Weekly Report,* May 1, 1993, p. 1060.

97. Al Kamen, "Tax Dollars and Common Sense," *Washington Post,* May 27, 1994, p. A23. For example, in the early months of the Clinton administration there was a gap in the appointees at the Department of Defense and in the armed services. This very well may have affected the president's ability to pursue his proposed changes in the status of gays in the military. Having people in place to confer with military leadership would have at least have facilitated communication, even if the outcome was not changed. With only a few appointees in place, most military people followed the debate in the newspapers instead of being briefed and consulted by their own superiors and colleagues. Of the twenty-four PAS positions in the Department of Defense, only ten had been filled by the end of June 1993, and of the twenty-two positions in the armed services only one had been confirmed; "The Pentagon's Missing Civilians," editorial, *Washington Post,* June 27, 1993. By December 12, 1993, the Department of Defense had 19 of 46 jobs filled; Justice had filled 15 or 29, and Commerce, 10 of 28; Al Kaman, "Help Wanted, Call Clinton (EOE)," *Washington Post,* October 12, 1993.

98. Ann Devroy, "Late for Appointments," *Washington Post,* March 2, 1993, p. 1.

99. *Time,* December 13, 1993, p. 42.

100. Interview with Harrison Wellford, Washington, D.C., March 27, 1995.

101. Drew, *On the Edge,* p. 36.

102. Interview with Bowman Cutter, Washington, D.C., April 13, 1995.

103. Drew, *On the Edge,* Chapter 3.

104. See Drew, *On the Edge,* p. 46.

105. Dan Balz and Ruth Marcus, "The Windup for the Pitch," *Washington Post,* March 7, 1993, pp. 1, 16.

106. William Lammers, "Policy Achievements in the First Year: Carter, Reagan, and Clinton" (Paper presented at the American Political Science Convention, New York City, September 1994, p. 27). See also Woodward, *The Agenda,* p. 140.

107. See the accounts in Drew, *On the Edge,* pp. 114–122; and Woodward, *The Agenda,* pp. 151–174.

108. For tactical details see *Congressional Quarterly Weekly Report,* April 3, 1993, p. 818.

109. David Broder and Dan Balz, "Clinton Finds Change Harder than Expected," *Washington Post,* May 14, 1993, p. 1.

110. For an analysis of the politics and policy of the "reinventing government" initiative, see James P. Pfiffner, "The National Performance Review in Perspective," *International Journal of Public Administration,* vol. 10, no. 1 (December 1996).

111. *Washington Post,* October 11, 1994, p. A6. See also Daniel Yankelovich, "The Debate That Wasn't: The Public and the Clinton Plan," *Health Affairs,* vol. 14, no. 1 (Spring 1995), p. 11. See also Bert A. Rockman, "The Clinton Presidency and Health Care Reform," *Journal of Health Politics, Policy, and Law,* vol. 20, no. 2 (Summer 1995), pp. 399–402.

112. For further elaboration of this advice see James P. Pfiffner, "The President's Legislative Agenda, *The Annals,* vol. 499 (September 1988), pp. 22–35. On the need to focus, see Paul C. Light, *The President's Agenda* (Baltimore: Johns Hopkins University Press, 1991); and Light, "The Focusing Skill and Presidential Influence in Congress," in *Congressional Politics,* ed. Christopher J. Deering (Chicago: Dorsey Press, 1989), pp. 239–61.

113. Quoted by Joshua D. Feuerstein, "Hitting the Ground Running on Different Tracks: A Reagan-Clinton Comparison" (Senior thesis for the Department of Politics at Princeton University, written under the direction of Fred I. Greenstein). This thesis is an insightful comparison of the two transitions; his source for the quote was Thomas L. Friedman, "Amid Setbacks, Clinton Team Seeks to Shake Off the Blues," *New York Times,* April 25, 1993, p. 28.

114. Gwen Ifil, "Clinton Sees Need to Focus His Goals and Sharpen Staff," *New York Times,* May 4, 1993, pp. 1, B9.

115. Ann Devroy and Ruth Marcus, "Clinton's First 100 Days," *Washington Post,* April 29, 1993, pp. 1, A18.

116. Quoted by Ruth Marcus, "Administration Now Sees Its Record at Risk," *Washington Post,* January 24, 1995, pp. 1, 6.

117. See James P. Pfiffner, "President Clinton and the 103rd Congress: Winning Battles and Losing Wars," in *Rivals for Power: Presidential-Congressional Relations,* ed. James Thurber (Washington, D.C.: CQ Press, 1996).

118. David Broder, "Round-the-Clock Operative," *Washington Post,* December 1, 1993, p. A25.

119. George C. Edwards, *At the Margins* (New Haven, Conn.: Yale University Press, 1989); Jon Bond and Richard Fleisher, *The President in the Legislative Arena* (Chicago: University of Chicago Press, 1990); Mark A. Peterson, *Legislating Together: The White*

House and Capitol Hill (Cambridge, Mass.: Harvard University Press, 1990); Lance T. LeLoup and Steven A. Shull, *Congress and the President* (Belmont, Calif.: Wadsworth, 1993); Charles O. Jones, *The Presidency in a Separated System* (Washington, D.C.: Brookings Institution, 1994).

120. Mark A. Peterson, "Clinton and Congress: What Would You Expect?" *Extension of Remarks,* Fall 1993, p. 3.

121. Lammers, "Policy Achievements in the First Year."

122. George Edwards, "Reforming the 'President': The Individuals as Leader," *PS: Political Science & Politics,* vol. 20, no. 3 (Summer 1987), p. 623; see also Edwards, *At the Margins.*

123. For a prescient analysis of the historical limits to Bill Clinton's political opportunities, see Hugh Heclo, "The Clinton Presidency as Political History," unpublished (January 16, 1993); and "The Clinton Style," *The Atlanta Journal & Constitution,* November 8, 1992, p. G1.

CONCLUSION: THE STRATEGIC PRESIDENCY

1. See John Kessel, *Presidential Parties* (Chicago: Dorsey Press, 1984), Chapter 3.

2. Charles O. Jones, *The Presidency in a Separated System* (Washington: Brookings, Institution, 1994), p. 3.

3. *Los Angeles Times,* January 9, 1983, part 1, p. 19. Quoted in Howard Shuman, *Politics and the Budget* (Englewood Cliffs, N.J.: Prentice Hall, 1984), p. 247.

4. For a discussion of the strategic approach of the Reagan administration, see Hugh Heclo and Rudolph Penner, "Fiscal and Political Strategy in the Reagan Administration," in *The Reagan Presidency,* ed. Fred I. Greenstein (Baltimore: The Johns Hopkins Press, 1983).

5. See Theodore Lowi, *The Personal Presidency* (Ithaca, N.Y.: Cornell University Press, 1985).

6. Much of this discussion is based on an interview with Richard Beal, primary author of the Initial Actions Project report and director of the Office of Policy Development for the Reagan administration, Washington, D.C., July 21, 1983.

7. For an analysis of the division of roles between White House staff and the departments and agencies, see James P. Pfiffner, "Can the President Control the Government? Should He?," in *The Managerial Presidency,* ed. James P. Pfiffner (Pacific Grove, Calif.: Brooks/Cole, 1991), pp. 1–16.

8. See Richard Neustadt, *Presidential Power* (New York: John Wiley & Sons, 1980), Chapter 11, "Hazards of Transition," p. 231.

9. Jones, *The Presidency in a Separated System;* Jones, "From Campaigning to Governing: The Challenge of Taking Over," in *Understanding the Presidency,* ed. James P. Pfiffner and Roger Davidson (New York: HarperCollins, forthcoming); and Jones, "Meeting Low Expectations: Strategy and Prospects of the Bush Presidency," in *The Bush Presidency: First Appraisals,* ed. Colin Campbell and Bert Rockman (Chatham, N.J.: Chatham House, 1991). See William Lammers, "Domestic Policy Leadership in the First Year," in *Understanding the Presidency,* ed. Pfiffner and Davidson; and "Policy Achievements in the First Year: Carter, Reagan and Clinton" (Paper presented at the 1994 American Political Science Convention).

10. See Hugh Heclo, *A Government of Strangers* (Washington, D.C.: Brookings Institution, 1977); and "The In-and-Outer System: A Critical Assessment," in *The In-and-Outers,* ed. Calvin Mackenzie (Baltimore: Johns Hopkins University Press, 1987).

11. See Stephen Barr, "When the Job Gets Old after Only 2 Years," *Washington Post,* June 2, 1994, p. A21.

12. National Commission on the Public Service (the Volcker Commission), *Leadership for America: Rebuilding the Public Service* (Washington, D.C.: National Commission on the Public Service, 1989), p. 18. This recommendation of the final report is based on the more detailed analysis contained in the Task Force Report to the Commission, "Politics and Performance: Strengthening the Executive Leadership System"; the task force was chaired by Elliot Richardson and staffed by project director James Pfiffner, printed in *Task Force Reports* (Washington, D.C.: National Commission on the Public Service, 1989), pp. 157–190.

13. *Leadership in Jeopardy: The Fraying of the Presidential Appointments System,* Final Report of the Presidential Appointees Project (Washington, D.C.: NAPA, 1985). The research analyses growing out of the project are printed in *The In-and-Outers,* ed. Mackenzie.

14. *Science and Technology Leadership in American Government: Ensuring the Best Presidential Appointments* (Washington, D.C.: National Academy Press, 1992).

15. Patricia W. Ingraham, James R. Thompson, and Elliot F. Eisenberg, "Political Management Strategies and Political/Career Relationships: Where Are We Now in the Federal Government?" *Public Administration Review,* May/June 1995, pp. 263–272. See also Judith Michaels, "A View from the Top: Reflections of the Bush Presidential Appointees," *Public Administration Review,* May/June 1995, pp. 273–283; James P. Pfiffner, "Political Appointees and Career Executives: The Democracy-Bureaucracy Nexus in the Third Century," *Public Administration Review,* January/February 1987, pp. 57–64; and Pfiffner, "Can the President Control the Government? Should He?" *The Managerial Presidency,* ed. Pfiffner; Elliot L. Richardson and James P. Pfiffner, "Political Appointees: Fewer Is Better," *Government Executive,* June 1991, pp. 58–59. For arguments that the number of political appointees is not a problem and that there are too few appointees, see Robert C. Rector and Michael Sanera, eds. *Steering the Elephant: How Washington Works* (New York: Universe Books, 1987).

16. Paul Light, *Thickening Government* (Washington, D.C.: Brookings Institution, 1995), Table A-2, pp. 190–82.

17. Light, *Thickening Government,* p. 167.

18. G. Calvin Mackenzie, "Appointing Mr. (or Ms.) Right," *Government Executive,* April 1990, p. 32.

19. Interview by Ken Adelman, "Summing Up," *The Washingtonian,* July 1995, p. 28.

20. For detailed analysis of the problems with some of our conflict of interest laws, see G. Calvin Mackenzie, "'If You Want to Play, You've Got to Pay': Ethics Regulation and the Presidential Appointments System, 1964–1984," in Mackenzie, *The In-and-Outers;* National Academy of Science, *Science and Technology Leadership in American Government* (Washington, D.C.: National Academy Press, 1992); National Commission on the Public Service, *Leadership for America* (Washington, D.C.: National Commission on the Public Service, 1989), pp. 15–16. See also *Report of the President's Commission on the Federal Appointments Process,* and the statement by James P. Pfiffner (Washington, D.C.: Executive Office of the President, December 1991), pp. 41–48.

21. For an analysis of the Senate role in the appointments process, see Christopher J. Deering, "Damned If You Do and Damned If You Don't: The Senate's Role in the Appointments Process," in Mackenzie, *The In-and-Outers.*

22. Stephen L. Carter, *The Confirmation Mess* (New York: Basic Books, 1994).

23. Quoted in Elizabeth Drew, *On the Edge* (New York: Simon and Schuster, 1994), p. 258.

24. *Washington Post,* June 25, 1993, quoted by Charles Ross, "The Tory Elite: President Bush's Executive Branch Appointments" (Ph.D. diss., George Mason University, 1994), p. 217.

25. See Carter, *The Confirmation Mess,* pp. 191–206.

26. See the final report, NAPA Presidential Appointee Project.

27. These data are drawn from the NAPA Presidential Appointee Project. See G. Calvin Mackenzie, ed., *The In and Outers* (Baltimore: The Johns Hopkins Press, 1987).

28. For a proposal to institutionalize orientations for new political appointees, see James P. Pfiffner, "Strangers in a Strange Land: Orienting New Presidential Appointees," in *The In and Outers,* ed. Mackenzie.

29. Interview with John Ehrlichman, Santa Fe, June 3, 1983.

30. Interview with Jule M. Sugarman, Washington, D.C., July 3, 1983.

31. Jones, *The Presidency in a Separated System,* p. 281.

32. For an analysis of the legal issues involved with impoundments, see James P. Pfiffner, *The President, the Budget, and Congress* (Boulder, Colo.: Westview Press, 1979).

About the Author

James P. Pfiffner received his Ph.D. in political science at the University of Wisconsin at Madison and is now professor of government and public policy at George Mason University. He has taught at the University of California, Riverside, and California State University, Fullerton.

He worked in the Director's Office of the U.S. Office of Personnel Management in 1980–1981 and has served on panels or project staffs of the National Commission on the Public Service (Volcker Commission), the National Academy of Public Administration, the National Academy of Sciences, and the Center for Strategic and International Studies. He has lectured widely on the presidency throughout the United States and in Europe, and he has been a research fellow and visiting scholar at the Brookings Institution.

He has written or edited seven books on the presidency, including *The Modern Presidency* (1994), *The Managerial Presidency* (1991), *The Presidency in Transition* (1989), and *The President, the Budget, and Congress: Impoundment and the 1974 Budget Act* (1979). He received the Distinguished Faculty Award at George Mason University in 1990 and the Army Commendation Medal for Valor in Vietnam and Cambodia in 1970.

Index